W9-DGJ-189

INSPIRATION AND THE OVERSELF

LARSON PUBLICATIONS

To keep updated on our new publications, please fill in your name and address (and/or names of interested friends or book dealers) and drop this card in the mail. You'll be hearing from us on a regular basis.

Name _____

Address _____

_____

Name _____

Address _____

_____

Interested in _____ Philosophy/Spiritual Lifestyle

_____ Education/Parenting _____ Children of all ages' spiritual literature

☐ Please send brochure on *The Notebooks of Paul Brunton* series.

Topics of special interest to me in *The Notebooks* are:

Larson Publications
4936 Route 414
Burdett, NY 14818

THE NOTEBOOKS OF PAUL BRUNTON

(VOLUME 14)

INSPIRATION AND THE OVERSELF

PAUL BRUNTON

(1898–1981)

An in-depth study of
category number twenty-two
from the notebooks

Published for the
PAUL BRUNTON PHILOSOPHIC FOUNDATION
by Larson Publications

International Standard Book Number (cloth) 0-943914-40-X
International Standard Book Number (paper) 0-943914-41-8
International Standard Book Number (series, cloth) 0-943914-17-5
International Standard Book Number (series, paper) 0-943914-23-X
Library of Congress Catalog Card Number: 88-81481

Manufactured in the United States of America

Published for the
Paul Brunton Philosophic Foundation
by
Larson Publications
4936 Route 414
Burdett, New York 14818

Distributed to the trade by
Kampmann and Company
9 East 40 Street
New York, New York 10016

89 91 92 90 88
2 4 6 8 10 9 7 5 3 1

The works of Paul Brunton

A Search in Secret India
The Secret Path
A Search in Secret Egypt
A Message from Arunachala
A Hermit in the Himalayas
The Quest of the Overself
The Inner Reality
(*also titled* Discover Yourself)
Indian Philosophy and Modern Culture
The Hidden Teaching Beyond Yoga
The Wisdom of the Overself
The Spiritual Crisis of Man

Published posthumously

Essays on the Quest

The Notebooks of Paul Brunton

(*continued next page*)

CONTENTS

EDITORS' INTRODUCTION

Since the fall of 1981, when a working photocopy of Paul Brunton's personal notebooks was first made available in the library of Wisdom's Goldenrod Center for Philosophic Studies, the sections with notes on *Inspiration and the Overself* have been read more, and with more enthusiasm, than any other section in the *Notebooks* series. Their remarkable beauty, their rare atmosphere of intimacy with the divine presence, quicken our spiritual vigor and clarity; their practical, simple, and efficacious guidance on how to recognize, cultivate, and make the most of those brief moments of reawakening to our spiritual reality inspires long-range confidence and optimism.

The previous volume in this series (volume thirteen, *Relativity, Philosophy, and Mind*) addressed the limited reliability of sense-knowledge and ordinary reasoning. It concluded with a convincing case for the point of view that the kernel of durable value and intelligent guidance in this purposive game of living is to be discovered directly, in the depths of one's own individual mind. *Inspiration and the Overself* now sets out to enhance dramatically the conscious relationship between our ordinary selves and that deeper level of our own minds.

Chapter one discusses *intuition*. Here is a faculty midway between our mundane identity and our true selfhood— intrinsically superior to ordinary sense, emotion, and reasoning, yet subject to misinterpretation, distortion, and consequent misapplication. This chapter stresses the importance of developing the intuitive faculty as the beginning of a conscious relationship between the ego and the soul; it also gives important and useful instructions on how to recognize and accept authentic intuitions, how to cultivate, test, and develop them, and how to apply them intelligently as the most reliable source of fruitful conduct in daily living.

Chapter two concerns *inspiration*—both inspiration in itself and several levels and directions of its operation. Whereas the first chapter emphasizes the *knowledge* available through intuition, this chapter emphasizes the soul's *power* to elevate both the ego's consciousness and the level of operation of its developed skills. The chapter's concluding section on the "Interior Word" discusses the extraordinary power with which specific words and sentences can be charged when the lower mind awakens to this unique faculty of the soul.

Chapter three makes clear that the source of these intuitions and inspirations is one's own best self, the true individuality, which P.B. most frequently calls the Overself. Because it *is* one's own true self, it is never absent but is always accessible . . . even though usually ignored. This chapter is devoted to awakening us to that constant Presence and inspiring us to make it the conscious context of every detail in our lives.

In this chapter, P.B. insists that we cannot strictly define or even adequately describe in words the total nature of this "Overself." How can that which is the ever-prolific source of *all* our inspired ideas and intelligent actions be encompassed by any single idea, any grouping of ideas or activities that are themselves but memories by the time we finish formulating the definition? Yet this position arose not from a *poverty* but from an *abundance* of ideas about and experiences of it—not from a lack of detail but from a wealth of detail. Dwelling as frequently—in early life, and as continuously in his later years—in full consciousness of its Presence as he did, P.B. saw both the validity and the limitations of concepts formed about it through human intellect and feelings. Many writers and teachers on this topic have felt constrained to produce or discover a strict definition or system, which they then spend much of the rest of their lives repeating and defending. They live, consequently, more and more in their memories of and thoughts about an earlier spiritual event whose living presence is increasingly replaced by dogmatism. In contrast, P.B. freely, affirmatively, and emphatically chose to center his attention and identity more in the living Presence itself than in his thoughts about it. This choice meant being reverentially awake to its ongoing mystery *and* intellectually precise concerning what can be spoken accurately about it. The indomitable mental freedom arising from such a position is the core of what is unique about his account of what he learned through constant attentiveness to its workings within him.

An issue of lively debate among serious students of this "true individuality" concerns whether it should be described as singular or multiple. Does each individual have his or her own unique Overself, or is the Overself one and the same in every human being? In several places, P.B. addresses the problems involved in planting both feet inflexibly in either camp. In the eighth chapter of *The Wisdom of the Overself* he wrote, "If there be a slight technical confusion in using the singular number alone, there would be immeasurably more confusion if, in using the plural, this dire error of any radical difference existing between them were to be authenticated." For this reason, P.B. chose throughout his later writings to emphasize the oneness of rather than the diversity within the Over-self—the sameness of the core of the divine consciousness rather than the variety of its expressions in different individuals. To readers concerned with the details of P.B.'s thought on this technical issue, we recommend— in addition to the present volume—study of *The Wisdom of the Overself* (especially chapter eight) and the section *World Mind in Individual Mind* in volume sixteen of *The Notebooks*.

The remaining chapters of *Inspiration and the Overself* are devoted to attracting, savoring, and following through on moments of authentic spiritual inspiration. It is this material in particular that readers in the Wisdom's Goldenrod library have found specially inspiring and valuable. Its wealth of detail about the what, how, when, and why of spiritual "glimpses," permeated by a rich atmosphere of intimate experience and crystal-clear understanding, is both poetically beautiful and uniquely informative. The final chapter, contrasting these ennobling but all-too-fleeting glimpses with the durable goal of philosophic realization, could have come from few other sources.

Editorial conventions with regard to quantity and structuring of material, spelling, capitalization, and other copy-editing practices for this volume are the same as have been outlined in earlier introductions. As in earlier volumes, (P) at the end of a para indicates that the para also appears in *Perspectives*, volume one of *The Notebooks* series.

We would like to take this opportunity to thank again the many friends at Wisdom's Goldenrod and the Paul Brunton Philosophic Foundation who are responsible for another volume's being ready for press. We would also like to thank again, on behalf of the foundation, all those dedicated readers throughout the world whose additional financial support is helping to make it possible for these books to be published at their current rate.

For further information about publication schedules and related projects, please write to the

Paul Brunton Philosophic Foundation
P.O. Box 89
Hector, NY 14841

INSPIRATION
AND THE
OVERSELF

When he first faces the mystery which is at the heart's core and in the mind's essence, he knows nothing about it other than that it is the source of his being and that it possesses a power and intelligence utterly transcending his own. Yet he feels that it draws his love and, in his best moments, inspires his character.

He feels the Presence of something higher than himself, wise, noble, beautiful, and worthy of all reverence. Yet it is really himself—the best part come at last into unfoldment and expression.

1

INTUITION THE BEGINNING

The spiritual nature can only be discovered spiritually—not intellectually, not emotionally, and certainly not physically. Such a spiritual discovery can only be attained intuitively.

2

The mystery into which we have been born is not penetrable by weaving fancy or logical intellect. But intuition, if we are patient enough and willing enough to follow it, can lead us into an overwhelming experience where we discover that IT is there, always there.

3

It is not through any intellectual process of reasoning from premise to conclusion that we come to know we exist, but through an immediate and spontaneous intuition.

4

Intuition moves thought and penetrates feeling, so that it is often mistaken for them. Yet its true nature is something other than both theirs.

5

Intuition is the mind's inner light.

6

Where ego merely believes, intuition definitely knows.

7

There is an intermediate entity, compounded of the ego's best part and the point of contact with the Overself. Call it the higher mind, the conscience, or the intellectual intuition, if you wish.

8

The discovery of its presence makes possible a form of communication between person and Overself which is passive, not active. That is, he is directed guided or corrected in and through his human faculties, intuitively. The person acts, does, thinks, speaks, and decides as if he were doing so completely alone. But he is not: he is responding to the Overself, to the effects of its presence, now unhindered by his ego.

9

Whether we call an intuition a "thought-feeling" or an "emotive thought," it is still something that is deeper than thinking, different from ordinary feelings.

10

There is a sacred oracle within, to which the problems of life and living can be carried in our calmer moments. Its laconic answers may or may not need interpretation.

11

In this matter we mistake the common type for the normal type. The mystically minded person is not usually met with, but he is nearer *true* normality than the materially minded one. For one part of his human psyche—the intuitive—is at least functioning, whereas it is "dead" in the other man.

12

There is a faculty in man which knows truth when it sees it, which needs no argument, reflection, or cogitation to attest or prove what it knows.

13

There is another way of knowing beside the ordinary way, through the channels of eyes or thoughts, a way which can be found only by quietening the mind and stilling the emotions.

14

Here is this wonderful potency in man lying largely unused, this faculty of intuition that links him with a higher order of being.

15

However arguable his theories may be, the scientific facts which Freud produced are less debatable. And he must be praised for having included among them the important fact that highly complicated mental acts are sometimes performed unconsciously. An immense accumulation of facts and experiences is contained within the deeper level of the mind as in a storehouse upon which we may unknowingly draw. The possibility—nay, the certainty—of intuition becomes perfectly explicable when the existence of this deeper level is accepted. The successful transference of any of these facts or any lessons of these experiences from the hidden to the conscious region constitutes one particular form of what we call an intuition.

16

The need for advancing individuals is to go beyond the intellect, to draw from the intuition or to find inspiration.

17

How many minds have pondered over life and searched for its meaning, only to feel baffled in the end, and held back by their own limitations? For although the active intellect naturally asks such questions, only the intuition can answer them adequately. But the latter is the least cultivated of all our faculties and the most torpid, and this is why we have no access to the answers, and why the questions remain troublesome or even torturing.

18

The same mind which men use to understand that two added to three totals five cannot be used to understand that he who loses himself finds himself.

19

The messages which come to the human race from the kingdom of heaven, mercifully come through different channels of its psyche. The Word may be received in abstract mental activity as well as utter mental stillness, in passive aesthetic appreciation as well as active creation.

20

The intuition is a mystical faculty, whose messages may dawn slowly on the conscious mind or emerge into it suddenly.

21

These intuitive feelings tell us that a deeper kind of Being is at the base of our ordinary consciousness.

22

It is almost impossible to put into thoughts that which is above thoughts. But hints, suggestions, and symbols may render some service. Only intuition, which comes up by itself, can come closer still to the truth and deliver what is more like it.

23

If intellect fails to touch Reality, what can? The answer is intuition and inspiration.

24

That intuition is often mistaken for insight reveals one of the defects of mysticism. There are some who even question the validity of all insight, and, indeed, this is a sensible question to raise. The whole problem needs threshing out in a paper on the subject. Meanwhile, I must remind those who were troubled by what was written in the appendix to *The Hidden Teaching Beyond Yoga* that insight is not concerned with mundane matters, but only with what is beyond our time-space dimensions. Quite obviously, no one has the right to apply such a term to views concerning such matters as intellectual theology or physical diet. Intuition can, however, deal with these quite effectively—when it is, itself, checked by reason.

25

If we lack the capacity to comprehend, gauge, or perceive the Infinite, we do have the capacity to feel its presence intuitively.

26

Spirit—impenetrably mysterious, without form or figure, yet as real to the mystic as matter is to the materialist—finds its voice in man and Nature, in art and circumstance.

27

Faint glimmerings fall upon our sight from above through furtive gleams of intuition.

28

These delicate intuitive impulses can produce no impression on ordinary minds.

29

We can convince the intellect that the soul exists—but the only really adequate proof is intuitive personal experience of it.

30

The discovery of the soul's existence is not a result of intellectual analysis or of emotional feeling but of intuitive experience.

31

The intuition should be accorded the highest place among man's faculties. It should always lead or direct them.

32

Knowledge of the facts concerning man and his nature, his general destiny and spiritual evolution, can be gained by the intuition; but information concerning the details of his personal history must be gleaned, if at all, by the psychical faculty.(P)

33

The intuition appears indirectly in aesthetic ecstasy and intellectual creativity, in the pricking of conscience, in the longing for relief from anxieties, or peace of mind. It appears directly only in mystical realization.(P)

34

The intuition comes from, and leads to, the Overself.(P)

35

It is the strength or feebleness of our intuition which determines the grade of our spiritual evolution. What begins as a gentle surrender to intuition for a few minutes, one day resolves into a complete surrender of the ego to the Overself for all time.(P)

36

The intuitive method should not be asked to solve problems which can easily be solved by the reason; otherwise it may fail to respond. On the other hand, when intuition is working, intellect should retire.

37

To find your way to the major truths it is not enough to use the intellect alone, however sharpened it may be. Join intuition to it: then you will have intelligence. But how does one unfold intuition? By penetrating deeper and hushing the noise of thoughts.

38

Intuition tells us *what* to do. Reason tells us *how* to do it. Intuition points direction and gives destination. Reason shows a map of the way there.(P)

39

To the inexperienced or ignorant the conclusions of reason and the discoveries of intuition may clash, but to the matured they accommodate and adjust themselves harmoniously.

40

We may oppose one thing to another if both are on the same plane, but not if they are on unequal planes. Intuition is not anti-intellectual but super-intellectual.

41

When intuition guides and illuminates intellect, balances and restrains the ego, that which the wise men called "true intelligence" rises.

42

The intuition never needs to hunger for truth. While the intellect is seeking and starving for it, the intuition already knows and feels it.

43

Intuition is truth drawn from one's own self, that is, from within, be it a practical or a spiritual truth, whereas intellect squeezes its conclusion out of presented evidence, that is, from without.

44

Calculation may be pushed by the ego to the point of cunning. The first is quite proper to the business world and the mathematical sphere, but in the area of spiritual seeking it has only a limited applicability. The second is quite useless here. What is here of greater worth than both is intuition. But because this latter faculty is little developed in most people, they have to be content for the time with simple trust. But this is not a faculty; it is a trait of character. It may mislead a person if he puts it into the wrong channel, or it may serve him well if he places it properly.

45

While the intellect argues waveringly at length, the intuition affirms confidently in an instant. While the one gropes among the appearances and shadows of truth, the other walks straight toward truth.

46

Ordinarily, ample time is needed to accumulate data and deliberate properly before correct decisions or judgements can be made. None of this is necessary to make them intuitively, for the intuition itself operates out of time and beyond thought.

47

An intuitive idea is quite different from one derived from the customary process of logical thinking. Unless it is distorted or muddled by the man himself, it is always reliable. Can we say the same of an intellectual idea?

48

The best wisdom of a man does not come out of acuteness of thinking; it comes out of depth of intuition.

49

The danger of intellectualizing these intuitions is that they flee while we prepare to examine them. This is why our theological seminaries produce so many competent religious orators, but so few inspired religious prophets. This is why the art schools produce so many people who can draw good lines and space drawings so well, but so few who can draw something that is individual and outstanding. The intellect is necessary to the complete person, but it should be kept in its place and made to realize that when it approaches such an intuition, it treads on holy ground.

50

Reasoned thinking can only check the guidance or revealing of intuition, whereas the latter can actually guide and illumine the path of the former.

51

Where the shrewdest judgement finds itself bewildered, the mysterious faculty of intuition moves unhesitatingly and surely.

52

It was a period of absolute clarity, when the thought of a problem was welded into one with its solution, when there was no gap of time between question and answer.

53

If anyone has a clear intuition about a matter, it would be foolish of him to trust intellect alone in the same matter.

54

The intellect is one medium of understanding, the intuition is another.

55

The intuition should give orders which the intellect should carry out. The reasoning and practicality needed to do so and to attend to their details will then be provided by the intellect itself. But the original function of giving direction and the authority of giving command will be vested in the intuition alone.

56

Intuition reaches a conclusion directly, without the working of any process of reasoned thinking.

57

What the thinking intellect in him cannot receive, the mystical intuition can.

58

The secret has yielded itself again and again, but not to man's logical thinking; it has yielded itself only to man's subtle intuition.

59

"After long thought and observation I became aware of a second brain or gland, locked in the region of the heart, which commanded with authority. I discovered that most of the difficulties of life were the result of the head-brain attempting to do the work of the heart-brain. It was like a skilled laborer trying to assume the place of a high-powered engineer." (source unknown)

Cultivating, developing intuition

60

His first step is to detect the presence of the higher Power consciously in himself through vigilantly noting and cultivating the intuitions it gives him.

61

He must educate himself to recognize the first faint beginnings of "the intuitive mood" and train himself to drop everything else when its onset is noticed.

62

Intuitive feelings are so easily and hence so often drowned in the outer activity of the body, the passions, the emotions, or the intellect, that only a deliberate cultivation can safeguard and strengthen them.

63

We may ardently want to do what is wholly right and yet not know just what this is. This is particularly possible and likely when confronted with two roads and when upon the choice between them the gravest consequences will follow. It is then that the mind easily becomes hesitant and indecisive. The search for the wisest choice may not end that day or that month. Indeed, it may not end until the last hour of the last day. This is how the aspirants are tested to see if they can humble the ego with the realization that they are no longer capable of making their own decision but must turn it over to the higher self and wait in quiet patience for the result. But when finally the intuitive guidance does emerge after such deep, sincere, and obedient quest of God's will, it will do so in a formulation so clear and self-evident as to be beyond all doubt.

64

He has to bring his problems and lay them at the feet of the higher self and wait in patience until an intuitive response does come. But this is not to say that he has to lay them before his timid fears or eager wishes. The first step is to take them out of the hold of the anxious fretting intellect or the blind egoistic emotional self.

65

One of the first steps is to watch out for those infrequent moments when deeply intuitive guidance, thoughts, or reflections make their unexpected appearance. As soon as they are detected, all other mental activities should be thrown aside, all physical ones should be temporarily stilled, and he should sink himself in them with the utmost concentration. Even if he falls into a kind of daze as a result, it will be a happy and fortunate event, possibly a glimpse.

66

The secret is to stop, on the instant, whatever he is doing just then, or even whatever he is saying, and reorient all his attention to the incoming intuition. The incompleted act, the broken sentence, should be deserted, for this is an exercise in evaluation.(P)

67

The whole of this quest is really a struggle towards a conception of life reflecting the supreme values. Hence throughout its course the aspirant will feel vague intuitions which he cannot formulate. Only a master can do that.

68

It is better to wait, if intuition is not at once apparent, till all favourable facts are found and till full knowledge is gained of the unfavourable ones before deciding an issue.

69

The intuition grows by use of it and obedience to it.

70

The intuitive faculty can be deliberately cultivated and consciously trained.(P)

71

Intuitive guidance comes not necessarily when we seek it, but when the occasion calls for it. It does not usually come until it is actually needed. The intellect, as part of the ego, will often seek it in advance of the occasion because it may be driven by anxiety, fear, desire, or anticipation. Such premature seeking is fruitless.(P)

72

When one has reviewed a problem from all its angles, and has done this not only with the keenest powers of the mind but also with the finest qualities of the heart, it should be turned over at the end to the Overself and dismissed. The technique of doing so is simple. It consists of being still. In the moment of letting the problem fall away, one triumphs over the ego. This is a form of meditation. In the earlier stage it is an acknowledgment of helplessness and weakness in handling the problem, of personal limitations, followed by a surrender of it (and of oneself) to the Overself in the last resort. One can do no more. Further thought would be futile. At this point Grace may enter and do what the ego cannot do. It may present guidance either then, or at some later date, in the form of a self-evident idea.(P)

73

The commonest error is to try to produce and manufacture intuition. That can't be done. It is something which comes to you. Hence don't expect it to appear when concentrating on a problem, but if at all *after* you've dismissed the problem. Even then it is a matter of grace—it may or may not come.(P)

74

He must watch vigilantly for the impulses of self-interest which interfere with the truth of intuitions or reflections.

75

We must be ready to fly in the face of worldly wisdom if our inner mentor so bids it. We shall not rue the day we acted so.

76

The giving up of all earthly desires, the liberation of the heart from all animal passions, the letting go of all egoistic grasping—these attitudes will arise spontaneously and grow naturally if a man is truly quest-minded, so that his intuition will assert itself little by little.

77

Often intuition does not advise him until the time for an action or a decision or a move is nearly at hand. So he must wait patiently until it does and not let intellect or imagination construct fanciful plans which may be cancelled by intuition's arisal.

78

Will he be willing to follow its lead if it bears him in a contrary direction to the one he thought it ought or would do?

79

Without this constant listening for intuitive guidance, and submission to it, we waste much time putting right the mistakes made or curing the sickness which could have been prevented or bemoaning the calamity which willpower could have averted. None of these are God's will, but our own causation.

80

Being guided intuitively does not mean that every problem will be solved instantly as soon as it appears. Some solutions will not come into consciousness until almost the very last minute before they are actually needed. He learns to be patient, to let the higher power take its own course.

81

"We can thank intuition for many of the inventions that surround us every day," said C.G. Suits, General Electric Company's chief of research. "I know that intuition has invariably set me on the right track. My hunches come to me most frequently in bed, in a plane, or while staring out of a pullman window. . . . When a problem really has me stumped I'm apt to write down all the details as far as I can go, then put it aside to cool for forty-eight hours. At the end of that time I often find it's solved itself. . . . In any case, the most interesting sensations are the elation that accompanies the hunch and the feeling of certainty it inspires that the solution which has been glimpsed is right. Learn to relax. Intuition can't operate when your conscious mind is tied up in knots. Among the best ways to relax are hobbies, provided they are not taken too seriously."

82

These intrusions from a realm beyond conscious thinking may be heavenly ones. If so, to resist them would be to lose much and to accept them would be to gain much. But they have to be caught on the wing. Their delicate beginnings must be recognized for what they are—precious guides.

83

The more he follows this intuitive leading the more he not only learns to trust it but also develops future response to it.

84

It is a loss, and a grave one, to let himself remain torpid to intuitive feeling so much of the time, while alert and alive to every lesser and lower feeling.

85

There are times, however, when, in a hard problem, reason will come into conflict with intuition but when the latter is so overwhelmingly strong that it seems he must perforce yield to it. In that case he should do so. Time alone can show the truth of such a matter. Let him therefore not fall into the peril of dogmatizing about it. Let him rather withhold judgement and await its issue patiently.

86

Intuition does not always flash suddenly out of the depths of the mind into consciousness: quite often it forms itself very slowly over a period of hours, days, or even weeks.

87

Who hears this quiet whisper of intuition? Who, hearing, obeys? Not only is it mostly unnoticed but its guidance is also unsought; men prefer, and follow, the ego's direction.

88

It begins as an uncertain and intermittent feeling: it ends as a definite and persistent intuition.

89

If men followed their intuition more there would be fewer tragedies that could have been prevented or regrets that could have been avoided.

90

The student should make his own research and observation on the need of accepting first intuitive impressions as being the best guidance.

91

The unregarded feeling which first comes when an object, a person, or an event confronts one is mostly the correct intuition about it. But it must be caught on the wing or it will be gone.

92

If we understood this capacity to receive first impressions better, we should value them accordingly.

93

The subtlety and depth of his intuitions will increase with quickness, readiness, and obedience of his response to them.

94

Intuition must be caught quickly and inspiration must be followed up at once if they are to remain and not vanish away.

95

If we respectfully meet each intuitive feeling and give it our trusting collaboration, it will little by little become a frequent visitor.

96

First, we have to become *willing* to receive these divine intuitions.

97

These intuitive feelings do not respond to direct frontal demands for their appearance. They must be gently coaxed out of their deeper levels where they reside, quietly lured out of their shy seclusion.

98

To open ourselves and receive an intuition we must surrender the ego and submit the intellect to it.

99

If he is to interpret it aright and not miss its importance, he should let himself go when he feels this inner prompting. Let it absorb his being, draw him inwards to a deepening sense of its self.

100

The deeper mind is so close to the source of our karma that we may at times get its right guidance not only intuitively from within but also circumstantially from without.

101

The interval between the coming and the going of an intuitive thought is so short that he must immediately and alertly respond to it. If he misses it, he will find that the mind can go back to it only with difficulty and uncertainty.

102

We can receive a new truth more easily in the mind's quietude than in the mind's agitation. When thinking is stilled, intuiting begins. Such internal silence is not useless idleness, it is creative experience.

103

The Overself may use some event, some person, or some book as a messenger to him. It may make any new circumstance act in the same way. But he must have the capacity to recognize what is happening and the willingness to receive the message.

104

To *let* the intuitive feelings come through requires an inner passivity which meditation fosters but which extroversion inhibits.

105

Submit yourself as an empty vessel to be filled with the intuitive leading of Overself. Do not stop short of this goal, do not be satisfied with a half-and-half sort of life.

106

The intuition first presents itself to us as a fine delicate filament which we must treat tenderly if we do not wish to lose it.

107

His need is to recognize these half-formed intuitions for what they are, to rescue them from their vagueness, develop, nurture, and formulate them.

108

When this first faint intrusion is sensed, the need is for utter relaxation, for becoming passive and yielding. Only so can the aspirant follow intuitive prompting more and more inwards until it becomes stronger and stronger, clearer and clearer.

109

His early development of intuition is largely a matter of confused and uncertain impressions.

110

When seeking intuitional light upon a subject, the aspirant is advised to put his body in a recumbent position. This, passive as it is, will correlate with the passivity of mind that he should cultivate at such a time.

111

Because an intuitive feeling is usually soft and delicate where egoistic ones are often strong and passionate, it is too many times not recognized for what it is, until someone else formulates it and offers it from outside, as a statement of truth or a suggestion for action.

112

An intuition which is vague and weak in the beginning may become clear and certain in the end—if allowed to grow.

113

With this beginning of the momentary "catch" in attention, he must follow by waiting with much patience, listening inwardly all the while.

114

Have faith in your inner promptings and accept their guidance. When you are uncertain about them, wait and they will gradually clarify themselves.

115

He is to defend himself against false intuitions, not only by silencing wishful thoughts, but also by purifying the personal emotions.

116

They are messages brought from the infinite for the blessing and guidance of finite man. But he must recognize their value and esteem their source.

117

Often he will not respond and allow an intuition to form itself within his mind, because he does not immediately realize what is happening, does not feel a birth is beginning.

118

In the search for guidance when we have to make a momentous decision, or take an important step, it is well to go into the "Silence" with our problem. We may not get the answer quickly or even directly but if we are well experienced in this kind of seeking, a light may eventually emerge from the dark and shine down on the problem.

119

He should not form a preconception of what the answer ought to be, for thereby he imposes the ego's dubious solution in advance upon the higher mind's. Instead he should be entirely unbiased and try to receive the answer, as well as respond to it, in a perfectly free way.

120

What is sometimes so hard to do is to trust this intuitive monitor when it contradicts the voices of those who are monitorless. But in the end he will discover by results that this is practical wisdom.

121

Sometimes an intuition appears as a vague feeling which haunts a man and which he cannot shake off.

122

If he firmly believes in his own hidden intuitive powers, he will be able to ascribe much of his success to his readiness to follow their guidance, despite the opposition of logic and circumstances.

123

When we keep ourselves busy with everything external and our minds with thoughts about everything external, the intuition is unable to insert itself into our awareness. Even if it whispers to us, we will not realize what is happening. If we continue to ignore it, we may lose the capacity to hear it at all. It is then that we have to retrain ourselves to do so. The practice of meditation is one such way of training our receptivity.

124

The source of intuitive knowledge lies outside the conscious mind. The vehicle which conveys that knowledge need not necessarily be within us. It may be without us, in the form of a book, a person, or an event to which we are led, guided, or prompted.

125

We blunder in life and make endless mistakes because we have no time to listen for the Overself's voice—Intuition.

126

A change of attitude towards his problems may help to clear the way for intuition to operate on the conscious level. These inner promptings—when authentic and not ego-biased, and when double-checked by reason—can guide him to wiser decisions concerning both outward work and inner life.

127

If we would heed our intuitions as much as we heed our desires, the trick would be done. Illumination would come in not too long a time.

128

Alexander Graham Bell, inventor of the telephone: "Of course, it will be a little thing, but do not ignore it. Follow it up, explore all around it; one discovery will lead to another, and before you know it you will have something worth thinking about to occupy your mind. All really big discoveries are the results of thought."

129

In trying to get an intuitive answer, it is important to formulate the problem or the questions clearly and as sharply as you can.

130

Let him wait tranquilly for the intuitive feeling to warm and enlighten him, as flowers wait tranquilly for the morning sun to warm them.

131

We leave the word to go away to the thought (which the mind does almost at once) but we ought to leave a wordless intuitive feeling only to go deeper into it.

132

Again and again his thoughts should return to whatever memorable experience brought him an intuitive feeling that he was on the right track, or to whatever sudden lighted understanding of mentalism flashed into his head after study or reflection.

133

If he feels the intuition but does not attend to it then, however slightly, the very faculty which produced it begins to lose strength. This is the penalty imposed for the failure, and this shows how serious it is.

134

If he is always alert for this intuitive feeling, he will throw aside whatever he is doing and meditate upon it at once. He will depend more and more on these casual exercises, in contrast to the dependence on fixed routine exercises in the Long Path.

135

Treasure every moment when the intuition makes itself felt and, most especially, when it takes the form of a glimpse into higher truth; it is then that other things should be well put aside in order to sustain and prolong the experience.

136

If his own scepticism, sensualism, or materialism does not offer too hard a resistance, the intuition which is working its way to formulation, expression, and understanding may finally gain acceptance. This opens a new cycle for him.

137

If only he heeds its intuitive message, the higher self will not fail him. He will make his way to true balanced sanity and deep inner calm. Without searching for others, knowing that in himself God's representative resides and that this can give the right kind of help, he will depend for self-reliance on an ever-presence.

138

If one cultivates sufficient faith, out of the cosmic mind will come the response to his aspirations and, eventually, the answers to his questions. To receive this, one must learn to keep a constant vigil for intuitive feelings and messages of the most delicate nature, and to trust his inner promptings. His attention should always have God at its centre.

139

By constant prayer and aspiration to his higher self, the student will get intuitive promptings from time to time. He should catch them when they appear and yield himself to them: in this way he will get the necessary guidance from within.

140

Once you learn to recognize the intuitive voice, follow its dictates; do not hesitate to conform with them or try to make up an excuse for failing to do so if the guidance is unpalatable.

141

If the seeker will heed this intuitive feeling it may lead him to a clue, a thread by holding which he may grope his way to clearer and stronger feeling until it becomes a certainty.

142

Whatever be the personal problem, if reason, experience, and authority cannot solve it, carry it inwards to the deep still centre. But you must learn to wait in patience for the answer, for the blockage is in you, not in it. A day or a month may pass until the response is felt, thought, or materialized.

143

There is a feeling of sacredness, of holy peace at such moments, and they should be cherished for the precious moments that they are. They contain hints of the communion with the Higher Self, elements of something beyond the ordinary self, and possibilities of transcending the past with its debris of memories and mistakes.

144

In every important move he will seek guidance from the intuitive levels of being as well as from the intellectual.

145

These messages are all formulated by the faculty of intuition. Hence their lofty tone. But the emotions, desires, and intellect—being on a lower level—ignore the message in practice and action. Hence, disobeyed, they bring suffering or disappointment.

146

Sometimes the intuitive bidding of Overself will be in favour of his own private interests but sometimes it will be at variance with them.

147

Where the wakeful consciousness is not easily reached owing to its preoccupations, then the dream consciousness will be more receptive to the message.

148

Sometimes an intuition does not stay behind. It flashes through consciousness for a small fraction of a second and is gone. Unless it is detected and recognized during this quick passage while it is still fresh, we are hardly likely to do so afterwards.

149

Amid the toils and agitations of everyday living, through all the boiler pressure of crisis events, such intuitions can gain entry only with difficulty. Yet we need their help and solace more than we know: we need their stimulus to enkindle fresh hope and more faith.

150

Either a man possesses this intuitive sense or he does not. It cannot be created by argument or analysis.

151

They betray the higher part of themselves every time they resist, reject, or merely ignore the intuitive feelings which come so delicately into consciousness.

152

In the seeming self's activity, personal willpower is used and personal effort is made. In the Overself's activity, both these signs are absent. Instead there is a passive receptivity to its voice—intuitions—and obedience to its guidance.

153

The intuitive feeling or the seminal idea may be planted in a man's heart today but it may need twenty to thirty years before it comes to sufficient growth in his conscious mind.

154

When the inner voice says what we do not like to hear, we are apt to ignore it.

155

In its first manifestation, an intuitive idea is too often such a tiny spark that we are more likely to miss it than not.

156

It is more prudent to obey warning premonitions than to ignore them.

157

Take time over problems, let your final decisions wait until they are fully ripe.

158

Where is the wisdom in forcing a quick decision, which could easily be a wrong one, merely to get a decision at all?

159

Intuition is the voice which is constantly calling him to this higher state. But if he seldom or never pauses amid the press of activity to listen for it, he fails to benefit by it.

160

Such intuitions manifest themselves only on the fringe of consciousness. They are tender shoots and therefore need to be tenderly nurtured.

161

The more he follows a course contrary to intuitive leading, the more will errors and mishaps follow him.

162

These feelings may be cultivated as a gardener cultivates flowers. Their visitation may be brought on again, their delight renewed.

163

In the end he will rely on this little inner voice which, if he listens humbly, speaks and tells him which way to turn.

164

Do not deny your intuitive self as Judas denied his master, as Peter denied him.

165

"There is also his subconscious mind, his brilliant and seemingly effortless hunches. His judgements come forth spontaneously like lightning, with no supporting brief of argument. He follows his own subconscious with blind faith but insists that to have a hunch, you must first have all the facts at your command, and your intelligence must be working at full speed. Then suddenly and without conscious effort you think of a solution which is really based on facts, but is not achieved by deliberate cerebrations. With it comes an unexampled feeling of well-being."—author unknown

166

He will learn sooner or later by the test of experience to defer to this intuitive feeling whenever its judgement, guidance, or warning manifests itself.

167

Edison said that all his inventions grew out of initial flashes which welled up from within. The rest was a matter of research.

168

The intuitive element has to be awaited with much patience and vigilant attention.

169

Is he fully open to intuitive feelings that originate in his deeper being, his sacred self? Or does his ego get in the way by its rigidities, habits, and tendencies? The importance of these feelings is that they are threadlike clues which need following up, for they can lead him to a blessed renewal or revelation.

170

The capacity to respond to spiritual intuitions is latent in all men but trained and developed in few men.

171

From this hidden source comes at times guidance, warnings, attractions, or aversions which ought to be construed as intuitive messages. But for this they must first be recognized and believed: they pass too quickly.

172

It is not that he puts out the antenna of his intuition, so much as that he insulates its ends and thus provides clear receptivity.

173

We may not forecast how quickly or how well every student will progress in this art. For one may naturally possess much sensitivity but another may possess little. And even when an intuition is recognized immediately, the will may respond to it very slowly.

174

It is true that conscience is the voice of the Overself in the moral life of man, but it is also true that he seldom hears its pure sound. Most often he hears it mixed with much egotism.

175

The suppositions and anticipations, the attractions and repulsions of the ego enter into its intuitive experiences and impede or change them.

176

Most inner guidance is rarely purely intuitive but more often a mixture of genuine intuition with wishful thinking. Hence it is right in parts and wrong in others.

177

The original intuition itself may be a correct one but its reception is so inexpert and so biased that the version accepted in consciousness has deformed and somewhat falsified it.

178

The intuitive is so fine and sensitive a faculty that the emanations of another mind may well disturb its activity or distort its truth.

179

The intuitive approach is the most effective of all, provided it is not clouded by suggestion from outside sources or blurred by bias from inside ones.

180

Before a man complains that he is unable to get intuition, he should remember that his own moral fault may be responsible for this. It can prevent him not only from receiving true intuitions but also from responding to them in action.

181

Amid the general rush of today's events it is easy to miss an intuitive feeling.

182

Nor when the answer first comes, may we understand it aright. We may mix it up with our own ideas or wishes, our own expectations or fancies, and the result will be that the help received will not work out quite as it should have done. We may have to spend further years straightening out the message and, incidentally, ourselves. But again, it is worth doing and nothing else is so much worth doing.

183

He will come to find that the guidance he receives is perfect but his reception of it may still be imperfect.

184

The genuine intuition gets mixed up with guesses and speculations about the matter, with reasonings and ruminations about it.

185

His intuition is unavoidably conditioned by his own personality, inevitably shaped as it is because he is the kind of man he is.

186

It is not only his wishes and hopes which interfere with correct receptivity to intuition but also his fears and suspicions.

187

His normal everyday mind is slow to heed the Higher Power and confused in interpretation of the prompting received.

188

One whose mind is too sharply critical to be sensitive to finer mental radiations may fail to recognize the inner happening. This may be because he himself is not sufficiently in tune with the high frequency represented by Overself, or it may be because he is too impatient and wants something which in his case can only be had with sufficient time.

189

When intuition points to something unwelcome to the ego, the intellect looks for and usually finds an excuse to reject it. A man who really and sincerely wants to find the Truth should be on the lookout for hints, clues, and signs which would be useful to his Quest, for they constitute the response from the Overself to his aspiration. The Overself can furnish him with the Truth and puts these signals in his way.

Intuition and pseudo-intuition

190

No counsel could be safer and better than that which proceeds from a man to himself by way of intuition. But first let him be sure that it *is* intuition.

191

Intuition carries its own assurance with it. Those skilled, proficient, and accustomed to it, who are able to recognize the authentic signs, can safely accept and trust themselves to it. But the beginner and the inexperienced need to check and test it, lest they are led astray by some impostor posing as the real thing or by some impulse sincerely presuming itself to be the real thing.

192

To accept the ever-rightness of these intuitions is one thing; to separate them from their imitators is another.

193

Intuition will not mislead you but your conscious mentality, which is its receiving agent, may do so. For your consciousness may partially deviate from its message, or even wholly pervert it, in giving deliverance to exaggerations or extravagances, impossibilities or delusions, thus filling you with useless hopes or groundless fears. Consequently, at the very time when you suppose that you are being infallibly guided by intuition you may in fact be strongly guided by pseudo-intuition—which is something quite different. You may believe that you are honouring higher guidance when in actuality you are dishonouring it. The situation is therefore much less simple and much more complex than most people know. To get intuitive direction when, for example, two or more conflicting courses of action confront you is not so easy as it seems and less easy still during a time of trouble. For during such a time you will naturally catch at anything already unknowingly or knowingly pre-determined by some complex to be the best way out of it. The very desire for a particular thing, event, or action may put a pseudo-intuition into your mind. If you want to be wary of this you should seek corroboration from other sources and especially from right reason. Again, the first thought which enters your consciousness after you have decided to seek such direction and have committed your affair to the deeper mind, is not necessarily an authentic intuition. Nor is the second thought such a one, nor the third, and so on. If the impression is to be rightly received, it must be patiently received, and that quite often means that you must sleep on it, and sleep on it perhaps for several days, sometimes weeks. The trustworthy intuition is really there during all this time but the obstacles to knowing it are also there in yourself. Do not, therefore, lose the inner direction through haste nor set up a stone image to be worshipped by mistake in its place. Nor is it enough to say that intuitive truths are self-evident ones. What appeared to be self-evident to you twenty years ago may now appear self-delusive to you. Edit your intuitions with your reason.

194

All men at some time or other receive intuitive suggestions from within, whilst a few men receive them constantly. It is not therefore that intuition is such a rare and extraordinary manifestation. What is rare and extraordinary is its pure reception, its correct comprehension. For on the one hand we receive along with an intuition the suggestions of environment, education, heredity, and self-interest no less than the distortions of desire, fear, and hope, while on the other hand we receive the doubts and questionings of reason. Even if we correct the suggestions and adjust the distortions of the first group, we remain uncertain and unclear because reason naturally wants to know *why?* It wants to *understand* why an intuitive prompting should be accepted. And by the very nature of an intuition it is often something which neither past experience nor present logic can justify. This is not only because all the facts of the case are not at our command but, because of their endless ramifications or superphysical character, cannot possibly be at our command. These are some of the difficulties which confront man at his present stage of evolution and which render so many so-called intuitions unreliable or undependable even though their original birth was genuinely what it claimed to be. What is the remedy? Only careful, ruthless, and impartial analysis of each and every intuition, constant vigilance over and checking of the results which ensue when they are accepted, and long self-training through several years can finally bring us to the clear recognition of what is or is not authentic intuitive guidance, suggestion, or information.

195

He would not be so bad a judge of value as to prefer reason over intuition, whenever he had the absolute certainty that it *was* intuition. But past experience has shown how difficult it is to arrive at such certitudes, how deceptive are the masks which impulse, desire, rashness, and selfishness can assume. Until, therefore, his development has reached the point where a genuine intuition is at once recognized as such and a pseudo-intuition quickly detected for what it is, he must not abandon the use of reason but rather regard it as a most valuable ally.

196

How can he tell if inner guidance is truly intuitive or merely pseudo-intuitive? One of the ways is to consider whether it tends to the benefit of all concerned in a situation, the others as well as oneself. The word "benefit" here must be understood in a large way, must include the spiritual result along with the material one. If the guidance does not yield this result, it may be ego-prompted and will then hold the possibility of error.(P)

197

An intuitive feeling is one untainted by the ego's wishes, uncoloured by its aversions.(P)

198

Wrong personal intention may be negated by right intuitive guidance, but it is not easy to recognize the latter as such. The difference between a mere impulse and a real intuition may often be detected in two ways: first, by waiting a few days, as the subconscious mind has then a chance to offer help in deciding the matter; second, by noting the kind of emotion which accompanies the message. If the emotion is of the lower kind, such as anger, indignation, greed, or lust, it is most likely an impulse. If of the higher kind, such as unselfishness or forgiveness, it is most likely an intuition.(P)

199

You may recognize the voice of wisdom when having to make a decision by the fact that it proceeds out of deep inner calm, out of utter tranquillity, whereas impulse is frequently born in exaggerated enthusiasm or undue excitement.(P)

200

A compelling inner conviction or intuition need not necessarily collide with cold reason. But as an assumed intuition which may be merely a bit of wishful thinking or emotional bias, it is always needful to check or confirm or discipline it by reasoning. The two can work together, even whilst recognizing and accepting each other's peculiar characteristics and different methods of approach. Hence all intuitively formed projects and plans should be examined under this duplex light. The contribution of fact by reason should be candidly and calmly brought up against the contribution of inward rightness made by "intuition." We must not hesitate to scrap intuitively formed plans if they prove unworkable or unreasonable.(P)

201

The promptings that come from this inner being are so faintly heard at first, however strong on their own plane, that we tend to disregard them as trivial. This is the tragedy of man. The voices that so often mislead him into pain-bringing courses—his passion, his ego, and blind intellect—are loud and clamant. The whisper that guides him aright and to God is timid and soft.(P)

202

So subtle is the oncoming and so mysterious is the working of the true intuition, so open and blatant is the fantasy that is false intuition, that the first test of authenticity is indicated here.(P)

203

The corrective separation of true from false intuitions, and of impersonal from personal impressions, follows a careful disciplining of the consciousness and a cautious vigilance over the feelings.

204

He can learn with time, and from the visible results it always brings, a better estimate of the truth or falsity of these impressions and intuitions. When the results injure him, he may know that the acceptance of that which led to them was an error; a careful study of such errors will point the way to their avoidance in the future.

205

The intuitive consciousness eludes common sense at some times but aligns with it at other times.

206

The day will come when constant effort and long practice will permit him to recognize true from pseudo-intuition with the speed and certainty with which a musically trained ear recognizes notes and times (tunes) in a played piece.

207

When a strong intuitive feeling contradicts—much more if it nearly swallows up—a conventional sense-impression, it is wise to become alert and reconsider the report.

208

Intuition is always sure of itself, but few persons are always sure whether what they feel is actually intuition or not. They may test it against reasoned analysis.

209

It is not surprising that after the Hitler fiasco thoughtful minds which were once prone to believe sincerely in the existence of such a faculty as intuition and willing to accept its revelations, as made by others, found their confidence in it gravely shaken. We ventured to point out that egoistic emotions and unconscious complexes frequently masquerade as mystical intuitions, that criticism should be directed solely against such pseudo-intuitions and should not be casting doubts upon the existence of genuine intuition itself.

210

It is admittedly hard to distinguish intuition from its counterfeits, but one way to do so is that it often opposes personal emotions. Thus we may feel strongly and naturally prejudiced against a certain course of action yet a gentler feeling may be in its favour.

211

If it is authentic intuition, he will feel increasingly convinced by it as days and weeks pass until in the end its truth will seem unarguable to him.

212

When his self-training and checked experience have gone far enough, the doubts and uncertainties regarding these intuitive feelings will vanish. By that time, they will appear in his consciousness as peculiar and unmistakable.

213

What intuition reveals the deepest thought confirms.

214

The notion that the Overself's voice is necessarily accompanied by occult phenomena or heard clairaudiently inside oneself is a very limited one. It may be totally unaccompanied by anything strange or, as if it were conscience, felt rather than heard. Or it may speak to one indirectly through any other person or any circumstantial event that touches one's path.

215

The passing of time will either disprove his judgements or prove them correct. He ought to note carefully this eventual result and compare it with the feelings which possessed him at the time of making his original decisions. In this way he can learn to see for himself the difference between the marks of a true intuition and those of a false one.

216

An intuition comes into the mind suddenly. But so does an impulse. Therefore it is not enough to take this mark alone to identify it. It is strong; so is an impulse. It is clear; so is an impulse. To separate the deceptive appearance from the genuine reality of an intuition, look for the trail of assurance, relief, and peace to follow in its wake.

217

It is never present without certain qualities being present with it, too. There is first an utter serenity, then a steady joy, next an absolute conviction of its truth and reality, finally the paradoxical feeling of a rock-firm security despite any appearance of adverse outer circumstances.

218

The process is partly an unconscious one, they know, because something is being done to them by this higher power. They cannot exactly define why they must accept its truth, but its mental effect is almost hypnotic. It is an intuition which is self-supporting, which must be accepted upon its own mysterious authority. Nor do they accept it because of its inherent strength alone. They accept it also because of its inherent beauty.

219

Intuitive feelings hover in him, half-guessed at, half-doubted: he does not know what to accept, what to reject, because he does not feel certain whether they are mere ordinary thoughts or authentic messages from heaven.

220

If it be asked how to prevent oneself from being deceived by these pseudo-intuitions, it can be said that a useful rule is to check them against other sources on the same subject and see if they all harmonize. If, for example, fifty inspired men who have written on the subject teach what contradicts the alleged intuition, then there is something wrong on one side or the other and careful investigation is called for. It is always safer to ascertain what the great scriptural texts or the classic mystical testaments have to tell on the matter and not depend solely on what one's intuition tells.

221

There are four chief ways in which guidance may be given. They are: intuitive feeling, giving in a general way approbation or rejection of a proposed course of action; direct and precise inner message; the shaping of outer circumstances; and the teaching of inspired texts. If all four exist together, and if they all harmonize, then you may step forward in the fullest assurance. But if there are contradictions between them, then great caution and some delay is certainly advisable.

222

It is also needful to remember that the higher self can only be known by the higher part of the mind, that is, the intuition. The emotions are on a lesser and lower level, however noble or religious they may be. The immense satisfaction which the ecstatic raptures give is no indication that he is directly touching reality, but only that he is coming closer to it. They may seem purely spiritual, but they still belong to the ego's feeling nature and if he believes otherwise he will fall into self-deception. Only through the pure intuition, freed from emotional egoism and transcending intellectual illusion, can he really make a contact with the Overself. And that will happen in a state of utter and perfect tranquillity; there will be none of the emotional excitement which marked the successful practice of the earlier stage of meditation exercises.

223

When the deliverance of intuition cancels the deliverance of reason, he may trust himself to the first, but only when he is sure it is what it purports to be.

224

When he finds some of his own intuitions formulated and printed in someone else's book, he feels their truth is confirmed and his own mind comforted.

225

He has the right to judge an intuition rationally before submitting to it, but what if his judgement is itself wrong?

226

Intuition may support reason but must supplant it only on the gravest occasions.

227

The sudden revelation of correct understanding, whether in certain situations or about uncertain problems, may come unexpectedly or abruptly anytime during the day. It springs up of its own accord or it appears in a dream as a message.

228

If the intuitive feeling leads him gently at some times, it also leads him firmly at other times.

229

An intuition is directly self-revealing; it does not depend on what kind of thought and study were done before it appeared. It is also self-evident: the correctness of the guidance given or information imparted becomes obvious and doubt-dispelling.

230

A truth is intuitively discerned when it is so lit up that it appears perfectly self-evident, when the receiving consciousness is very calm, and when the lapse of time tends to strengthen its authority.

231

The intuitive answer may come in one of several ways, but the commonest is either a self-evident thought or a deep heartfelt feeling.

232

It is a truth so plainly self-evident that he cannot help thinking it. This is how intuition usually appears and is usually recognized for what it is.

233

Develop theme that another sign to recognize intuitions is their unexpectedness.

234

The mysterious appearance of an intuition may well make us ask where it comes from. At one moment it is not there; at the next it is lodged in the mind.

235

Sometimes we are wiser than we know and utter involuntary answers which surprise us with their unexpected wisdom or unknown Truth. This is one way intuitions are born.

236

Because it comes from within, it comes with its own authority. When it is "the real thing," the seeker will not have to question examine or verify its authenticity, will not have to run to others for their appraisal of its worth or its rejection as a pseudo-intuition. He will know overwhelmingly what it is in the same way that he knows who he is.

237

Education and experience alone do not make the mind; there is something higher that mixes itself in now and again with disconcerting incomprehensible spontaneity.

238

One reason why an intuition is so often missed is that it flashes into the mind as disjointedly, as abruptly, and as inconsequentially as a person or a thing sometimes comes momentarily into the field of vision through the corner of an eye.

239

The marks of an authentic intuition include conclusiveness and finality.

240

When a man hesitates too long over taking a course which intuition tells him he should take, and in which his higher life is concerned, it may be that destiny will intervene and make him suddenly realize that this *is* the way, and that all doubts should be thrown out.

241

An intuition may be sudden and unexpected, quite contrary to the line of previous thought about the matter. This is certainly true of many appearances but it is not true of other ones.

242

An intuition may come into the mind apparently by hazard, unsummoned, unexpected.

243

Every thought which comes down to us from that serene height comes with a divine authority and penetrating force which are absent from all other thoughts. We receive the visitant with eagerness and obey it with confidence.

Let intuition rule

244

Intuition is not the equal but rather the superior of all other human faculties. It delivers the gentlest of whispers, commands from the Overself, whereas the other faculties merely carry them out. It is the master, they are the servants. The intellect thinks, the will works, and the emotion drives towards the fulfilment of intuitively felt guidance in the properly developed spiritually erect man.

245

The philosopher is simultaneously a thinker and a believer, but his ruling role is neither. It is that of an intuitionist.

246

The intuition must lead all the rest of man's faculties. He must follow it even when they do not agree with its guidance. For it sees farther than they ever can, being an efflux from the godlike part of himself which is in its way a portion of the universal deity. If he can be sure that it is not pseudo-intuition, truth in it will lead him to life's best, whether spiritual or worldly.

247

The man who is not thrown off his balance is the man who lets intuition rule all his other functions.

248

The passage in time before his intellect will yield and acknowledge the rightness of what his intuition told him about a person at their first meeting, may be a long one.

249

He will have to maintain his loyalty to the intuition against the cautions, the excessive prudence, of a frightened intellect.

250

In the fully trained philosopher, intuition is the most active faculty.

251

The intuition is to collate all these different functions of the personality, and direct them towards its truest welfare.

252

A man is really free when his intuition directs his intellect and rules his energies.

253

The verdict of intuition may be vindicated by time but he cannot always afford to wait for it.

254

Feeling is as much a part of true insight into the Real as knowing. It gives life to the end result. It is evoked by enlightened writings and inspired art works. Thinking may not rightly claim overlordship here, but intuition, the silent voice of the Overself, may do so.

255

Here, just on the very frontiers of wakeful consciousness, amidst daydreams and intuitions, thoughts and premonitions, lies hidden treasure. It is precisely in this inward region which ordinary men dismiss as worthless, unreal, and false that the mystic finds worth, reality, and truth.

Fruits of living intuitively

256

There is an inner light in all people which could, with time, convert their perplexed questionings into solid certitudes. There is this remarkable fact that hard problems which the unaided intellect cannot solve, gnawing anxieties upon which our past experiences throw no helpful light, may become illumined and solved with ease if we adopt this practical method of applying intuition to them. Among all the varied powers of the mind, a properly unfolded intuition is indeed one of the most priceless anyone could have. It always warns against wrong courses and often counsels the right ones. "I sometimes have a feeling, in fact I have it very strongly, a feeling of interference . . . that some guiding hand has interfered," confessed Winston Churchill in a speech during October, 1942. On the other hand, intuition may help us and allay our fears where reason alone merely increases them.

257

The intuitively governed mind is the undivided mind. It does not have to choose between contrasts or accept one of two alternatives. It does not suffer from the double-facedness of being swayed this way or that by conflicting evidence, contradictory emotions, or hesitant judgements.

258

However bitter a situation may appear, the accepted prompting of the Overself can bring sweetness into it; however trying it may be, the same prompting can bring fortitude into it.

259

The man who has trained himself to listen for the voice of intuition, which means trained himself to wait for it to speak and disciplined himself to be inwardly alert yet also inwardly quiet for it, does not have to suffer the painful conflicts and tormenting divisions which others do when confronted by issues demanding a choice or a decision.

260

He will find, if he accepts this intuitive leading, that although the unfavourable circumstances may remain the same, unchanged, his attitude towards them does not. Out of this inner change there will be given him the strength to deal with them, the calm to deal with them unmoved, and the wisdom to deal with them properly.

261

There is no single pattern that an intuitively guided life must follow. Sometimes he will see in a flash of insight both course and destination, but at other times he will see only the next step ahead and will have to keep an open mind both as to the second step and as to the final destination.(P)

262

One of the functions of intuition is to protect the body against unnecessary sickness by warning the man in it when he is transgressing the laws of its hygiene, or by showing the right road. In this, intuition is pitted against the body's past habits and animal appetites, the emotional nature's desires, as well as the mind's ignorance immaturity and inexperience—a combination of enemies which usually triumphs over it. Another of its functions is to protect the man against avoidable calamity or preventable loss, by consciously warning him of its impending existence or subconsciously moving him out of its reach. But here it has opposed to it the egoistic desires and habits or the emotional impulses and negative feelings which perceive only the immediate and not the impending, the semblance of things and not the actuality.

263

The intuitive life does not always know how or why it acts, for it is often spontaneous and unconscious. But when it does become at times intellectually self-conscious, its power in the world to affect men is heightened, not lessened.

264

Like Socrates we possess an inner warning voice which forbids certain courses of action but does not recommend better ones. It is negative and not positive.

265

Intuition—which Bergson called the surest road to truth—eradicates hesitancies. When you are in contact with the Overself in solving a problem, you receive a direct command what to do and you then *know* it is right. The clouds and hesitancies and vacillations which arise when struggling between contrary points of view, melt. Whereas, if you are not in contact with the Overself, but only being carried along through karma, then you swing back and forth with emotion or opinion.

266

He is indeed fortunate whose intuition shows itself in one impelling thought strong enough to outclass all other conflicting thoughts.

267

The uncomfortable feeling that something is wrong may combat the smooth plausible appearance of everything being right.

268

He can depend on one thing alone to show him the right roads and the right master. It is intuition.

269

A man's life will be less troubled and his happiness more secured, if his reason governs his body and his intuition governs his reason.

270

If a man acts according to intuitive wisdom, all will go well with him. This is not to say that he will be free from external misfortunes. But if they come, they will be of the unavoidable kind and therefore less in number than if they included those of his own direct making. And even the others will be turned to profit in some way by the search for their underlying meanings, so that although humanity calls them evil, he will nevertheless gain some inner good from them.

271

If he is sensitive enough and can touch the intuitive element within himself, either deliberately by sheer power of deeply introspective concentration or spontaneously by immediate acceptance of its suggestive messages, his decisions will be filled with utter conviction and followed with resolute determination.

272

He may be sure of this, that whatever action the Overself's leading causes him to take will always be for his ultimate good even though it may be to his immediate and apparent detriment.

273

There is the feeling of being led, but not the ability to see where, and to what, one is being led.

274

To the degree that the intuitive element can displace all others for the rulership of his inner life, to that degree can a healing and guiding calm displace the emotion of moods and commotion of thought.

275

The most satisfying proofs will come to him that the Overself is really guiding the course of his outer life and really inspiring the course of his inner life.

276

There will be decisions that he does not think out logically, moves that he does not plan calculatingly. Yet the sequence of further events will prove the one to be right, the other wise. For they will have come intuitively.

277

He may have no idea how to get out of his predicament. Yet suddenly he will make some unreasoned and unpremeditated act which will do this for him.

278

His best moves are mostly the unplanned ones.

279

He would be wise to do nothing drastic unless there is a clear and positive urge from the deepest part of being approving the deed.

280

Such efforts will eventually open the way for intuition to come into outer consciousness and, absorbing all lesser elements, give him the great blessing of its guidance.

Intuition and the Glimpse

281

Jesus likened the Kingdom of Heaven to a grain of mustard seed, which was a simile among the Jews for anything exceedingly small. Why did he do so? Because, in its first onset, the Kingdom is not an experience but an intuition—and the latter begins as an exceedingly faint and tiny leading.

282

Whereas we can reach the intellect only through thinking, we can reach the spirit only through intuition. The practice of meditation is simply the deepening, broadening, and strengthening of intuition. A mystical experience is simply a prolonged intuition.(P)

283

The prettily vague and poetically general statements of spiritual truth, the woolly, sentimental, or foggy revelations and communications, are heard or intuited only in the outer courts. When the neophyte approaches the central inner court, what he receives is very precise clear and exact. This is so until he reaches the inmost shrine, the holy of holies itself. Here, words must come to an end for here he must "Be still and know that I am God."

284

It is important that the feeling of "inward drawing" which comes to him at times be at once followed up, whenever possible, by a withdrawal from external affairs for a few minutes and a concentration on what the feeling leads to. This practice is like a thread which, if followed up, will lead to a cord, that to a rope, and so on. Thus he will benefit by the grace which is being shed upon him, and not turn away unheedingly. But the mind, at the beginning, leaves this intuitional plane all too quickly, so extreme vigilance is called for to bring it back there.

285

What is more private, more intimate, than intuition? It is the only means they possess wherefrom to start to get mystical experience, glimpses, true enlightenment. Yet they insist on seeking among those who stand outside them, among the teachers, for that which must be searched after and felt inside themselves.

286

The hierophant in the Mysteries of Isis told the aspirant at initiation: "In the dark hour that thou shalt find thy true self, follow him and he will be thy true self, follow him and he will be thy genius, for he holds the secret of thine existence."

287

The teaching that is most worthwhile comes directly from your own inner being, not from another's.

288

To develop these brief intuitions and bring them to maturity in lengthier moods, is his task.

289

That which guides him to the god within his own being, that slender thread of intuitive feeling and intelligence, may at first appear and disappear at intervals.

290

At first intuition is like a frail thread, almost impalpable, of which he is just faintly aware; but if he heeds it, rivets attention stubbornly to it, the visitations come more and more often. If he follows the thread to its source, the message becomes clearer, stronger, precise.

291

If you can attentively trace this subtle feeling back to its own root, you will get a reward immeasurably greater than it seemed to promise.

292

It is only by constant use that intuition can mature into mystical enlightenment.

293

If one learns to cultivate these brief intuitive moments aright, there can develop out of them in time mystical moods of much longer duration and much deeper intensity. Still later, there could come to maturity the ripe fruit of all these moods—an ecstatic experience wherein grace descends with life-changing results.

2

INSPIRATION

Turning to the meaning of that word "inspiration," what more can one say than that it is "in-breathing"—the in-breathing of a spiritual quality that raises a work or a person above the common order of things? I do not mean a work is inspired when it is cheaply glamorous, or that a man is inspired when he is rhetorically aggressive, or that a mind is inspired when it indulges in clever intellectual jugglery. It is my standpoint that all inspired art is the expression at most or a product at least of spiritual experience, although the latter may not be well understood by its experiencer. The experience must come first. Art is movement and noise, whereas the spirit out of which it arises is hushed stillness and invulnerable silence.

2

When the goddess Athena, in Greek mythology, says that "some things you will think of for yourself, and others a god will put into your heart," this is her way of describing what we, more simply, would call inspiration.

3

Only the direct experience of this exalted state will supply the sense of actuality and the feeling of vividness in spiritual writing.

4

When this exalted feeling is transferred to the intellect and there turned into thought, whether for expression in words for one's own understanding or for communication to others, it is termed a truth. In this form it becomes a source of renewed inspiration, a help in darker times, and a guide to live by in ordinary times.

5

Inspiration can come to any person. It is not reserved for artists and mystics alone.

6

When intuition expresses itself through, or enters into, the creative arts, we call it inspiration. The two are the same in root, but different in leaf.

7

It would be absurd to believe that the creative power of inspiration exhausts itself with the arts alone. It can appear in any and every kind of human activity, in the making of a home or of a decision.

8

It is the difference between real beauty and mere prettiness, between divine inspiration and practised competence, between a flower and the painting of it.

9

There is a hidden light within man himself. Sometimes its glow appears in his most beautiful art productions, his loftiest religious revelations, his most irreproachable moral decisions.

10

There are swift elusive moments which every real artist knows, and every deep lover experiences, when the faculty of concentration unites with the emotion of joy and creates an indescribable sense of balanced being. Such moments are of a mystical character.

11

None of us can play with the pen for some years, or wield the painter's brush, or practise any of the arts, without in time letting our minds dwell on the processes of inspiration. The mysteries of man's being must then necessarily occupy us. And if we dare to be truly frank in our facing of the self, if we will put aside preconceived notions and ready-made theories in order to watch what really happens during those processes, we discover our feet upon the verge of a great discovery. For we shall discover—if we are both patient enough and yet persistent enough—that there is a Source within us which promises astonishing possibilities to the human race. That Source is loosely called the soul.

12

That part of us that responds to truth and ideals is the best part.

13

Great importance is to be placed on the guidance to be got from what psychoanalysis calls the unconscious elements within man. How many a prominent orator's delivery during public speeches shows that when he speaks out of his head he is quite undistinguished and uninspiring, whereas when he speaks out of his heart, without previous preparation and under the sway of his innermost feeling, he strongly impresses and affects his audience.

14

It happens on a plane above men's heads; most of them don't know of it explicitly at the moment. Yet they are truly rendering service through being used as channels.

15

There are moods or periods when the ideas stream through his mind in swift succession or come in slow stately revelations.

16

What is true of the world's work is true also of the arts. The secret of inspired action is also the secret of inspired art. The temporary inspirations of the artist can become permanent, if he or she will take the divine path. Intermittent inspiration develops ultimately into continuous contact with the sublime, when genius discovers the mysterious source which inspires it.

17

He is as intensely alive in the spirit as most men are insensely alive in the flesh.

Its expression and development

18

What begins as a mysterious presence ends as a clear influence.

19

To the extent that we can keep and hold our awareness of this divine consciousness, we can also express something of its knowledge and power.

20

Once "tuned in," the longer you can stay with the Overself, the greater the depth penetrated; and this in turn means the more general benefit will be gained, the more creativity will be possible in ideas, in arts, and in intuitions.

21

The glimpse becomes the creative source, the inspirer, of his intellectual or aesthetic pursuits—if he is an artist or writer—or of his moral aspirations and conduct if he is not. First there is the turning-within and opening to that which is his finest being; then there is the reversal of direction, the turning-without and giving or serving his small or large world. This humanistic way is a grace for those whom it touches.

22

There are men who may be high in talent but low in character. Notice that I use the word talent. I can not believe that it is possible to possess true inspiration and yet deny it or fail to express it in one's conduct.(P)

23

Whatever talent of creative quality he brings to meditation could come out inspired, renewed, and exalted.

24

What he gets from these delectable inner meetings he tries to give the world in whatever way his situation allows, in an artistic creation or a simple smile, or otherwise.

25

To the extent that a man is conscious of the presence of the Overself, he becomes inspired. To the extent that he is also talented in any of the arts, his work also becomes inspired.(P)

26

If he feels this presence, and can do his work without deserting it, then his is a sacred function, no matter whether it be an artist's or an artisan's.(P)

27

Even while working in an office or factory or field, a man is not prevented from continuing his search for the inner mind. The notion that this quest requires aloofness from the commonplace utilitarian world is one which philosophy does not accept. Distraction and action are not so mutually inclusive as we may think. The student may train himself to maintain calm and serene poise even in the midst of strenuous activity, just as he also avails himself of the latest discoveries of scientific technique and yet keeps his mind capable of browsing through the oldest books of the Asiatic sages. He can discipline himself to returning from meditation to the turmoil, go anywhere, do anything, if truth is carried in the mind and poise in the heart. He may learn to live in reality at all times. The sense of its presence will need no constant renewal, no frequent slipping into trance, no intermittent escape from the world, if he follows the philosophic threefold path.(P)

28

It is not enough to obey and follow the prompting which draws him inward through formal meditation. It is equally needful to sustain spiritual activity through all the many hours of external business, to learn the art of not being of the world although in it, to achieve the wonderful state of inspired action.

29

The whole of life must be inspired, not merely action alone, not merely thinking alone, not merely feeling alone. Inspired living must be the keynote of the disciple's efforts.

30

He will carry its inspiration into all his activities. Every department of his life will be divinized.

31

If his inspiration is of the highest kind, it will be a fruitful one. It will manifest in external achievement by the personal ego and in altruistic service, enlightenment, and uplift of the world community in which he lives.

32

Those critics who assert that we have lost our mystical values because we teach that mystical contemplation is not an end in itself but rather a means to action, have not understood our teaching. The kind of action we refer to is not the ordinary one. It is something higher than that, wiser than that, nobler than that. It is everyday human life divinized and made expressive of a sublime FACT. We have indeed often used the phrase "inspired action" to distinguish it from the blind and egotistic kind. He who practises it does not thereby desert the contemplative path. This inner life is kept deep full and rich, but it is not kept refrigerated and isolated. He reflects it deliberately into the outer life to satisfy a twofold purpose. First, to be on the earth, so far as he can, what he is in heaven. Second, to work actively for the liberation of others. This cannot be achieved by inertia and indifference—which are virtues to the mystic but defects to the philosopher.(P)

33

The mind stilled, the self surrendered, a divine awareness possesses him. For there can be three forms of possession: divine, human (as in artists or writers), and diabolic. In the ideal sage, divine possession has become a permanent state.

34

He finds within himself not merely a passive repose but also a veritable fountain of wisdom and strength, inspiration and bliss.

35

When spirituality shines through a man, it makes him great, even though he be bereft of talent in any other direction.

36

It should heighten, and not destroy, his creative capacities in the world of art or intellect, in public service or technical endeavour, in the businesses and professions.

37

In ancient times the very idea of inspiration, of being under the influence of a higher power, connoted an accompaniment of extremely strong stirring of the feelings. This is clearly on a mystical level, for there is deep calm during inspiration on a philosophical level.

38

It is not quite correct to say that in literary inspiration the pen races ahead of the mind, that thoughts are too swift and too numerous to get written down without missing any. This is one kind of inspiration. There is another wherein thoughts are slow and few, but deeper.

39

The priest and the guru, the artist and the writer have to carry a small flock or a million minds with them by means of their work. The talent if they possess it is theirs, but the inspiration comes from a higher level.

40

The disappointed escapist seeks compensations for life, the inspired activist seeks life.

41

To make the mood of inspiration a haphazard affair, is imprudent.

42

Whether it comes as an inspirational idea or as an intuitive feeling, it should be treasured and nurtured and developed.

43

A good deal of achievement goes on in the silent solitude of our own hearts, unnoticed and unknown to other men; one day it blossoms into irresistible action, and then the world wonders why.

44

In the end, thought and conduct, ideal and action, truth and being, must be coordinated, fused, and united.

45

We fulfil life when we find ourselves in the divine presence unendingly, aware of it and expressing it.

As act of Overself

46

Finding the Overself is one thing, and the first thing, but letting it take over is another thing.

47

The first reality of universal existence must become the first thought of human consciousness. Only then is our life rightly orientated and properly sustained. All action will then become sublime, inspired, and wise, leading to the true success at all times and despite adverse outward appearances.

48

It is one secret of the inspired individual that he *lets* himself be led: he does not try to do with his ego what can be better done for him by the intuition. But this will be possible only if he pauses and waits for the inner leading to come to him.

49

Give the ego back to the Overself and then the Overself will use it as it should be used—in harmony with the cosmic laws of being. This means that the welfare of all others in contact with the ego will be considered as well as the ego's own.

50

When these wonderful inspirations come on him, when the Overself draws him inward to involvement in its glorious being, even his physical gait, movement, and activity are affected by the change. They become quite relaxed, slowed down and very leisurely. It is as if time is no longer as important as it ordinarily seems. Yet if the intellect protests against the change, the intuition replies that the higher power will take care of the real duties.

51

His behaviour is spontaneous, but not through mere impulse nor through unused intellect. It is the spontaneity, the forthrightness of an inspired man who knows where he is going and what he is doing, who is directly guided in his relations with other men by a higher will than his own ego's.

52

When the Overself's will is the motivating power in his life, all strain and all effort to act rightly cease.

53

When the ego is displaced and the Overself is using him, there will be no need and no freedom to choose between two alternatives in regard to actions. Only a single course will present itself, directly and unwaveringly, as the right one.(P)

54

His activity as a merely selfish person comes to an end; his activity as a divinely inspired one begins. It is a transformation from "works of the flesh" to "fruits of the spirit" in the Bible's phrase.(P)

55

To gain such an inspiration in all its untarnished purity, his egoism must be totally lost and absorbed in the experience.(P)

56

He has to penetrate to the inner workings of the mind, to discover where the spark of contact with the Overself is glowing, and with that find that a finer being, a nobler outlook, and a collaboration with the World-Idea can be created.

57
Inspired action becomes possible when, to speak in spatial metaphors, every deed receives its necessary and temporary attention within the foreground of the mind whilst the Overself holds the permanent attention of the man within the background of his mind.(P)

58
As the consciousness of the Overself seeps into him, the power of the Overself expresses through him.

59
Over and above the pressure of our individual wills there is this sublimely gentle yet ever-insistent pressure of the Overself's will.

60
He has access to infinite wisdom and infinite support in every situation and under every given circumstance. But he has it only so far as he submits the ego to the higher self.

61
The next characteristic of the inspired life is that it is an effortless one. No striving in any direction is necessary. Neither the weight of external compulsion nor the pressure of interior desires is ever again felt. He acts with the lightest touch.

62
Even if he has found an intermittent inspiration, it will desert him in the end if he tries to glorify himself.

63
The wise man *lets* the Overself's presence flow through his life, never blocks it by his ego nor turns it aside by his passions.

64
The ego can no longer foresee what will happen to the outer course of its personal life when the Overself takes the lead, nor can it dictate what that course should be.

65
With all his humility before the Overself, he will bear himself among his fellow human beings with serene self-assurance and speak with firm conviction of that which he knows.

66
When these experiences increase and multiply to such an extent that they accumulate into a large body of evidence, he will become convinced that some power is somehow using him as a beneficent channel. It is the

real originator of these experiences, the real bestower of these blessings, the real illuminator of these other people. What is this power? Despite its seeming otherness, its apparent separateness, it is really his own higher self.

67

Only when we act in and from the Overself can we really be said to act aright, for only then shall our deeds be wise and virtuous, most beneficial in the ultimate sense both to our own self and to others.

68

What the ego thinks and feels and does is to reflect the Overself's dominion. The ego itself is now to be subsidiary. Every thought or feeling or act is to be a dedicated one, every place where it finds itself a consecrated one.

69

The Overself is not merely a transient intellectual abstraction but rather an eternal presence. For those who have awakened to the consciousness of this presence, there is always available its mysterious power and sublime inspiration.

70

It is the divine moment; no longer does speech come forth humanly nor action individually: the god within has taken over.

71

At some mysterious moment a higher power takes possession of him, dictates his thoughts, words, and acts. Sometimes he is amazed by them, by their difference from what he would normally have thought, spoken, or done.

72

The unfoldment of intuitive action, intuitive thinking, and intuitive feeling means that the Overself and the personality are then in accord and working together. The little circle of the ego then lies within the larger circle of the Overself, in harmony and in co-operation. It does not matter then whether a man lives as a monk or as a householder, whether he is engaged in the world's activity, or whether he is in retirement. Of course, such a condition is not attained without a full and deep transformation of the man. It is necessary to point out that the mere removal of thoughts by itself is not enough and could only give an illusory illumination and the kind of peace which one feels after a dreamless sleep—passive, but not positive. There are various tricks. Some are of a hypnotic nature, whereby thoughts can be kept out of the mind and an apparent stillness obtained; but the meditator who only uses these tricks and nothing more deceives himself. He might as well go to sleep and then wake up. The spiritual value is about the same, while the psychological value is definitely adverse to him. He will then be in danger of becoming a dreamer with a dulled mind.

73

He must look forward hopefully to the day when he can actually feel the higher self present within all his activity. It will reign in his inner world and thus be the real doer of his actions, not the ego in the outer world.

74

It is not easy to subordinate oneself to this inner voice. But where can one hide from it? We are to exalt life, not to degrade it.

75

There are times when the Overself accepts no resistance, when it acts with such compelling force that the man is unable to disobey. But such happenings are special ones.

76

Some self other than his familiar one will rise up within him, some force—ennobling, masterful, and divine—will control him.

77

When a man's consciousness, outlook, and character are so exalted as this is, altruistic duty becomes not a burden to be carried irksomely but a part of his path of self-fulfilment from which he would not wish to be spared.

78

There is a strange feeling that not he but somebody else is living and talking in the same body. It is somebody nobler and wiser than his own ego.

79

The feeling of being possessed for a while by a holy other-worldly presence comes over him.

80

He is now under the influence, and later may be under the control, of a superior power.

81

He becomes a vessel, filled from time to time with a spiritual presence.

82

His words, his feeling, and his actions will then not only be expressions of his human self but also of that self united indissolubly with his divine self.

Its power and limitations

83

Whoever finds his Overself and draws from it the will and desire to serve others, will radiate joy, confidence, and peace to them.

84

From that high source of inspiration may come great actions, immense inner strength, superb artistic creativity, and a beautiful, delicate inner equilibrium.

85

What inspired artist ever creates a new work except in joy? Is this not a clue to the fact that the inspirational or best level of his mind is a happy one?

86

He lives in the sunny light of his own inspired thoughts.

87

Even the best of men are subject to the peculiarities of their temperament, to the form of their individuality; and even if they always seek to stay upon the level of inspiration they cannot help expressing the channel through which the inspiration has to come, which is a human channel subject to human limitations.

88

The inspiration may be pure Spirit but, because it must come into a particular man, he receives it in a particular way, interprets, expresses, and communicates it in a personal way, so that the purity is at best a little adulterated, the integrity a little lost. His character may be as selfless as he can make it, but the colouring of his mind can only fade out to a particular extent because his body is still there, his entire past history is there graven in the subconscious, and body is interfused with mind. All this will vanish with death, or some while after death if he is not fully advanced.

89

Regardless of the fears and dreads, the hesitancies and timidities of the lower ego, he must carry out whatever his newly found commander bids him do. But this will not be so hard and unpleasant a task as it might seem to others. For he will now feel at least the same satisfaction in yielding to the higher self's bidding that he formerly felt in yielding to the lower one's desires. And with the bidding will come the needed strength, courage, and wisdom to obey it. The world's opposition and danger may be recognized but will not deter him. It is not by his own will that he engages himself in such work, but by a will that supports and guides him better than ever he could support or guide himself. This he clearly comprehends and gladly accepts.

90

It is a mistake to believe that to find the Overself is to find eternal monotony and boredom. On the contrary, it holds out the promise of life more abundant—of joy, happiness, and satisfaction physically as well as spiritually.

91

All great poetic utterance is discovery. Its moments are angels' visits.

92

He will be an inspired man in his labours of spiritual service or artistic expression. He will be aware that a power greater than his own is working through him and affecting others. And he will know that this power comes from the secret God within himself.

93

So immense is the security which the Overself enfolds him with that he will not hesitate to take chances which prudence, caution, discretion, or fear would never take. But he will do so only if the Overself guides him to.

94

He who commands his thoughts and senses from his divine centre, commands life.

95

The wonder and joy of finding himself to be a channel of blessing, teaching, healing peace, and uplift to others will increase as the results themselves increase.

96

The inspiration may be made manifest in a production, so that others may have the chance to feel its reflection; but there can be no guarantee that they will do so.

97

It is true that inspiration comes at unpredictable times. But if we prepare conditions advantageous to it we are more likely to receive its visitation.

98

In the literature of disappointment, such as the modern writings of Schopenhauer and the ancient recorded sayings of Buddha, we may trace one part of the history of man's search after truth. But there is another part, a joyous and happier part.

99

The forces of heredity and the dominion of environment would appear to be the overwhelming impulsions of a man's actions. But let the Soul arise in its masterful urgency, and they vanish!

100

Inspiration brings the mind to its most exalted pitch, whether it be a mystic's mind or an artist's.

101

Such is the power of true inspiration that it lifts men to the plane of hero in action, genius in art, or master in renunciation.

102

This is the power that coaxes the unwilling personality to enter the fires of expiation; this is the urge that makes a man swim through bitter waters to find wisdom.

103

The truth is that the source of man's inspiration is always there, but his awareness of it is intermittent.

104

Most of us cannot turn on the tap of inspiration at will, cannot put Pegasus between the shafts. Often we deceive ourselves and imagine the presence of inspiration when it is really absent. The works we do then are our humble own, not fiery gifts from heaven.

105

Through whatever medium he uses—artistic or not, physical form or silent thought—his inspiration will be transmitted, his perception of truth disseminated.

106

The intensity of his awareness will measure the degree of his influence.

107

Inspiration comes and goes as it will, staying a few minutes or abiding for quite a while.

108

Work done under the Overself's inspiration can never be tedious but will always be satisfying.

109

To do something really worthwhile, to become creative and constructive in an inspired way, aware of the Overself, is to become godlike. We then fulfil the purpose of human existence on earth.

110

Whoever keeps this divine flame burning brightly within his heart, radiates the spirit of his purpose to all whom he contacts.

111

Where do such feelings come from? Certainly not from his ordinary self. They come from his higher self.

112

Inspired work will always bear the glow of inner life.

113

The Overself is not merely a pleasant feeling—although it arouses such a feeling—but a veritable force. When it possesses a man, he is literally and actually gripped by a dynamic energy. A creative power henceforth pervades his atmosphere, enters his deeds, permeates his mind and charges his words, and runs through his history.

114

At this stage he feels its presence as being very active and very real: he is not alone.

Examples, anecdotes

115

Brahms explained his method of finding inspiration as beginning with a pondering on lofty universal spiritual truths which led him into a deeper dreamlike semi-trance condition. After this prelude he felt inspired with the ideas for his work.

116

Constantin Stanislavski, who founded the Moscow Art Theatre at the turn of this century, and whose brilliant directing work was honoured by members of his profession throughout Europe, studied enough of yoga to believe that the inspired state could be brought about deliberately. He further believed that when that happened upon a stage, the actor's own nature fused with his role and that he was then unable to distinguish between the two. He said that this was the mark of the genius but admitted that it was unlikely to last more than a short time.

117

"He cannot stay here long. Nature pulls him back from this ethereal atmosphere; body and world insist that he come back, duty and responsibility buzz in his ears. Reluctantly he returns." Harsh words! They come from an artist, from Richard Wagner. They are one-sided, yes, exaggerated no doubt, but it was to one of these turnings-away that the world owes his finest, noblest opera, *Parsifal*.

118

Geoff Hodson on Krishnamurti: "When he spoke to an audience, there was a moment when you saw the expression on his face change: at that moment I saw clairvoyantly a great being began to overshadow him. He became inspired."

119

Why did the crowds press into the lecture halls wherever Emerson came? Why did they listen in awe and silence to this man in whose mind glowed a divine lamp? Emerson gave them inspiration.

120

I remember one day when A.E. (George Russell), the Irish poet and statesman, chanted to me in his attractive Hibernian brogue some paragraphs from his beloved Plotinus that tell of the gods, although the number of words which stick to memory are but few and disjointed, so drugged were my senses by his magical voice. "All the gods are venerable and beautiful, and their beauty is immense. . . . For they are not at one time wise, and at another destitute of wisdom; but they are always wise, in an impassive, stable, and pure mind. They likewise know all things which are divine. . . . For the life which is there is unattended with labour, and truth is their generator and nutriment. . . . And the splendour there is infinite. . . ."

The Interior Word

121

The fruit of meditation may include messages conveying general teaching or specific guidance but the student will recognize that they emanate from his own mind at its best or from his own intuition. But he will know the Interior Word seems to come to him from a source outside himself, from some higher being or master. It uses his own thought to speak to him but the inspiration for each thought is not his own. This is the Interior Word.

122

The feeling of some presence inside his heart will become so powerful at intervals, so real and so intense, that he will quite naturally enter into conversation with it. He will implore it, pray to it, express love for it, and worship it. And he will find that it will answer him in words, the sentences forming themselves spontaneously within his mind as speech without sound. It will give him pertinent didactic instruction—often at unexpected moments—and formulate higher points of view.

123

Interior Word. When he succeeds in penetrating the still depths of his being, another mind will appear to superimpose itself on his own, directing, teaching, and inspiring him. It will speak to him out of the silence within himself yet it will not be his own voice. Its tone will be friendly, and when he becomes familiar with it he will know it to be none other than the voice of the Holy Spirit, the word of the Higher Self.

124

As the interior word delivers its message to him day by day, as he advances in understanding through receiving it and in character by obeying it, he will have the best evidence that this quest which he first tried as an experiment is becoming a priceless experience.

125

It is the soul speaking truth to the intellect out of its larger range of life. Its voice is best and easiest heard when the consciousness is turned inward away from the sense-existence and brought as near to stillness as we can make it.

126

Interior Word. It speaks not through uttered words clairaudiently heard as in spiritistic phenomena but through the higher form of spontaneous intuitively formulated thoughts.

127

A voice comes to his hearing but not with the ordinary kind of audibility. It is within him for it is only a mental voice yet it speaks with a strange authority. It says to him, "I am the Way, the Truth, the Life."

128

Interior Word: Something within begins to speak to him, some mind begins to find its own expression. It is his, and yet not his.

129

The Overself issues its commands and exacts its demands in the utter silence and privacy of a man's heart. Yet they are more powerful and more imperious in the end than any which issue from the noisy bustling world.

130

He may count himself fortunate if he comes under the tutelage of the Interior Word. But his good fortune will last only as long as he faithfully obeys it. The failure to do so will bring painful but educative retribution.

131

It is as if no one existed but these two—the listening mind and the soundless voice. This is real solitude; this is the true cloister to which a man may retire in order to find God; this is the desert, cave, or mountain where, mentally, he renounces the world's business and abandons friends, family, and all humanity.

132

The Interior Word: When another personality speaks from the en-
tranced or semi-entranced body, be the latter a spiritualist medium, a
hypnotized person, or a psychologically auto-suggested one, we have a
phenomenon in which no true mystic would take part. When this same
personality announces itself to be Jesus, Krishna, Saint Francis, Mrs.
Eddy, or Mme. Blavatsky, it may immediately be labelled as spurious.
Whether the phenomenon be produced by actual spirit-possession (when
usually a lying spirit is the operating agent) or by psychological self-
obsession, with the wakeful personality unconscious of what the other has
said, in both cases it is one which ought to be avoided. The Catholic
Church, with its very wide experience in such matters, has cautioned its
adherents against being seduced either into allowing the thing to happen
or into believing the teaching given by the mysterious visitor. Pope Bene-
dict XIV went so far as to ascribe a diabolic origin to the voice. From the
standpoint of philosophy it may be said that the Inner Word speaks only *to*
a man, never *through* him to others. Nor is it heard clairaudiently and
therefore psycho-physically; it is heard only mentally and inwardly.

133

The phenomenon of the Interior Word does not ordinarily appear before one is able to carry the mind to a certain depth or intensity of concentration, and to hold it there continuously for not less than about a half
hour.

134

In that state of inspired communion when the Interior Word is heard,
thoughts keep coming into consciousness from a source deeper than the
personal mind. The ego is not directly thinking them but instead experiences them as being impressed upon it or released into it.

135

The utterance of the Interior Word can be heard only in heaven, only in
a state detached from the animality and triviality of the common state.

136

It is as if another being spoke inside me—not with audible voice but
with mental voice—and imposed itself strongly on my own mind.

137

Interior Word: Out of this blankness something will begin to speak to
him. It will not be a sound heard with the body's ears. That would be a
low psychic manifestation which must be stopped at once, if it happened.

138

Until the internal Word speaks in him he is really incapable of helping others spiritually. He may be able to do so intellectually or to comfort them emotionally but that is a different and inferior thing.

139

If the Interior Word bids him move in any direction which seems encompassed by difficulties or blocked by obstacles so that he can see no way before him, let him not doubt or fear. A way will be made by the power of the Overself. He need only obey, relax, and trust the guidance.

140

When the Inner Word begins to speak to him, he may begin to speak to others—not before. For only then will what he says bear any creative power, spiritual inspiration, enlightenment, or healing in it.

141

The Interior Word carries an authoritative and commanding tone.

142

The Interior Word is not heard with the reasoning mind, even though its statements may be very reasonable. It is not connected with the intellect at all, as are all our ordinary words. It is received in the heart, felt intensively and deeply.

143

Now that he has developed the capacity to hear, there sounds forth out of the obscure recesses of his being a silent voice, a messenger without name or form. It is the Word.

144

The Interior Word is never enigmatic and puzzling but always direct and simple. Only the revelations of occultism are obscure, never the revelations of truth itself.

145

What the German mystics called "the Interior Word" is precisely the same as what two thousand years earlier the Chinese mystics called "the Voice of Heaven."

146

The Interior Word cannot speak frequently until there is complete silence within the man's being.

147

The ideas which come to his mind through the Interior Word come stamped with the certitude of truth.

148

Internal Word: In the New Testament, John introduces the idea of the *logos*, the Word which speaks in every man who comes into the world. Every man is not able to hear it although it is always there, always immanent.

149

The Interior Word is referred to in the Bible: "I will hear what the Lord God will speak in me." (Psalms 84:9)

150

The *Interior Word* revealed itself in Socrates as his *daimon*.

151

Saint Teresa defined the Interior Word thus: "The words were clearly formed and not to be mistaken though not heard by the body's ear."

152

A mystical phenomenon which may develop out of this communion with his "holy ghost" is that of inspired writings. Helpful teachings that will be addressed to humanity in general or to the few seekers in particular may come through his pen. Or guidance in his personal life and instruction in his spiritual life may be addressed to the writer himself through occasional notes. In most cases the words will be impressed spontaneously upon his mind as though telepathically received from the dictation of his unseen but much-felt other self. In some cases, however, his hand and pen may move across the paper by automatic compulsion at a high speed, his mind being forced to move as quickly. He will then distinctly feel that he is merely an instrument which is being used to produce this inspirational script.

153

It would be a dangerous blunder for anyone to confuse this last phenomenon with the automatic writing of spiritualism and psychism. The similarities are only external ones. For in the one case there is the clear consciousness of a divine exalting ennobling presence whereas in the other there is, at best, only a blind submission to an unknown entity, usually purporting to be another human, if discarnated, being.

154

The words spoken by this unseen but much-felt presence are not heard by the physical ears yet they are strongly impressed upon the mind. They do not come from the spirits of deceased persons but from the holy spirit of one's own diviner self, from a deep mystical source, not a shallow "astral" one.

155

This is the same phenomenon which Emanuel Swedenborg experienced and described and called "internal speech with the Lord."

156

The experience of the Interior Word brings with it, or is heard in, an intensely concentrated state. With it there is a positive feeling of being the assured master of one's mind, emotions, and body.

157

What it amounts to is that the Interior Word becomes in effect the Inner Teacher and meditation itself the gateway to an inner school where instruction is regularly obtained.

158

It is the great Silence, yes, but also through the Interior Word it is to us humans the ever-speaking higher Self.

159

"To hear the Voice of the Silence is to understand that from within comes the only true guidance; to go to the Hall of Learning is to enter the state in which learning becomes possible. . . . For when the disciple is ready, the Master is ready also."—*Light on the Path* by Mabel Collins (Interior Word)

160

It is a process of inner dialogue, of mental conversation with the other self and of emotional communion with it, flowing under his thoughts to and fro.

161

Interior Word: "And in the deep silence the mysterious event will occur which will prove that the way has been found. Call it by what name you will, it is a voice that speaks where there is none to speak—it is a messenger that comes, a messenger without form or substance; for it is the flower of the soul that has opened."—*Light on the Path*

162

The instrument of reception must be accurately tuned, if God's messages are to be heard aright (Interior Word).

163

To bring others a message which elevates them and a truth which inspires them, the Interior Word will speak through him as him. This is a wonderful phenomenon when it happens.

164

The Interior Word must not be mistaken for any of the psychic voices cultivated by spiritists and mediums. The two are on entirely different planes, even though they are both within.

165

For Interior Word draw on my own experiences in 1918 when I also heard it for many months.

166

The Interior Word did not speak to me for myself alone, to prepare, teach, and direct me. It spoke also for others. It required me to write down its messages for them even more than for me.

167

There is a wisdom deep deep within man but alas! it finds no voice until he turns from himself and calls on the higher power. Then, from within, it—the deputy of that Power—when the conditions are right, can make itself heard and therefore speaks.

168

Let him humbly acknowledge that he does not have the wisdom and purity to know what is right for him to have and what is right to do. Let him turn in silent waiting to the Interior Word, and listen for it to tell him these answers.

169

When he has travelled to this stage of his journey; when he can close the door of his chamber, lie down, and listen to the Interior Voice; when the silence within becomes audible with clearly formulated instructions, then only is he ready to speak to others or write for others, and teach them. Until then he is a deaf mute, unable to hear and untrained to speak the sacred language. Now the Pentecostal power has descended on him and he is able not only to see the truth through the surrounding darkness but also to give it to those among his people who can take it.

3

THE OVERSELF'S PRESENCE

In each, in all, always

The spiritual self, the Overself, has never been lost. What has happened is that its being has not been recognized, covered over as it is with a multitude of thoughts, desires, and egocentricities.

2

The day will inexorably come when this pen shall move no more and I wish therefore to leave on record, for the benefit of those who shall come after, a sacred and solemn testimony that I know—as surely as I know that I am not this pen which scribes these lines—that a being, benign, wise, protective, and divine, whom men call the Soul, whom I call the Overself, truly exists in the hearts of all; therefore all may discover it.

A day will break surely when every man will have to bend the knee to that unknown self and abandon every cell of his brain, every flowing molecule of his heart, his blood, into its waiting hands. Though he will fear to do so, though he will fear to give up those ancient idols who had held him in bond so long and have given him so little in return, though he will tremble to loose his moorings and let his soul drift slowly from them with sails set for that mysterious region whose longitude few men know and whose shores most men shun, yet he will do so all the same. For the presence of man's own innermost divinity is the guarantee that he must inescapably seek and find it.

3

Whoever has been led into the cave of timeless life will poise his pen in a futile attempt to find words which will accurately measure this sublime experience. He rises renewed from the exquisite embrace of such a contemplation. He learns in those shining hours. That which he has been seeking so ardently has been within himself all the time. For there at the core of his being, hidden away underneath all the weakness, passion, pettiness, fear, and ignorance, dwells light, love, peace, and truth. The windows of his heart open on eternity, only he has kept them closed! He is as near the sacred spirit of God as he ever shall be, but he must open his eyes to see it. Man's divine estate is there deep within himself. But he must claim it.

4

The other part of the answer is that the Overself is always here as man's innermost truest self. It is beginningless and endless in time. Its consciousness does not have to be developed as something new. But the person's awareness of it begins in time and has to be developed as a new attainment. The ever-presence of Overself means that anyone may attain it here and now. There is no inner necessity to travel anywhere or to anyone in space or to wait years in time for this to happen. Anyone, for instance, who attends carefully and earnestly to the present exposition may perhaps suddenly and easily get the first stage of insight, the lightning-flash which affords a glimpse of reality, at any moment. By that glimpse he will have been uplifted to a new dimension of being. The difficulty will consist in retaining the new perception. For ancient habits of erroneous thinking will quickly reassert themselves and overwhelm him enough to push it into the background. This is why repeated introspection, reflective study, and mystical meditation are needed to weaken those habits and generate the inner strength which can firmly hold the higher outlook against these aggressive intruders from his own past.

5

Those who are unable to grasp this explanation the first time may do so at a later attempt, while those who *will* not grasp it and refuse to consider it further thereby indicate that they are not subtle enough to receive its truth. They will continue to seek reality among the cozening deceivers of superficial experience, but it will ever elude them there.

6

Although It is at the very heart of human beings, the Overself is very far from their present level of consciousness. Nothing could be closer yet this is the supreme paradox of our existence and the strangest enigma confronting our thought.

7

The Overself is implicit in all humanity but explicit only in a few solitary figures.

8

Its golden note of harmony falls dead upon our muted ears.

9

The Overself is not a goal to be attained but a realization of what already is. It is the inalienable possession of all conscious beings and not of a mere few. No effort is needed to get hold of the Overself, but every effort is needed to get rid of the many impediments to its recognition. We cannot take hold of it; it takes hold of us. Therefore the last stage of this quest is an effortless one. We are led, as children by the hand, into the resplendent presence. Our weary strivings come to an abrupt end. Our lips are made shut and wordless.

10

No situation in human life lasts totally unchanged forever, just as no condition on the very planet which harbours that life lasts forever. It is folly to demand changelessness. And yet we do. Why? Because beneath this conscious desire for fresh experiences there is the unconscious longing for That which is the permanent core of selfhood. The stilled, one-pointed, and reverent mind may know it, the self may dissolve in it.

11

We carry the divine presence with us everywhere we travel. We do not *directly* profit by it simply because we are not directly conscious of it. The effort to arouse such awareness is a worthwhile one, bringing rich reward in its train.

12

The soul is always with us but our sense of its presence is not.

13

There is a spiritual element in every man. It is his essence.

14

Although we are divided in awareness from the higher power, we are not divided in fact from it. The divine being is immanent in each one of us. This is why there is always some good in the worst of us.(P)

15

Goethe: "You give me space to belong to myself yet without separating me from your own life."

16

The Overself is always present but man's attention seldom is.

17

Because the soul is present deep down in each human heart, none is so depraved that he will not one day find the inward experience of it.

18

There is a zone of utter calm within man. It is not only there but always there. Those who suffer, fret, or are confused may doubt or deny this—understandably and pardonably.

19

It is always possible for a man to gain enlightenment anytime anywhere even though it may not be probable, for he has within himself the Light itself as an ever-present Reality. What does happen and what is probable is that some moment during the course of a lifetime a glimpse may happen, and the glimpse itself is nothing less than a testimony to that ever-presence, a witness telling him that it is true and real.

20

Just then, as thoughts themselves stop coming into his mind, he stops living in time and begins living in the eternal. He knows and feels his timelessness. And since all his sufferings belong to the world of passing time, of personal ego, he leaves them far behind as though they had never been. He finds himself in the heaven of a serene, infinite bliss. He learns that he could always have entered it; only his insistence on holding to the little egoistic values, his lack of thought-control, and his disobedience to the age-old advice of the Great Teachers prevented him from doing so.

21

These rare moments of spontaneous spiritual exaltation, which cast all other moments in the shade and which are remembered ever after, could not have been born if that divine element into which they exalted us did not already exist within us. Its very presence in our hearts makes always possible and sometimes actual the precious feeling of a non-material sublimely happy order of being.

22

It is not really a goal to be reached, nor a state to be attained, nor something new to be added to what he now has or is. But if he insists on thinking that it is any of these things, there is no other course open than to take the appropriate action, make the necessary effort, for such achievement. His labours are really self-imposed, a consequence of incorrect thought about himself.

23

Is this benign state a past from which we have lapsed or a future to which we are coming? The true answer is that it is neither. This state has always been existent within us, is so now, and always will be. It is forever with us simply because it is what we really are.

24

It is not as if he has to find something foreign, making communication too distant and too difficult, for this is his very native being, giving him meaning and awareness.

25

If the real Self must have been present and been witness to our peaceful enjoyment of deep slumber—otherwise we would not have known that we had had such enjoyment—so must it likewise have been present and been witness to our rambling imaginations in dream-filled sleep and to our physical activities in waking. This leads to a tremendous but inescapable conclusion. We are as near to, or as much in, the real Self, the Overself, at every moment of every day as we ever shall be. All we need is awareness of it.

26

A man's refusal to allow spiritually intuitive feelings to awaken in him cannot obliterate the presence of the source of those feelings. He bears that presence ever within him and one day must reconcile himself willingly, knowingly, even yearningly, with it.

27

The Overself is always within call, for its hiding place is no farther than a man's heart. But if the call does not go forth, or goes forth without faith, or is not sustained with patience, the response will not come.

28

God is ever present with us but we are ever turning away from him. No one is forsaken except those who look only to, and into, the ego, and even then only for a time.

29

In one sense that world of the Overself remains always inaccessible and inexpressible, but in another sense it is as close as breathing and as palpable in the highest art forms or in the illuminated man's presence as a fragrant perfume.

30

By his ignoring of the Overself's presence, man commits his greatest sin and shows his worst stupidity.

31

If God did not exist then we humans would not exist. A divine ray, atom, soul, call it what you wish, is present in each of us. Some are aware of this, others must one day come to this knowledge.

32

The Overself is always present in man's heart. If he does not receive awareness of this fact in his mind, that is because he makes no proper and sustained effort to do so.

33

You may be an insignificant creature in the vastness of the cosmos, but the divine life—of which that cosmos is but a channel—is in you, too. Have enough faith in your divine heritage, take it into your common everyday life and thought, and in some way, to some people, you will become very significant and important.

34

We live all the time in unfailing, if unconscious, union with the Overself.

35

Perhaps the most wonderful thing which the illuminate discovers is that his independence from the infinite life power never really existed and was only illusory, that his separation from the Overself was only an idea of the imagination and not a fact of being. Even the desire to unite with the Overself was only a dream, and consequently all lesser desires of the ego were merely dreams within a dream.

36

I began to enter consciously into the real "I" and to comprehend by realization that it was always there, that nothing new had been found, and that this was eternal life.

37

The truth is this second self—or rather the feeling of its presence—has been shut up so long, that we have come to look upon it as non-existent and to regard the rumours of its actual experience as hallucinations. This is why religion, mysticism, and philosophy have so hard a battle to fight in these times, a battle against man's inevitable incredulity.

38

For centuries theologians have argued about the meaning of Jesus' declaration that the kingdom of heaven was at hand. Most of them have given it a historical interpretation. Only those who could approach the mind of Jesus have given it a mystical interpretation. For only they can see that he meant that the kingdom of the Overself is really as close to us as is our own hand. All such argument is useless when it starts from different planes of knowledge and the arguers never really meet each other.

39

Everywhere we see people in bondage to their egos. Everywhere, too, the sage sees the Overself waiting, always present, for them to turn from themselves to It.

40

The overlooked part is his consciousness; the forgotten self is his knowing power. These exist uninterruptedly, even in apparently subconscious forms like deep sleep and swoon. Yet he denies this share of his in the Real Being, identifies with the body instead of making it merely an object of awareness.

41

The Overself is in the heart of every man but few care to seek it out until pressure of its grace from within, or fatigue with the world-life without, drives them to do so.

42

The Overself exists in all of us—the bad as well as the good, the stupid as well as the clever.

43

When the divinity in his own self is found at last, he will afterwards find its light reflected upon every other man and woman he encounters.

44

Every man is sacred did he but know it.

45

If we say that the Overself resides in each man we say something that is not quite true nor quite false. It would be better to say that each man first feels the Overself—when he does have the good fortune to feel it—as residing within his heart, but the result of further development is to show him that the contrary, although a paradox, is also correct, which is that he resides in the Overself!

46

The godlike abides in each of us but only the master knows and feels its glory.

47

The mind keeps on moving about until sleep overcomes it ... and because it never stopped to collect itself, it still does not know the higher and better part of itself—the Overself.

48

The divine presence is constant, it does not go away: but man himself is too often absent, heedless, interested elsewhere. But each return gives him a glimpse which he calls a grace.

49

The soul is present and active in every man. This is why it is quite possible for every man to have a direct glimpse of the truth about his own inward non-materiality.

50

Nothing can ever exist outside God. Therefore, no man is bereft of the divine presence within himself. All men have the possibility of discovering this fact. And with it they will discover their real selfhood, their true individuality.

51

This is the truth that must be proclaimed to our generation, that the

Soul is with us here and now—not in some remote world or distant time, not when the body expires—and that it is our joy and strength to find it.

52

There is no pint of seawater in which salt is not present in solution. There is no human entity in whom a divine soul is not present in secret.

53

Not even a solitary Crusoe passes through life alone. Everyone passes through it in fellowship with his higher self. That such fellowship is, in most cases, an unconscious one, is not enough to nullify it. That men may deny in faith or conduct even the very existence of their soul is likewise not enough to nullify it.

54

This, the real I, is always accessible to him in meditation and always is the half-known background of his conscious self at other times.

55

So long as the Overself is sought elsewhere than where It is, as apart from the seeker himself, so long will the quest for it end in failure.

56

The divine being is present in all people, from the crudest to the most cultured.

57

It is present in every person but only dim echoes may succeed in emerging from the hinterland of consciousness.

58

The absence of the ego is the presence of the Overself. But this is only a surface impression in the person's thought, for the Overself is *always* present.

59

We may have the intuitive assurance that this higher power *does* exist even when we have no personal experience of it and no direct knowledge of its nature.

60

Amid all the perplexities and oscillations of life, the witnessing and understanding Overself waits with infinite patience. No one is ever left out. This is the only God we can hope to know, the true Teacher for all. Those who yearn to unite with it should plead persistently for its Grace.

61

The Overself's power to alter circumstances, create opportunities, and uphold persons is available to anyone who fulfils the requisite conditions. These include some amount of mental preparation and moral purification, some clear perception of the fact that the Overself is present here and now, an instant and constant remembrance of this fact, and finally a willingness to trust completely to its providential help, supply, and support no matter how undesirable or intolerable a situation seems to be.

62

In every grade of life's manifestation, from every quality of human character, the divine is always present and never absent.

63

There are resources within man's grasp that could redeem his character and transform his life, yet they lie untouched and undeveloped.

64

The silent secret part of the self is forever there, forever asking a little surrender of attention. But few give it.

65

All the time it is silently asking: "Will you not turn toward Me, accept Me, for I am your other self?"

66

In one sense, we have never left the divine Source, never lost our divine identity.

67

The Presence is inseparable from human existence, even though so many human beings may find the statement incredible, imaginative, or merely tied to a religious faith. If it would only announce itself more loudly! But mankind has to accept its ways on its own terms. Those who wish may learn what they are.

68

There is something godlike in every person. By finding it in ourselves, we rise above the common human life as that in turn rises above the animal.

69

And you will perceive that the Overself is always there, albeit you will have repeatedly to raise your eyes from earth and your mind from ego to come into realization of this truth.

70

Because we draw our very life from the spiritual principle within us, we can only *ignore* the truth that this principle exists but can never *lose* its reality.

71

Retreat into his mystical home is ever open to him, withdrawal into the blissful privacy of the Overself is his blessed right.

72

God is both outside and inside us, is everywhere around and deep within. It is there but waits to be recovered by the individual consciousness.

73

Where can he find this peace or practise this presence except in himself? This done, he can go about his daily business anywhere and everywhere.

74

Jesus spoke in simple crisp sentences about this great fact that heaven—the state of real happiness—is within man even here and now.

75

Deep within man there is Something which waits for his discovery, something which reveals itself when he has penetrated far enough or when grace grants it or karma favours it.

76

This divine soul never withdraws from man's life, is never absent from man's fate. For the very purpose of these last two is to draw him to seek and find the soul.

77

The truth is that never for a moment are we really separate from our inner self.

78

It is simply asking man to accept himself for what he is.

79

A single train would still be too large to carry all the men in America who are living in the awareness of the Overself.

80

There is a centre in every one's Self which is divine and radiant.

81

The same Overself is behind us all, contains us all.

82

This is the divine element whose continuing presence in man confers a guarantee of eventual salvation.

83

In all of us there is this resplendent being dwelling in the deepest concealment, linking us with the Supreme Being.

84

In its own perfect silence and with its own perfect patience, the Overself awaits us.

85

Look where you will, go where you will, the higher power is there, whether in silence or in action.

86

The Sufi-Muhammedan sage-poet, Ibn al-Arabi:

> O Pearl Divine! While pearl that in a shell
> Of dark mortality is made to dwell,
> Alas, while common gems we prize and hoard
> Thy inestimable worth is still ignored!

87

The Overself can become very real to him when feeling its ever-presence in all his experience, when awake to its *now*-ness.

88

The revelation of truth may come directly from within himself because of the presence of the divine spark within himself.

89

Since the higher individuality is a stable thing, it is not to be achieved by any efforts but is to be discovered as present.

90

The doorway to truth stands wide open throughout the day.

91

If men would, or could, believe that with every breath they are acting in concert with the cosmic rhythm, that in clinging to the self they are actually sharing the divine presence!

92

It is a presence which can be felt directly in daily active life, although not so vividly as when removed from the world and concentrated upon in solitary meditation.

93

The Overself appears to all alike, regardless of colour or race, when they have made themselves ready for It. Anybody who has so misunderstood the message in my books as to believe differently, is mistaken.

Value, effects of its presence

94

To be satisfied with anything less than this egoless Self is to worship at the shrine of an idol.

95

The Overself is neither a cold metaphysical concept nor a passing wave of emotion. It is a *Presence*—sublime, sacred, and beneficent—which grips your heart, thought, and body by its own mysterious power, making you regard life from a nobler standpoint.

96

The divine soul is the real essence of each person. If we do not come into the full experience of its existence, all our religion is a mere surface emotionalism, all our metaphysics a mocking intellectualism.

97

Once you are clearly aware of the presence of the Overself, you will find that it will spontaneously provide you with a rule of conduct and a standard of ethics at all times and under all circumstances. Consequently you will never be at a loss to know what to do in difficult moral situations, nor how to behave in challenging ones. And with this knowledge will also come the power to implement it.

98

When this contact with the Overself is established, its power will work for you: you will no longer go through the struggles of life alone.

99

This is not to say that the spiritual contact will remove all difficulties and perplexities from your inner life, but that it will give you added power to deal with them.

100

From this seeming nothingness deep within he draws a peace of mind, an emotional freedom, a sense of God's living presence that the world's harshness cannot dislodge.

101

The appearance of the sacred presence automatically extinguishes the lower desires. The holding on to that presence wherever he goes and whatever he does as if it were his real identity, will help to establish that release as a lasting fact.

102

As he becomes more sensitive to the Overself's presence, he knows that he has only to turn to it to receive divine strength and nourishment.

103

When all other sources of help have been tried, there is no other source left to man than the divine Overself, by whatever name he calls it or under whatever symbol he pictures it.

104

Once the Overself is felt in the heart as a living presence, it raises the consciousness out of the grip of the egoistic-desire parts of our being, frees it from the ups and downs of mood and emotion which they involve. It provides a sense of inner satisfaction that is complete in itself and irrespective of outside circumstances.

105

The extraordinary thing is not that he will feel the divine self is with him but that it has always been with him.

106

"How quiet it is!" exclaimed Lao Tzu, in describing the Overself. "Yet it can transform all things."

107

The stillness has magical powers. It soothes, restores, heals, instructs, guides, and replaces chaos and tumult by orderliness and harmony.

108

There is much confusion of understanding about what happens to the ego when it attains the ultimate goal. Some believe that a cosmic consciousness develops, with an all-knowing intelligence and an "all-overish" feeling. They regard it as unity with the whole universe. Others assert that there is a complete loss of the ego, an utter destruction of the personal self. No—these are confused notions of what actually occurs. The Overself is not a collective entity as though it were composed of a number of particles. One's embrace of other human beings through it is not in union with them but only in sympathy, not in psychic identification with them but in psychic harmony. He has enlarged the area of his vision and sees himself as a part of mankind. But this does not mean that he has become conscious of all mankind as though they were himself. The true unity is with one's own higher indestructible self. It is still with a higher individuality, not a cosmic one, and it is still with one's own self, not with the rest of mankind. Unity with them is neither mystically nor practically possible. What we discover is discovered by a deepening of consciousness, not by a widening of it. Hence it is not so much a wider as a deeper self that he has first to find.

With the rectification of this error, we may find the correct answer to the question: "What is the practical meaning of the injunction laid by all the great spiritual teachers upon their followers, to give up the ego, to renounce the self?" It does not ask for a foolish sentimentality, in the sense that we are to be as putty in the hands of all other men. It does not ask for an utter impossibility, in the sense that we are never to attend to our own affairs at all. It does not ask for a useless absurdity, in the sense that we are to become oblivious of our very existence. On the contrary, it asks for what is wise, practicable, and worthwhile—that we give up our lower personality to our higher individuality.

Thus it is not that the aspirant is asked to abandon all thought of his particular self (as if he could) or to lose consciousness of it, but that he is asked to perceive its imperfection, its unsatisfactoriness, its faultiness, its baseness and its sinfulness and, in consequence of this perception, to give it up in favour of his higher self, with its perfection, blessedness, goodness, nobility, and wisdom. For in the lower ego he will never know peace whereas in the diviner one he will always know it.

109

What this harmony means is that the hidden centre of consciousness within the other person will be alike to the centre within himself.

110

Through his higher self, a man can attain the highest good.

111

The concept of the Overself is foundational. It provides meaning for life.(P)

112

That man is verily ignorant who does not know that what the Overself can give him is immeasurably greater than what he can gain from any other source. For on the one side there is infinite power, on the other only limited capacity.

113

Lots of words are not needed to communicate what the Overself has to say. From its presence the truth, the power, and the virtue can make themselves felt.

114

In that benign atmosphere, negative thoughts cannot exist.

115

He who has discovered how to live with his higher self has discovered a serenity which defies circumstance and environment, a goodness which is too deep for the world's understanding, a wisdom which transcends thought.

116

Even in the midst of worldly distresses, he will feel the Overself's support to such an extent and in such a way that they will seem to be someone else's, with himself as a merely continuous spectator of them.

117

He lives in the gratifying consciousness that he is supported by the divine will, the divine power.

118

To find the Overself is to eliminate fear, establish harmony, and inspire living.

119

The power of the Overself to enlighten, protect, and exalt man is as actual a fact as the power of electricity to illumine his home—or it is nothing.

120

It is quite possible to open doors of inner being without the aid of a teacher. One's own higher self will give him all the guidance he needs, provided he has sufficient faith in its existence and its assistance.

121

Alone and depending on his little, personal ego, a man can do the merest fraction of what he can do when he becomes an instrument of the Infinite Power.

122

When the star of a man's Overself rises into ascendancy, he will no more feel lonely even if he be often alone. A sense of the universe's friendliness will surround him, enfold him.

123

He always turns for his first defense against the perils and troubles of this world to brief meditation upon the all-wise, all-powerful Overself, and only after that for his secondary defenses to the ego's human resources.

124

From the outside, by means of events, persons, or books; from the inside, by means of intuitions, thoughts, feelings, and urges—this is how the way is shown him by the Overself.

125

Out of this deep mysterious centre within himself, he will draw the strength to endure distresses with fortitude, the wisdom to manage situations without after-regrets, the insight to keep the great and little values of everyday living in proper perspective.

126

The correct understanding of what man really is is both self-humbling and self-glorifying.

127

If the consciousness of God in him makes him very strong, the consciousness of his dependence on it keeps him very humble.

128

Its wisdom is a perfect solvent of human perplexities, its tranquillity a perfect balm for human bruises.

129

Because he has access to this inward source, he may live the loneliest of lives but it will not be loveless. The joy and warmth of its ever-presence will abide with him.

130

In very truth the Overself becomes his beloved companion, bringing an intense satisfaction and profound love which no external friendship could ever bring.

131

The ever-presence of the Overself is to him life's greatest fact. There is nothing to compare with it; he takes his stand upon it. He rejoices in it. When the outside world does him injustice or slanders him or hurts him or defrauds him, he turns inward, deeper and deeper inward, until he stands in the presence of the Overself. Then he finds absolute serenity, absolute love. Every lesser thing must dissolve away in its divine atmosphere, and when he returns to mundane thought he feels no resentment against the wrong-doers; if anything, he feels pity for them. He has lost nothing, for good name and property are but the accidents of existence, whereas the presence of the Overself is a basic essential, and he has not lost that reality. So long as It loves him and so long as he loves It there can be no real loss.

132

We do not live self-sufficient and self-sustained lives but depend wholly on the Overself in every way and at every moment.

133

Under great strain and amid grave dangers, the aspirant will find courage and endurance in the talismanic power of remembering the Higher Self. It is always there.

134

It is from this source that he will draw both strength to rise above his own temptations and love to rise above other men's hatred.

135

It is a state where inner resistances are no more, inner conflicts are not known.

136

It is the presence of the Overself in us that creates the germ of our aspirations for a higher life. It is the warm sunshine and cold rain of experience that nurtures the germ. It is the influence of spiritual individuals that brings the growth through its varying stages.

137
All nerve tensions are lost in this holy quietude. An exquisite mood of well-being takes their place.

138
He who perpetually feels the presence of the divine soul within himself, thereby obtains an effortless control of himself.

139
The doubts and fears, the hesitations and suspicions, the jealousies and bitternesses, the enmities and hatreds of common life can never enter here.

140
Jallaluddin Rumi gave a beautiful and fitting name to the Higher Self in many of his poems. He called it "the Friend."

141
There is a sense of perfect safety, a sense which particularly and strongly reveals itself at times of danger, crisis, or distress.

142
It is a fact more real than we usually grant that the continuous presence of the Overself makes men's satisfaction with wholly material living both impermanent and impossible.

143
The extent of the peace and strength, the confidence and beneficence which lie stretched out beneath the little ego's troubled life is like unto the oceans: no other simile will suit.

144
Mysterious pools of wisdom and goodness are underneath the personality, if only we could find our way to them or else bring gushes from them to the surface.

145
In this higher part of his being he feels completed within himself, at-oned with Nature and as self-sufficient as Nature.

146
The Overself is present as the supreme Fact in his, and all, existence even as it is present as an emotional necessity in the religious man's existence.

147
All his finest emotions, his deepest wisdom, his creative faculties, his truth-discriminating intuitions come into being because of the Overself's central if hidden presence.

148
Many will dispute this possibility, but it is certainly possible for your higher self to guide and instruct you directly—through and within yourself. It is not an existence far apart from yourself.

149

If in your divinest being you are the Overself and if the rest of you is both path and goal, the way and the truth, what do you need a guru for, why step outside yourself? But people do not care for such questions. They look for teachers locally or in India and thus look always outside themselves, outside the Overself.

150

In it, in this gentle divine atmosphere, he lives and moves and has his being, and this is one reason he has to follow Shakespeare's counsel and be true to himself.

151

This is the really Real, its moral directions the rightest of the Right.

152

The joy that emanates from the Overself has a healing quality. It dissipates anxieties and eradicates neuroses.

153

Its power can carry him through a grave crisis with unfaltering steadiness.

154

Do not think so much of looking for outside help. Your Higher Self is with you. If you could have enough faith in its presence, you could look inwards. With persistence and patience, it would guide you.

155

Without this awareness he is not a whole man, for he is not functioning in all his being.

156

It is a truth by whose light a man lives nobly and in whose comfort he may die serenely.

157

Where the ego fails or falters, the Overself proves equal to every occasion.

158

Enfolded by that inner strength, one ceases to fear, to be anxious, or to dread the future.

159

For him the most worthy achievement is to live in this state of being and to love it.

160

It is always there, always present in him although not always easily reachable. It is the secret centre of his being. This conscious contact with it gives a feeling of marvellous security, of mountain-like strength.

161
He feels as sheltered by its presence inside him as the seed by the earth outside it.

162
In its warm glow, men find a holy therapy for their suffering, a healing remedy for their disordered and dismembered selves.

163
In its sacred presence fear and suffering must take their inevitable departure.

164
He can assert this protective truth against whatever evils and dangers may appear from time to time.

165
The Overself is there and in its presence he becomes indifferent to the praise of friends or the venom of enemies.

166
He dwells in some inner fortress—safe, protected, and sure of himself. He is hardly touched by the turmoil of passing events.

167
He will gain with time the sense of a Presence which walks with him and dwells in him. It is a guide with practical value, too, for it warns him what not to do if he would live ethically and avoid additional suffering. Even if he does not advance so far as perfect realization, he will advance.

168
The early Christian Fathers believed that only a few privileged souls ever received this Grace of direct divine illumination.

169
In this healing presence the past is washed away and old sins with it.

170
It is the part of his being which, being worth most to him, deserves most from him.

171
Quite a number get a mysterious support and consolation from simply knowing at second hand that the Overself is there, even though they themselves cannot make any contact with it.

172
It is real, it is present and active in our very midst, its power and its guidance can be felt and recognized.

173
Why look to any man who is outside you—when IT is inside you? And why forget that all men are imperfect whereas IT alone is perfect?

174

In our present plight we cannot give ourselves too many supports, and there is none better than that which is to be found in the Overself.

Toward 'defining' the Overself

175

There is some life-power from which we derive our capacities and our intelligence. It is hidden and intangible. No one has seen it but everyone who thinks deeply enough can sense that it is there, always present and always supporting us. It is the Overself.

176

This is the ultimate beauty behind life, which all people seek blindly and unknowingly in such varied external forms that merely and momentarily hint, suggest, or herald its existence.

177

Ernest Wood's *Yoga Dictionary* defines "Overself" as follows: "A term designed by Dr. P. Brunton to indicate that the holy fount of our being and root of our consciousness is still ourselves, is indeed our true self. The Sanskrit equivalent is *adhyatma* as in *Bhagavad Gita*, Chapter VII and VIII." To Dr. Wood's learned definition I would like to add *Kutastma*, what stands above or beyond illusion, and also the *Gita*'s picture of the higher element in man controlling the lesser self. Further I would not leave out Buddha's transcendent atmosphere of goodwill to all beings.

178

It is this grandeur of self that is the magnetic pole drawing us to the Good, the Beautiful, the Just, the True, and the Noble. Yet itself is above all these attributes for it is the Attributeless, the Ineffable, and the Infinite that human thought cannot grasp.

179

Both the inward and outward lives of every man are controlled by a concealed entity—the Overself. Could he but see aright, he would see that everything witnesses to its presence and activity.

180

He will feel that this nobler self actually overshadows him at times. This is literally true. Hence we have named it the Overself.

181

When man shall discover the hidden power within himself which enables him to be conscious and to think, he will discover the holy spirit, the ray of Infinite Mind lighting his little finite mind.(P)

182

If we could penetrate to the deeper regions of personality, the deeper layer of consciousness, we would find at the core a state that is utterly paradoxical. For it combines, at one and the same time, the highest degree of dynamic being and the extreme degree of static being.

183

This is the abiding essence of a man, his true self as against his ephemeral person. Whoever enters into its consciousness enters into timelessness, a wonderful experience where the flux of pleasures and pains comes to an end in utter serenity, where regrets for the past, impatience at the present, and fears of the future are unknown.

184

Nothing could be nearer to a man than the Overself for it is the source of his life, mind, and feeling. Nothing could be farther from him, nevertheless, for it eludes all his familiar instruments of experience and awareness.

185

Without the Overself no human creature could be what it is—conscious, living, and intelligent.

186

Although awareness is the first way in which we can regard the soul or Overself, the latter is also that which makes awareness possible and hence a sub- or super-conscious thing. This explains why it is that we do not know our souls, but only our thoughts, our feelings, and our bodies. It is because we *are* the soul and hence we *are* the knower as well as the act of knowing. The eyes see everything outside yet do not see themselves.

187

The Overself is certainly the Way (within man), the Truth (knowing the Real Being), and the Life (applying this knowledge and practising this way in the midst of ordinary everyday activity).

188

We cannot accurately and strictly define the Overself. It is really indescribable, but its effects are not. The feeling of the Overself's presence and the way to awaken it may both be described for the benefit of those who have neither experienced the one nor learned the other.

189

If the Overself could be expressed in words there would be no need for Its silence.

190

We can know the Overself only by *being* it, not by thinking it. It is beyond thoughts for it is Thought, Pure Mind, itself.

191

Everything else can be known, as things and ideas are known, as something apart or possessed, but the Overself cannot be truly known in this way. Only by identifying oneself with It can this happen.

192

From the ordinary human point of view the Overself is the Ever-Still: yet that is our own conceptualization of it, for the fact is that all the universe's tremendous activity is induced by its presence.

193

That out of which we draw our life and intelligence is unique and indestructible, beginningless and infinite.

194

Each of us feels that there is something which directs his will, controls his movements, and constitutes the essence of his awareness. This something expresses itself to us as the "I."

195

It is not only the hidden and mysterious source of their own little self but also the unrecognized source of the only moments of real happiness that they ever have.

196

At some time, to some degree, and in some way, everything else in human experience can be *directly* examined and analysed. But this is the one thing that can never be treated in this way. For it can never acknowledge itself without objectifying itself, thus making something other than itself, some simulacrum that is not its real self.

197

The Overself is a fountain of varied forces.

198

What does the coming of Overself consciousness mean to man? It means, first of all, an undivided mind.

199

Listen to the Roman Stoics' definition of the Overself: "the divinity which is planted in his breast" of Marcus Aurelius; "your guardian spirit" of Epictetus.

200

This is the "UNDIVIDED MIND" where experience as subject and object, as ego and the world, or as higher self and lower self, does not break consciousness.

201

At the centre of every man's being there is his imperishable soul, his guardian angel.

202

The Overself is not merely a mental concept for all men but also a driving force for some men, not merely a pious pleasant feeling for those who believe in it but also a continuing vital experience for those who have lifted the ego's heavy door-bar.(P)

203

No one can explain what the Overself is, for it is the origin, the mysterious source, of the explaining mind, and beyond all its capacities. But what can be explained are the effects of standing consciously in its presence, the conditions under which it manifests, the ways in which it appears in human life and experience, the paths which lead to its realization.(P)

204

It is a state of pure intelligence but without the working of the intellectual and ideational process. Its product may be named intuition. There are no automatically conceived ideas present in it, no habitually followed ways of thinking. It is pure, clear, stillness.(P)

205

The very essence of that Stillness is the Divine Being. Yet from it come forth the energies which make and break universes, which are perpetually active, creative, inventive, and mobile.

206

Let no one imagine that contact with the Overself is a kind of dreamy reverie or pleasant, fanciful state. It is a vital relationship with a current of peace, power, and goodwill flowing endlessly from the invisible centre to the visible self.(P)

207

Although it is true that the Overself is the real guardian angel of every human being, we should not be so foolish as to suppose its immediate intervention in every trivial affair. On the contrary, its care is general rather than particular, in the determination of long-term phases rather than day-by-day events. Its intervention, if that does occur, will be occasioned by or will precipitate a crisis.(P)

208

There is a knowing element in man, the real knower which makes intellectual knowing possible and which is Consciousness-by-itself.

209

It is that part of man which is fundamental, real, undying, and truly *knowing*.(P)

210

This is the element in the human being that is covered with mystery, which is why, to some extent, the ancient pagan religious secret or semi-secret organized institutional attempts to penetrate it were titled "The Mysteries."

211

What could be closer to a man than his own be-ing? What could be more inward than the core of his self-awareness?

212

Knowledge of law, language, or history can be collected and becomes a possession but knowledge of the Overself is not at all the same. It is something one must be: it owns us, we do not have it.

213

Stillness is both a sign that sense and thought, body and intellect, have been transcended and a symbol of the consciousness of the presence of the Overself.

214

Whatever is said or written about that august truth, reality, consciousness, and perception of the Overself, and no matter how eloquently, it will still be only a pathetic belittlement of its subject. That is why seers like Lao Tzu in China and Ramana Maharshi in India declared it was better to be silent and utter nothing at all.

215

To call this Overself "He" merely because the multitude ignorantly call God so, is to ascribe sex to what is formless and to give ego to what is impersonal, is to commit the disgusting blasphemy of anthropomorphism.

216

Just as the eye cannot see itself as a second thing apart, so the Overself (which you are) cannot objectify itself, cannot become an object to be looked at or thought about. For in that case you would be dealing with a pretender, while all your thinking could in the end only deliver another thought, not the reality itself.

217

The Holy Ghost was called by Origen "the *active* force of God."

218

This is its mystery, that seeing all, it is itself seen by none.

219

Whatever men may say about it will not be enough to describe it properly, justly, accurately. All such efforts will be clumsy but they will not be useless. They will be suggestive, offer clues perhaps, each in its own way.

220

What is its consciousness like? If we use our ordinary faculties only, we may ponder this problem for a lifetime without discerning its solution for it is evident that we enter a realm where the very questioner himself must disappear as soon as he crosses the frontier. The personal "I" must be like a mere wave in such an ocean, a finite centre in incomprehensible infinitude. It would be impossible to realize what mind-in-itself is so long as we narrow down the focus of attention to the personal "I"-thought. For it would be like a wave vainly trying to collect and cram the whole ocean within itself, while refusing to expand its attention beyond its own finite form.

221

All that he knows and experiences are things in this world of the five senses. The Overself is not within their sphere of operation and therefore not to be known and experienced in the same way. This is why the first real entry into it must necessarily be an entry into no-thing-ness. The mystical phenomena and mystical raptures happen merely on the journey to this Void.

222

It is a consciousness where the "here" is universal and the "now" is everlasting.

223

There is a sense of the total absence of time, a feeling of the unending character of one's inner being.

224

The being which he finds at the end of this inner search is an anonymous one. He may ask for a name but he will not get one. He must be satisfied with the obscure response: "I Am That I Am!"

225

The Overself is there, but it is hidden within our conscious being. Only there, in this deep atmosphere, do we come upon the mirage-free Truth, the illusion-free Reality.

226

There are deep places in men's hearts and minds into which they rarely venture. And yet treasures are hidden there—flashes of intuition, important revelations, extra strengths, and above all a peace out of this world.

227

It is Conscious Silence.

228

The Knowing or Self-awareness of the Overself is never absent; it is always seeing.

229

Yes, your guardian angel is always present and always the secret witness and recorder of your thoughts and deeds. Whether you go down into the black depths of hell or ascend to the radiant heights of heaven, you do not walk alone.

230

Wherever they happen to be, in wide-scattered countries, widely different climates, and far-apart centuries, men have experienced this divine presence. What does this show? That it is not dependent on place and hour, not subject to the laws of space-time.

231

Deep down in the mind and feeling of man is the mysterious godlike Essence seemingly too deep—alas!—for the ordinary man, who therefore lets himself be content with hearing from others about it and thus only at second hand.

232

If we believe in or know of the reality of the Overself, we must also believe or know that our everyday, transient life is actively rooted in its timeless being.

233

It is the life-giving, body-healing, or occult-power-bestowing force in man. It is not a theoretical conception but a quickening, transforming power.

234

The problem of our relation to the Overself is difficult to clear up satisfactorily in words. Hence the statements about it in my book must not be taken too literally and too precisely. Words pertain to a lower order of being. The Overself is not a discriminating observing entity in our human and ordinary sense. But its power and intelligence are such that the activities of discrimination and observation would *appear* to be at work merely through its presence. Everything in our lives happens *as if* the Overself took a direct interest and arranged its manifestation, and that is the wonder and mystery of the human situation. Only by comparing this situation with that of the dreaming man and his various dream egos can we even get a hint of what its reality is.

235

There is a godlike thing within us which theology calls the spirit and which, because it is also a portion of the higher power within the universe, I call the Overself. He is wise indeed who takes it as his truest guide and makes it his protective guardian.

236

In the end, after many a life on earth, he will find that much of what he looks for in others will have to be found in himself. But it will not be found in the surface self. It lies deeply submerged, in a region where the purest forms exist.

237

Those who want to prolong their ego's little existence into the Overself's life naturally draw back with shock or horror when it is explained that there all is anonymous and impersonal.

238

It is nothing frigid, austere, or inhuman but a warm serenity, a deep glowing peace.

239

The Overself is not only the best part of himself but also the unalterable part.

240

I am well aware that I have used the term Overself inconsistently and indifferently and that now a fresh definition is imposed upon the work in my new book. Does the cancellation of the earlier definitions render them false? By no means! They are perfectly correct when read *in their proper places*; their defect is that they are incomplete; they are not representative of the highest truth; they are true in the world of religion, or of mysticism, as the case may be, but not in the world of philosophy.

241

Although this does not think, its presence makes thinking possible, and although it does not register on our five senses, it makes all sense impressions possible.

242

We cannot see, hear, or touch without the mind. But the mind, in its turn, cannot function or even exist without the Overself.

243

It is from the Overself that every true prophet receives his power. "I of myself am nothing," confessed Jesus.

244

The point in consciousness where the mind projects its thoughts has been called by the ancients "the cave" or "the cave of the heart." This is because to the outside observer there is nothing but darkness in it and therefore the cave hides whatever it may contain. When, by an inward reorientation of attention, we trace thoughts, whether of external things or internal fancies, to their hidden origin and penetrate the dark shroud around it, we penetrate into Mind, the divine Overself. We cannot help remembering Gray's apposite lines: "Full many a gem of purest ray serene, The dark unfathomed caves of ocean bear."

245

The Overself does not evolve and does not progress. These are activities which belong to time and space. It is nowhere in time and nowhere in space. It *is* Here, in this deep beautiful and all-pervading calm, that a man finds his real identity.

246

Everything that exists in time must also exist in change. The Overself does not exist in time and is not subject to change.

247

Do not insult the Higher Power by calling it unconscious; it is not only fully conscious but also fully intelligent. Your real Self, which is this power, needs neither commands nor instructions from the physical brain.

248

The Overself is not anyone's private property.

249

Why did Jesus give the opening of the Lord's Prayer as "Our Father" and not as "My Father"? Was he not trying to get his disciples away from the self-centered attitude to the cosmic one? Was he not widening their outlook to make them think of mankind's welfare?

250

The Overself surrounds the borderline of the ego, its perfection stretching into infinity.

251

There is no way of showing the Overself for anyone's examination. Since the ego comes out of the Overself, the only way it can see it again is to go back into it.

252

Miguel de Molinos: "The Soul is a pure Spirit and does not feel herself. Its acts are not perceptible."

253

This beneficent, freedom-bestowing, character-transforming, soul-awakening, gentle Presence is Overself.

254

The interpretation of "Overself" which I have given in my book *The Wisdom of the Overself* is confirmed by the teaching of a former Sri Shankaracharya of Kolhapur (1912) as told by one of his disciples. He taught *Atman*—that part of the Absolute which is Man. He interpreted it as "higher self."

255

Whether out in this world of ugly happenings or deep within the mind in a heaven of beauty and peace, the observer is the same; but in the first case he is the little limited ego and in the second case he is THAT from which the ego draws its sustenance—the Overself.

256

If there is not to be an endless series of observers, which would be unthinkable, there must be an ultimate one, itself unobserved and self-illuminated.

257

Somewhere at the hidden core of man's being there is light, goodness, power, and tranquillity.

258

The infinite divine life dwells within all embodied creatures, therefore in all mankind. It is the final source of his feelings and his consciousness, however limited they are here in the body itself.

259

There is nothing else like it; nothing with which the Overself could be compared.

260

It has no form to be pictured and weighed, measured and numbered; it makes no movement to be timed and no sound to be registered on the ear drum.

261

It could be said that the innermost essence of a man, be it his heart or his mind, is the Overself.

262

No person can hope to discover what God is like since human beings do not possess the proper faculties for such an undertaking. The best one can do is to create for himself an idea or interpretation of God that will suit his understanding and help him. Some people call it by different names; in fact, in my writings, I have referred to it as the Soul, the Overself, the Higher Self, the True Self, and so on—all of which are quite correct.

263

The word Overmind should never have been introduced but now that it is here it must be explained. There is only one Reality. The nearest notion we can form of it is that it is something mental. If we think of it as being the sum total of all individual minds, then it is Overmind; if we can rise higher and know that it cannot be totalized, it is Overself. The first explanation was originally introduced to explain why abnormal phenomena can happen but not as a final explanation of what Mind and Reality are. People have confused the two aims. Actually there is only One thing, whatever you call it, but it can be studied from different standpoints and thus we get different results. That thing is Mind—unindividuated, infinite.

264

The planetary overmind is the active aspect of the Overself but still only an aspect. It works with space and time although the latter assumes dimensions far beyond that with which waking human capacity can cope. The Overself in its passive purity is timeless and spaceless.

265

The Overself has not expressed itself in matter simply because there is no matter! It has not improved itself by evolution, but finite, individual minds have done so. The universal gods are the Overminds, the sum totals of each system—that is, concepts of the human mind which are dropped by the adept when they have served their purpose in bringing him to That which is unlimited. Seek the kingdom first, and all these occult powers will be added unto you.

266

The point in the heart is a focus for meditation and also an experience during meditation. When, however, one rises to the ultimate path he disregards the heart because the Overself has nothing to do with localities or geography of any kind; it cannot be measured.

267

It is often asked why we have so little contact with the Overself, why it is so hard to find the clues which shall lead us to it.

268

There is more within him of the good than a man suspects, even though experience may make him believe otherwise. But it lies in a deeper layer, hence it needs a longer time to bring it up.

269

It is not the Reality found by speculation or thinking alone, for intellect can err. It is the Reality found by the mystic intuition of mystic experience, by Reason (as opposed to intellect) of Philosophy, and verified by a realization more immediate and intimate than the ego of ordinary life, with its passions, emotions, and thoughts, and deeper than anything ever before experienced.

270

There is no single term satisfactory on all points for use when referring to THAT. The name "Overself" is no exception to this situation. But to those who object to this coinage of a new word, the answer is best given by the editor of the latest edition of Fowler's *Modern English Usage*, Sir

Ernest Gowers: "I'm all in favour of new words. How else would a language live and flourish?"

271

It is the observer which is itself unobserved.

272

It is as difficult to trace the spiritual source of a man's life as it is to trace the mathematical source of *pi*, of 3.14159. . .

273

We may try to make this idea as clearly definable as we can, but nothing put into words can in the end be more than a hint, a clue, or merely suggestive.

274

Just as the pearl is well hidden within the oyster and not apparent until searched for, so the Overself is well hidden in man.

275

The Christ-self who was in Jesus is in us too.

276

It is like nothing that we know from experience or can picture from imagination. Space does not hold it. Time does not condition it.

277

There are some truths which are durable ones. Change cannot change them. This is one of them.

278

If most men fail to recognize the Overself, if they deny its presence in Nature or in themselves, can they be blamed? What else is so elusive?

279

It was, I believe, Matthew Arnold who first used this term "higher self," and it is certainly expressive enough for our present purpose.

280

Here is one thing which does not have to move with the times, although the communication of it and instruction in it, do.

281

Here is the concentrated ultimate essence of his being.

282

In this spiritual self we may find the origin of life.

283

That which is within us as the Overself, being godlike, is out of time and eternal.

284

There is something within him which is without personal existence, without a name, and without scrutable face. It is the Overself.

285

Here is the beginning, the middle, and the end of all wisdom.

286

All power and all intelligence reside within it.

287

It is "the sacred spirit dwelling within us, observer and guardian of all our evil and our good" of Seneca.

288

The Overself is shrouded in seemingly inaccessible and impenetrable mystery.

289

In the gravest depths of a man's being he will find, not fouling slime and evil, but cleansing divinity and goodness.

290

This is the irreducible essence of a man, where he *is*.

291

It is inaccessible to the intellect, unknowable by ordinary egoistic man. Yet there are some into whose consciousness It has entered.

292

It is a *felt* presence.

293

That from which the intellect's power recoils and the ego's pride suffers—that is the Overself!

294

He is not separate from his own experience, not an observer watching it. For there is only the inner silence, with which he is identified if he turns to examine the I, only the pure consciousness.

295

It is the presence of the Overself within us which makes more consciousness possible, whether it be the consciousness of the dream or the consciousness of waking.

296

There are two biblical quotations, one from the Song of Solomon and one from Saint Paul, that accurately refer to the Overself. This indeed is the real soul of man, whose finding here and now, during our life on earth, is the task silently set us by life itself.

297

That which finds itself and lives in him, works through him and is the God within: *a holy Presence.*

298

The real self is universal, in the sense that it does not belong to him or to his neighbour.

299

"The pristine nature of the Self is effortless, spontaneous *Tapas.* Incessant *Tapas* of that kind leads to the manifestation of all powers."—Sri Ramana Maharshi

300

This mysterious entity which dwells on the other side of our earthly consciousness is not as unperceptive of us as we are of it.

301

The Overself is truly our guardian angel, ever with us and never deserting us. It is our invisible saviour. But we must realize that it seeks primarily to save us not from suffering but from the ignorance which is the cause of our suffering.

302

This particular function of the Overself was known also to the more percipient among men of the Middle Ages and of antiquity. Thus Epictetus: "Zeus hath placed by the side of each, a man's own Guardian Spirit, who is charged to watch over him."

303

Atma = higher self; *Paramatma* = Mind; *Ishvara* = World Mind. Overself—all three generalized (preferred by Hiriyanna). *Jiva* = individual . . . (Tony's Center) "souls . . . behind the physicomental complex commonly called the individual . . . the eternal consciousness (*Atman*) as limited by the organism . . . the sense-organ, the *manas*, and the *antahkarana*."

Overself and World-Mind

304

We found it necessary, in the interests of greater precision and better exposition, to restrict the term "Overself" to represent the ultimate reality of man, and to introduce the term "World-Mind" to represent the ultimate reality of the universe.

305

The Overself is the representative of God in man.

306

The Overself is a part of World-Mind. Whereas World-Mind is beyond human capacity to know, the Overself is within that capacity.

307

That point *in* man where the two worlds of being—infinite and finite—can be said to touch, is Overself.

308

The gap between man's mind and God's mind is uncrossable. But the gap between his everyday mind and the Overself—which is close to God—is not. Through it he may penetrate a little deeper into the mystery.

309

The Overself is so close to God, so akin to the World-Mind, that no man need look farther, or aspire higher.

310

The Overself is the highest point in the human being; it is there where he can find himself "made in the image of God."

311

It is true to say that the Overself possesses properties which belong also to God. But because one man is *like* another, we do not claim him to be identical with that other. The Overself is Godlike in nature but not in identity.

312

The Overself is *our* knowledge, experience, or sight of the World-Mind, of God, and is the only one we shall ever get while we are still in the flesh.

313

There is a point where the human meets the divine, where the conscious ego emerges from the all-encompassing Void. That point we call the Overself.

314

There is some point in each individual being where the human and the divine must join, where man's little consciousness bends low before, or blends subtly with, the Universal Mind which is his ultimate source. It is impossible to describe that intersection in any terms which shall adequately fit it, but it can be named. In philosophy it is the Overself.

315

The essence of man is his Overself, which is an emanation from Mind.

316

Here is the focal point of all spiritual searching, here man meets God.(P)

317

The Overself is the point where the One Mind is received into consciousness. It is the "I" freed from narrowness, thoughts, flesh, passion, and emotion—that is, from the personal ego.(P)

318

That point where man meets the Infinite is the Overself, where he, the finite, responds to what is absolute, ineffable and inexhaustible Being, where he reacts to That which transcends his own existence—this is the Personal God he experiences and comes into relation with. In this sense his belief in such a God is justifiable.(P)

319

Overself is the inner or true self of man, reflecting the divine being and attributes. The Overself is an emanation from the ultimate reality but is neither a division nor a detached fragment of it. It is a ray shining forth but not the sun itself.(P)

320

It is true that the nature of God is inscrutable and that the laws of God are inexorable. But it is also true that the God-linked soul of man is accessible and its intuitions available.(P)

321

This divine self is the unkillable and unlosable soul, forever testifying to the source, whence it came.

322

Those who consider the hidden mind to be a mere storehouse of forgotten childhood memories or adolescent experiences and repressed adult wishes consider only a part of it, only a fraction. There is another and even still more hidden part which links man with the very sources of the universe—God.

323

That point of contact in consciousness where man first feels God and later vanishes into God, is the Overself.

324

The Overself is a part of the One Infinite Life-Power as the dewdrop is a part of the ocean.

325

In the normally covered centre of a man's being, covered by his thoughts and feelings and passions as a person, a self, IT IS. It is here that he is connected with the larger Being behind the universe, the World-Mind. In this sense he is not really an isolated unit, not alone. God is with him. It was a simple shepherd on Mount Horeb who, during a glimpse, asked "Who art Thou?" Came the answer: "I am He Who IS!"

326

With this grand consciousness, man reaches the APHELION of his orbit. He can go no higher and remain man.

327

Speaking metaphorically, we may say that the Overself is that fragment of God which dwells in man, a fragment which has all the quality and grandeur of God without all its amplitude and power.

328

The World-Mind's reflection in us is the Overself.

329

The thoughts and feelings which flow like a river through our consciousness make up the surface self. But underneath them there is a deeper self which, being an emanation from divine reality, constitutes our true self.

330

That which I call the Overself is intermediate between the ordinary human and the World-Mind. It includes man's higher nature but stretches into what is above him, the divine.

331

That which connects the individual man to the Universal Spirit, I call the Overself. This connection can never be broken. Its existence is the chief guarantee that there is hope of salvation for *all*, not merely for those who think their group alone will be granted it.

332

It is *his own* greater self, his Overself, that he thus experiences, although he may be so overwhelmed by its mysterious Power, so awed by its ethe-reality, that he usually believes—and names—it God. And in one mode of meaning, his belief is not without justification. For at the core of the experience, he, the atom within the World-Mind, receives the revelation that it is ever there and, more, ever supporting him.

333

It is this, the deepest part of his being, his final essential self, which is a man's Overself, and which links him with the World-Mind. It is this Presence within which evokes all his spiritual quality.

334

This is the essential being of a man, where his link with God lies.

335

Epictetus helps us to understand, and our intellect to define, the Overself. "Do you not know," he says, "that you carry a god within you? . . . You are a distinct portion of the essence of God and contain a part of Him within yourself."

Overself and ego

336

It is amazing paradox that the Overself completely transcends the body yet completely permeates it: both these descriptions are simultaneously true.

337

Although the Overself does not pass through the diverse experiences of its imperfect image, the ego, nevertheless it witnesses them. Although it is aware of the pain and pleasure experienced by the body which it is animating, it does not itself feel them; although detached from physical sensations, it is not ignorant of them. On the other hand, the personal consciousness does feel them because it regards them as states of its own self. Thus the Overself is conscious of our joys and sorrows without itself sharing them. It is aware of our sense-experience without itself being physically sentient. Those who wonder how this is possible should reflect that a man awakened from a nightmare is aware once again in the form of a revived memory of what he suffered and what he sensed but yet does not share again either the suffering or the sensations.

338

The Overself perceives and knows the individual self, but only as an imperturbable witness—in the same way that the sun witnesses the various objects upon the earth but does not enter into a particular relation with a particular object. So too the Overself is present in each individual self as the witness and as the unchanging consciousness which gives consciousness to the individual.

339

The "I" is immeasurably greater than the ego which it projects or than the intellect, which the ego uses.

340

The normal man thinks he is body plus mind, with emphasis on the body. But self-questioning and analysis show that, although he certainly has these two things and is certainly associated with them, the "I" is in fact neither of them. It is, by contrast, not changing and quite elusive. It is not in space, as the body is, nor in time, as the mind is. It is, in fact, a mystery. The attempt to find out what it is brings up the questions of existence, life, activity, and consciousness.

341

All that anyone basically possesses unlost through all his life is his "I." All that he really *is*, is this same "I." The physical body, although seemingly inseparable from it, is something lived in and used, as a house is lived in and a tool is used.

342

To look at a man and at his life from the outside is only to see half the man. To look at them from the inside is to see the other half. Put these two fragments together and there is the whole man. Or so it would seem. But what if behind his thoughts and feelings there were still another self of an utterly different kind and quality? And this exactly is his situation. He does not know all of himself, and he understands it even less. Those who have been privileged to look behind the veil can only urge him to recognize this incompleteness and teach him what steps to take to overcome it.

343

The divine soul in us is utterly above and unaffected by the sense impressions. If we become conscious of it, we also become conscious of a supersensual order of existence.

344

It is a higher self not only in a moral sense but also in a cosmic sense. For the lower one issued forth from it, but under limitations of consciousness, form, space, and time which are not in the parent Self.

345

When we come to see that it is the body alone that expresses the coming into life and the going into death, that in the true self there is neither a beginning nor an ending but rather LIFE itself, we shall see aright.

346

No men are without their sense of the Overself, but they miscomprehend and therefore misapply it. The result is that ego, the little part, is conceived to be the whole, the All.

347

Because the godlike is in each one of us, and because no two of us are alike, each has his or her separate gifts, capacities, or talents to express. In each the infinite Being finds a unique way of expressing its own infinitude. Even if we have no gifts we have our individual characteristics.

348

It is pure Being overlaid by many thoughts and much feeling.

349

Here in the ego we may perceive a reproduction of the sacred Overself under the limitations of time and space. Whoever grasps this great truth knows henceforth that this Overself is no more distant from him than his own heart and that what he calls "I" is inseparably united with what men call God.

350

We do not subscribe to the belief that the divine soul has somehow gone astray and got enslaved by the animal body.

351

His higher self is not polluted by his own pollutions any more than sunlight is affected by the foul places in which it often shines.

352

The higher self affects the ego but is not affected by it. Its existence goes on quite independently of the serialized earth appearances of the ego, and persists when the other ceases. The insensitive can never know it, and may roundly deny it, but the others sometimes receive unforgettable glimpses for which they give thanks to Allah for years afterwards.

353

Just as space is unaffected equally by the evil deeds or virtuous actions of men, so the Overself is unaffected by the character or conduct of the ego. It is neither made worse by the ego's wrong-doing nor better by its righteousness.

354

"I am the way, the Truth," announced Jesus. Who is this *I*? In the narrow and shallower sense it is the master. In the broader and deeper sense, it is the Christ-self within, the spiritual consciousness.

355

Why did Jesus say, "I and my Father are one," but yet a little later add, "The Father is greater than I"? The answer is that Jesus the man had attained complete harmony with his higher Self and felt himself one with it, but the universal Christ-principle will always be greater than the man himself; the Overself will always transcend the person.

356

Although it is still identified with him, since it is his own mind at its best level, it is immensely grander wiser and nobler than he.

357

It is an entity greater, nobler, wiser, and stronger than himself yet mysteriously and inseparably linked to himself; it is indeed his super-self.

358

Our bodies are born at some point of time and somewhere in space but their essence, the Overself, is birthless, timeless, and placeless.

359

This is a man's true individuality, not that mentally constructed "I" (which deludes him into acceptance as such).

360

It is never anything else than its own perfect self, never contrary to its own unique and infinite nature.

361

It is true that we are but poor and faulty, sadly limited, and miserably shrunken expressions of the divine spirit. Nevertheless, we *are* expressions of it.

362

The personal pronoun "I" really represents the Overself, the divine part of man. What people usually refer to as "I"—the body or the intellect or the emotions—is not the basic "I" at all.

363

You ask a question which (1) ought not to be asked and (2) is quite unanswerable. Nevertheless I shall try: "What good is a Consciousness of which we are unaware?" you argue. Answer: "No good!" But your question is in error. There *is* some awareness, although a limited one. This *appears* as your ego-consciousness, which is a reflection of the Consciousness you ask about. Because the Universal and Infinite cannot be packed into the personal and finite, your demand, natural though it be, is unreasonable. Erigena, the first British—I beg pardon, Irish—philosopher (ninth century) was much influenced by Dionysius the Areopagite (first century) and it was under such influence that he wrote: "God Himself knows not what He is, for He is not a 'what.'" So why ask a mere man?

364

Just as there is a sun hidden behind the sun, the divinity which animates it, so in the human being there is a Mind within the mind—and that is his Overself.

365

The personality is always limited and chained, the higher individuality always infinite and free.

366

Each man is the expression of this infinite life-power.

367

His awareness of life in the five senses will rest upon another and inner awareness. A second and hidden self will thus seem to support his outer one.

368

The true *I* yields quite a different feeling, experience, and consciousness from the familiar physical ego.

369

There is a deeper level of every man's mind which is not subject to his passions, not moved by his desires, not affected by his senses.

370

It is not possible for the timeless, spaceless, formless Overself to be degraded into activity by its time-bound, space-tied, form-limited offspring the person.

371

The essence of man is not his earthly body. Nor is it the ghostly duplicate of that body, as many spiritists and some religionists think.

372

The Overself is the Higher mind in man, his divine soul as distinguished from his human-animal nature. It is the same as Plato's "nous."

373

The true unchanging self is apart from any historical era and is not dependent on outer changes of custom and form.

374

The aim of the mystic is to know what he is, apart from his physical body, his lower emotion, his personal ego; it is to know his inner-most self. When this aim is successfully realized, he knows then with perfect certitude that he is a ray of the divine sun.

375

How shall he know and understand that this very awareness, of which so small is the fragment that he experiences, is a limited and conditioned part of the Great Awareness itself, of God?

376

The inhabitant of this fleshly body, including its accompanying invisible "ghost," is a sacred one.

377

There, within and yet behind his personal consciousness, is this other sphere of his own being into which he must one day be re-born as a chick from an egg.

378

This is his best self; this is what he really is under all the defects.

Central and universal

379

The higher self is a paradox. It is both central and universal. The two are together.

380

The knowledge that no two human beings are alike refers to their bodies and minds. But this leaves out the part of their nature which is spiritual, which is found and experienced in deep meditation. In that, the deepest part of their conscious being, the personal self vanishes; only consciousness-in-itself, thought-free, world-free, remains. This is the source of the "I" feeling, and it is exactly alike in the experience of all other human beings. This is the part which never dies, "where God and man may mingle."

381

There is only one Overself for the whole race, but the point of contact with it is special and unique, and constitutes man's higher individuality.

382

Whereas every human personality is different in its characteristics from every other one, no human Overself is different in its characteristics from any other one. The seekers of all times and all places have always found one and the same divine being when they found the Overself.

383

This Overself is everywhere one and the same for all men. The experience of rising into awareness of it does not differ in actuality from one man to another, but the purity with which he absorbs it, interprets it, understands it, does. Hence, the varieties of expression used about it, the clash of revelations concerning it.

384

This is the paradox, that the Overself is at once universal and individual. It is the first because it overshadows all men as a single power. It is the second because it is found by each man within himself. It is both space and the point in space. It is infinite Spirit and yet it is also the holy presence in everyone's heart.

385

This other being is outside the "I" yet, paradoxically, and in another sense, it is inside the "I." It is not himself yet also it is himself. If these statements cannot be understood at first reading, do not therefore denounce them. If you are really in earnest, approach them prayerfully or, if your feelings cannot be made to run on that line, aspiringly at the precise moments when you approach the mysterious moment that transmutes your waking state into the sleep state. But do not expect to receive satisfaction with the first trial nor even a twentieth—although this is always possible. If you do not desert the enterprise through impatience, you will find one day that you are at last able to read, clearly and correctly, the meaning of these mystical words. Other people have done it, have emerged from the mind's obscurity into the intuition's clarity, although at varying pace. They have succeeded because the constitution of man, being double, makes it possible.

386

The mysterious character of the Overself inevitably puzzles the intellect. We may appreciate it better if we accept the paradoxical fact that it unites a duality and that therefore there are two ways of thinking of it, both correct. There is the divine being which is entirely above all temporal concerns, absolute and universal, and there is also the demi-divine being which is in historical relation with the human ego.

387

It is possible for the fully illumined mystic to experience two different states of identification with his Higher Self. In one, he becomes conscious of the latter on IT's own plane; in the other, which he experiences in deep trance only, even that is transcended and there is only the ONE/Being. Yet this is not annihilation. What it is (*infinite*) is beyond human comprehension, and therefore beyond human description.

388

It is hard to tell in words about the wordless, hard to formulate in intellect-born phrases what is beyond the intellect. To say that the higher self is or is not individualized is to distort meaning and arouse miscomprehension. But a simile may help us here. The drop of water which, with the countless millions of other drops, makes up the ocean is distinct but not separable from them. It is both different from and yet the same as them. At the base of each man's being stretches the one infinite life alone, but within it his centre of existence rests.

389

At the end of all its adventures, the lower self may indeed have to go, but the indestructible higher self will not go. In this sense there is no utter annihilation of the individual, no complete mergence of it into an all-swallowing ocean of cosmic consciousness, as so many Western critics of Eastern wisdom believe to be the latter's last word.

390

Because of the paradoxically dual nature which the Overself possesses, it is very difficult to make clear the concept of the Overself. Human beings are rooted in the ultimate mind through the Overself, which therefore partakes on the one hand of a relationship with a vibratory world and on the other of an existence which is above all relations. A difficulty is probably due to the vagueness or confusion about which standpoint it is to be regarded from. If it is thought of as the human soul, then the vibratory movement is connected with it. If it is thought of as transcending the very notion of humanity, and therefore in its undifferentiated character, the vibratory movement must disappear.(P)

391

If we are to think correctly, we cannot stop with thinking of the Overself as being only within us. After this idea has become firmly established for its metaphysical and devotional value, we must complete the concept by thinking of the Overself as being also without us. If in the first concept it occupies a point in space, in the second one it is beyond all considerations of place.(P)

392

We may take comfort in the fact that the Overself never at any moment abandons or obliterates the human personality, however debased it becomes. Nor could it do so, whatever foolish cults say to the contrary, for through this medium it finds an expression in time-space.

393

When we say that the Overself is within the heart, it would be a great error to think that we mean it is limited to the heart. For the heart is also within it. This seeming paradox will yield to reflection and intuition. The mysterious relationship between the ego and the Overself has been expressed by Jesus in the following words: "The Father is in the Son, and the Son is in the Father."

394

The dictionary defines *individuality* as separate and distinct existence. Both the ego and the Overself have such an existence. But whereas the ego has this and nothing more, the Overself has this consciousness within the universal existence. That is why we have called it the *higher individuality*.

395

The fact that after awaking the mind picks up the thoughts of the day before, that the individuality connects with the old individuality of pre-sleep, proves the continuity of existence of a part of Self both during sleep as during waking.

396

Every situation in human life can be approached from two possible points of view. The first is the limited one and is that of the personal self. The second is the larger one and is that of Universal Self. The larger and longer view always justifies itself in the end.

397

Each Overself is like a circle whose centre is in some individual but whose circumference is not in any individual.

398

We must not imagine that the subordination of this sense of personal identity leads to any loss of consciousness—rather the reverse. Man becomes more, not less, for he emerges into the fullness and freedom of one universal life. He thinks of himself as: "I, A.B., am a point within the Overself," whereas before he only thought: "I am A.B."

399

The higher self keeps the same kind of individuality without being separate that each facet of a diamond keeps. The light which shines through it shines equally through all facets alike, remaining one and the same.

400

The individuality is beyond the personality—its level is higher. The one must prompt while the other must watch the pitiless destruction of its wishes and hopes, its values and desires, until only the pure being of individuality is left.

401

It is a kind of impersonal being but it is not utterly devoid of all individuality.

402

As a wave sinks back into the sea, so the consciousness which passes out of the personal self sinks back into its higher individuality.

403

This is the general mind behind our small personal minds, the one behind the many.

Responding to critics

404

There is no other way to settle doubts concerning the soul with incontestable certainty than the way of getting personal knowledge of it by a mystical glimpse.

405

Even when a man denies the Overself and thinks it out of his view of life, he is denying and thinking by means of the Overself's own power—attenuated and reflected though it be. He is able to reject the divine presence with his mind only because it is already in his mind.

406

Buddhism points out that although Nirvana *is*, there is no self to perceive it. As Buddhism denies a permanent self, the question of what Nirvana is *experimentally* does not arise. Nirvana is not a state of mind which is to be produced but is what is realized when the long-cherished notion of "I" is given up. Nirvana, in short, is the miracle of egoless being. The Buddha's doctrine of the soul was stated in negative terms because he was controverting current misconceptions. He explained this in *Alagadupama Majjhima*, 1, 135: "Even in this present life, my brethren, I say that the soul is indefinable. Though I say and teach thus, there are those who accuse me falsely of being a nihilist, of teaching the non-existence and annihilation of the soul. That is what *I am not and do not teach*."

407

There is a long line of testimony, to which I must add my own, that the Overself is no metaphysical abstraction or mystical hallucination but a living and inspiring, if uncommon, part of human experience. To know it is to know one's best self.

408

The Overself is not something imagined or supposed. Its presence is definitely felt.

409

If a man asks why he can find no trace of God's presence in himself, I answer that he is full of evidence, not merely traces. God is present in him as consciousness, the state of being aware; as thought, the capacity to think; as activity, the power to move; and as stillness, the condition of ego, emotion, intellect, and body which finally and clearly reveals what these other things simply point to. "Be still, and know that I am God" is a statement of being whose truth can be tested by experiment and whose value can be demonstrated by experience.(P)

410

When we realize that the intellect can put forth as many arguments against this theme as for it, we realize that there is in the end only one perfect proof of the Overself's existence. The Overself must prove itself. This can come about faintly through the intuition or fully through the mystical experience.(P)

411

Whoever needs proofs of the authenticity of this experience has not had it.

412

The difficulty of collecting and studying, sifting and describing the varieties of mystical experience which may be found today is a barrier to the expansion of scientific psychology. For those persons who are most eager to talk about their own experiences are the most dubious and unreliable source. Those who are the least eager, feeling the matter to be too private, personal, intimate, and sacred, are able to offer valuable evidence.

413

Testimony to the existence and reality of the glimpse will be found in the literatures of all peoples through all times. It is not a newly manufactured idea, nor a newly manufactured fancy. A man who denies it is foolish so to limit his own possibilities, but he may learn better with time.

414

These glimpses cannot rightly be dismissed by the scientist as merely self-suggested or wholly hallucinatory. Nor can they properly be regarded by the metaphysician as valueless for truth. As human beings we live by experience, and they are personal experiences which help to confirm the truth of the impersonal bases underneath them and which encourage us to continue on the same path.

415

The Overself is a living reality. Nobody would waste his years, his endeavours, and his energies in its quest if it were merely an intellectual concept or an emotional fancy.

416

The Overself is not only a necessary conception of logical thought. It is also a beautiful fact of personal experience.

417

There are three signs, among others, of the Soul's presence in a Soul-denying generation. They are: moral conscience, artistic imagination, and metaphysical speculation.

418

Criticism which knows only sensuous and intellectual experience can be little valid here if, indeed, it is not entirely irrelevant.

419

When a man confuses the nature of the mind with its own thoughts, when he is unable properly to analyse consciousness and memory, when he has never practised introspection and meditation successfully, he can know nothing of the soul and may well be sceptical of its existence.

420

That the Overself is not the product of an inflated imagination but has a real existence, is a truth which any man who has the required patience and submits to the indispensable training may verify himself.

421

It is not a dim abstraction but a real presence. Not a vague theory but a vital fact.

422

To the man of insight there is something strange, ironic, and yet pathetic in the spectacle of those who turn the consciousness and the understanding derived from Overself against the acknowledgment of Its existence.

423

Because he regards the theory and practice of his subject from the inside, the mystic can discuss it with a correctness and authority which most critics do not possess because they are outside it. They are largely in the dark about it—he is actually in the light.

424

Those who have never felt it in themselves nor seen it demonstrated in others cannot understand the blessedness of such a state.

425

Because they are unready for it, they cannot endure such an experience. The peace it imparts is too impersonal and would suffocate them. The detachment which it creates makes the worldly life seem less important and is too frightening.

426

The recognition that this experience does happen is increasing rapidly in Western countries but in the East it has never been doubted. The criticism that mystical experience is subjective and illusory is being dropped, as it ought to be.

427

Those who have never experienced this state yet venture to criticize it as illusory are dealing with mere words, not facts.

428

If the ordinary man seldom gets these subtler experiences it is because his nature is too coarse, his mind too physically based, his focus too personal to permit him to receive them.

429

Deep within his own heart, hidden within his own consciousness, every person carries all the evidence for the truth of these teachings that he or she is ever likely to need.

430

That arrogance which denies heaven to the unorthodox does not trouble the mystic. He finds heaven *here* in this life, *now* before the transition of death.

431

At such times, unexpected and unsought though they are, he feels the nearness of God, the love of God, the reality of God. Whoever ventures to call them delusions is himself deluded.

432

Do these moods of utter tranquillity have to repeat themselves again and again to convince doubting man that there is indeed a state of consciousness beyond the everyday so-called normal one? Is not such personal experience the best offering of testimony from the Soul to its own existence?

433

Not only philosophy, but the teaching of all seers like Krishna and Jesus, would have to be pronounced fraudulent if the Overself were not a fact.

434

In its oneness and sameness for participants the world over, the mystic experience proves its validity.

435

Men who pronounce judgements or write opinions upon mysticism without actual and personal experience of its mental states and phenomena, who interpret it only from the outside and only as observers, cannot be reliable authorities on the subject.

436

Those critics who are on the outside looking in, do not and cannot know as much about the truth of mysticism as those who are deep within its inside looking out.

437

There is only one way to settle his question of whether the Overself exists and that is the very way most moderns refuse to accept. Each must gain for himself the *authentic* mystical experience. Sugar can really be known only by its sweet taste, the Overself only by opening the doors of the mind to consciousness of its presence.

438

Those who have had this overwhelming experience require no arguments to make them believe in the soul. They know that they *are* the soul.

439

An experience which is so convincing, so real, that no intellectual argument to the contrary can stand against it, is final. Let others say what they will, he remains unswayed.

4

INTRODUCTION TO MYSTICAL GLIMPSES

A glimpse is a transitory state of mental enlightenment and emotional exaltation.

2

It is an experience of *self*-discovery, not the discovery of some other being, whether a guru or a god.

3

These brief flashes bring with them great joy, great beauty, and great uplift. They are, for most people, their first clear vivid awakening to the existence and reality of a spiritual order of being. The contrast with their ordinary state is so tremendous as to shame it into pitiful drabness. The intention is to arouse and stimulate them into the longing for re-entry into the spirit, a longing which inevitably expresses itself in the quest.

4

In the past these glimpse experiences were regarded as wholly religious. Today the truth about them is better understood. They may be aesthetic, psychological, intellectual, or creative—happening outside the religious circle.

5

All our ordinary experience comes to us through sense responses or intellectual workings. But here is a kind of experience which does not come through these two channels. It is not a series of sensations nor a series of thoughts. What is it, then? Philosophy says it belongs to the transcendental world.

6

The uniqueness of this moment shines out against the relatedness of all other moments. Words only limit it by their precision and their pressure, yet they are all some of us have with which to make a likeness of it to show friends, or to hold before ardent seekers, or even to return to ourselves in dark and difficult periods.

7

The glimpse may be best compared to a moment of wakefulness in a long existence of sleep.

8

These mystical glimpses have close parallels with the best features of the best types of religious conversion. Indeed, as might be expected, they are deeper and more developed and better controlled forms of them.

9

These glimpses, these transcendental visitations as the Hindu metaphysician calls them, bring joy, serenity, and understanding.

10

No rational explanation has been given of the seemingly eccentric character of these glimpses, no reasonable theory of their why, what, how, and when.

11

The mystical experience may be beyond reasoned analysis but it is not beyond reasonable description.

12

Putting words together on paper to tell how this glimpse lifts one out of the ordinariness of the common existence, is a work anyone must enjoy doing.

13

It is a brief and temporary enlargement of consciousness, in theological language, an improvement of its connection with God.

14

How is one to describe this experience? It is an expansion, and yet also a concentration, of consciousness.

15

It is not enough to say that someone has had a mystical experience. This phrase can cover the most opposite, the most widely different experiences.

16

The experience is so beautiful that no description can transfer the feelings it awakens from one heart to another.

17

These are the real waking moments of a man's life: for the rest he is asleep without ever guessing that he is.

18

It is *not* the highest point of the moral experience, although that approaches it, or can help to bring it on, or acts as a preparation for it. It is not the peak of the aesthetic experience, although that fulfils the same services.

19

Here are life's highest processes, an experience beyond thinking and an awareness beyond the sensual.

20

During this period he is, as the Chinese say, "in the Way," or as we Westerners would say, "in God."

21

These rare moments lift him out of his animal self and detach him from his lower human self.

22

Only a poet could portray these experiences as they deserve; to write of them with outer photographic exactness only is to half-lose them.

23

In religious language he is in God, and in mystical language God is in him.

24

He has reached a world which is as much beyond good as it is beyond evil.

25

In the world's literatures there are many records left by persons who have had this glimpse, but each has interpreted it in his or her own way, each has reacted within the frame of his or her personal background.

26

These are sudden and unpredictable emergences from the ignorance and confusion of ordinary consciousness.

27

These visitations of grace are intimations of reality.

28

These moments of true consciousness free from the illusion unavoidable in ordinary experience are memorable.

29

It is to experience while still in the flesh what some others will not experience until they are in the spirit.

30

At such times he becomes aroused from the sleep of ignorance to the Overself's constant presence.

31

Put it into words as much as you can, this "Touch of the Untouch," but you will get nothing that is anything more than a whispered hint, a vague clue.

32

Those strange visitations, when one is suddenly aware of a presence—close, powerful, yet immaterial—are not easily explicable.

33

These are the moments which inspire a man, renew his dedication, strengthen his will, and give him integrity.

34

The years of spiritual fulfilment may be far off still, but presages and tokens may come momentarily to hearten him at times.

35

This is the sacred interlude when man transcends his isolation and feels the universe supporting him.

36

It is the highest possible form of self-recognition. It is the discovery of who and what we really are.

Part of natural life-experience

37

Although such glimpses are not common and do not happen every day, still they are more common and more frequent than is generally supposed.

38

That God is present in each person's life may seem unbelievable to so large a number of us. Yet it is for those undergoing the experience certitude, not theory. It is generally believed that hardly more than a few attain it, but as there are degrees of such an attainment one could say that in the lesser ones there are more successes than people generally know.

39

Even to ordinary persons moments can come which can pass very easily into glimpses. But their importance is not recognized and so the opportunities are missed. It is pitiful and pathetic that anyone should be so close to the diviner self and not take advantage of the propinquity by a pause of activity and a surrender to the delicate feeling which would develop of itself into a glimpse. It is pathetic, because these moments are in the nature of clues leading to the inward way; pitiful, because such people are living in a kind of blind alley and must one day retrace their steps.

40

This kind of thing is supposed to lie outside common experience, but the fact is that it comes more often through Nature, art, or music than most people suspect.

41

There is a moment in most men's lives when they are close to an understanding of the world's real nature.

42

Psychologists and psychoanalysts are beginning to find a minority among their ranks who put a high value upon these glimpses which they call "peak-experiences." Academically qualified, professionally trained, and science-oriented just like their colleagues, they yet differ in appreciating and studying such experiences as being important to an adequate knowledge of the human being.

43

Whatever conception of God a man may hold, his secret inner connection with God will disclose itself to him, whether in the pre- or post-mortem state, whether in the present or a future birth. This Revelation is his human right. The guarantee is that the World-Idea, which includes him too, must realize itself in the fullness of time in its irresistible and imperious course. He is bound to get the Glimpse for himself and no longer depend on others' say-so.

44

The glimpse in its most elementary form does not come only to specially gifted persons. It belongs to the portrait of every human being as a natural and not a mysterious part of his life-experience. It is simply a part of the feeling for Nature, to whose system he belongs, and for the Sun which is Nature's supreme expression. The sun's glory, beauty, power, and benignity arouse reverence. Oriental faiths mostly recognized this and made prayers obligatory at dawn and twilight.

45

The point which has yet to be made is that these glimpses are *not* supernatural superhuman and solely religious experiences. When scientific psychology has advanced to the point where it really understands the human being in all his height and depth, and not merely his surface, it will see this.(P)

46

Although he is normally quite unconscious of this connection with the Overself, once at least in a lifetime there is a flash which *visits* him and breaks the unconsciousness. He has a glimpse of his highest possibility. But the clearness and intensity of this glimpse depend upon his receptivity. They may amount to little or much.(P)

47

Many people without pretensions to mystical knowledge or belief have had this experience, this glimpse of timeless loveliness, through Nature, art, music, or even for no apparent reason at all.(P)

48

Those who have followed the Quest in previous lives will generally receive a glimpse at least twice during the present one. They will receive it in early life during their teens or around the threshold of adult life. This will inspire them to seek anew. They will receive it again in late life during the closing years of the reincarnation. This will be bestowed as a Grace of the Overself. Those aspirants who bemoan the loss of their early glimpse should remind themselves, in hours of depression, that it will recur before they leave the body. In addition to those glimpses which attend the opening and closing years of a lifetime, a number of others may be had during the intervening period as a direct consequence and reward of the efforts, disciplines, aspirations, and self-denials practised in that time.(P)

49

We ought not to mistake this for the exception; it is really the type. Most aspirants have experienced this mystical glimpse, brief and unexpected perhaps, which has started or kept them on this quest.

50

Even those men who assert or lament that they have never had a single glimpse during their whole lifetime will get it at the end. For it is a divinely ordained part of the process of dying.

51

When the genuine mystical experience comes, it presents the student with the rare chance to know for himself a state in the evolution of consciousness which still lies far ahead of mankind generally.

52

Such memorable glimpses of a higher state of being, which encourage and reassure him, may occur not only at the beginning of his spiritual career but also at the beginning of each new cycle within it.

53

A glimpse is apparently something that men rarely experience or something that most of them never experience. But the fact is that more people have had it than have recognized it for what it really is. And this has happened through their admiration of Nature or art, through falling in love, through sudden news.

54

This mystical glimpse comes to most men only at death, or at the fraction of a fraction of a second during the highest pitch of sexual intercourse.

55

At present this mystic experience is a fugitive one in the human species. But because it is also the ultimate experience of that species, there is no reason why it should not become a common one in the course of evolutionary development.

56

Dr. Richard M. Bucke's theory that the standard age of these illuminations is thirty-six is untenable. Mozart died in his thirty-sixth year but he had had glimpses long before. So did many other historically known men in the Orient. To this must be added quite a list of others in the West as well as the East, in recorded history and out of it, who have also had the experience.

57

We shall never know how many mystical experiences took place within those medieval cloisters and those Oriental ashrams but were lost to human record because those to whom they happened lacked the talent to write them down or the will to dictate them.

58

My records, gleaned from correspondence or got from interviews, show that some persons have been started off by glimpses during surgical anaesthesia and others just after a near miss of death.

59

What today is believed abnormal will, in a civilization ahead of ours, be regarded as quite natural. I refer to the transcendental experience.

60

There are individuals scattered here and there who have found the Overself. It is certain that they are types as well as individuals—therefore, it is certain that the whole race will also one day find the Overself.

61

Even one who is active, efficient, practical, and worldly may also be touched by this heavenly light: it is not reserved for the dreamers and poets, the artists and saints alone. I have known men who blue-printed public buildings, engineered factories, managed office personnel, filled the lowest and the highest positions in a nation, who themselves had known ITS visitations, who recognized and revered it.

62

An aspirant wrote in a letter: "I went into a lawsuit upon which depended the existence of an entire business and my own ability to continue to support my family. Judgement was given against me. I experienced the most curious sensation that the whole thing did not matter at all, that I seemed to be the witness of it all, and I was utterly calm. In fact, I had never felt so calm in my entire life, and did not feel the least bit depressed. It seemed to me Mr. . . . [himself] was almost a stranger to me, and I was just a witness of what was happening to him." He had a glimpse of the way in which a sage would have treated the same event, and that glimpse came to him at the right moment, the moment he needed it most.

63

Many people pass through these experiences of the glimpse and do not really know what is happening to them because they have never studied or been taught anything about such experiences.

64

If some have had a mystical glimpse before the age of ten, more have done so during adolescence, still more during their thirties or forties. If thereafter the experience is less known, it can still happen even in the seventies.

65

In the last year of her life, the Glimpse came to Simone Weil several times a week. Yet she was first in a hospital and then in a sanatorium during most of that time!

66

It is a result which several persons have experienced that the Glimpse which came while reading some inspired passages of a book or verses of a poem, returns again at a later time.

67

The belief that he must wait many years before he can find a glimpse of his godly self is not accurate.

68

Those frightened away from the Quest by the high qualifications de-manded, may find some comfort in the fact that these "glimpses" increas-ing in number depth and frequency can be had even at an early stage.

69

It is as silly to fix the age for such an experience at thirty-six, as the late author of *Cosmic Consciousness* did, as it is to assert that it always lasts about twenty-four hours merely because St. Francis Xavier was illumined for such a period.

70

How near to the glimpse do the mass of people come who claim they have never had one? Perhaps the feeling of awe to which certain buildings or persons or ideas may give rise is the nearest.

71

In ordinary life such glimpses are all too rare but they are not so rare as is generally believed. For their true nature may not be recognized. The external surroundings or the external situations which led to their internal appearance may disguise them so that their independent nature is not understood. Such surroundings as an impressive natural landscape or such situations as a perfectly relaxed physical body are not an absolutely indispensable condition of their existence.

72

Moments like this have come to many men who have not recognized the preciousness, the special value, and the uncommon nature of the experience.

73

Often there are only half-glimpses, but even they afford a vague satisfaction.

74

The time will come when it will be found that glimpses are a proper part of human existence, are within the area of a normal life, are valid topics for study and examination by science.

Their importance

75

Everyone has the experience of doing, few of being. Yet that is the most precious, most important of all life's experiences.

76

This is the experience which makes the fully mature man or woman happiest. It is usually short but its next advent will always be eagerly awaited. It is often isolated by long intervals of prosaic commonplace living, but they only serve to give it even greater value by contrast.

77

The inner need of man is forever demanding this experience, for it is heaven.

78

Whether it is born out of appreciation of beauty or an infinite humiliation of the ego, or out of some totally different occasion, this awareness of the Overself's presence is essential to the completion and fulfilment of human life.(P)

79

To enter into Heaven is to enter into the fulfilment of our earthly life's unearthly purpose. And that is, simply, to become aware of the Overself. This holy awareness brings such joy with it that we then know why the true saints and the real ascetics were able to disdain all other joys. The contrast is too disproportionate. Nothing that the world offers to tempt us can be put on the same level.

80

He will find that somewhere within there is a holy presence not himself, a sublime power not his own. He will understand then that no one is truly alive who has not made this discovery.

81

The glimpse lies at the core of religion, the precious gem which each devotee must find for himself underneath all the sermons, chantings, rituals, prayers, and observances of his creed.

82

A stillness which is not simply the absence of noise but which is rich, fruitful, and uplifting in beauty and refinement of its presence—this is the best.

83

No good fortune that comes his way will ever after be counted so great as the good fortune which he now feels to be his in the realization of the Overself.

84

Omar Khayyam: "Would but the desert of the Fountain yield One glimpse—if dimly, yet indeed revealed, To which the fainting traveller might spring."

85

Another significance of the glimpse is that of initiation.

86

We cannot know God in the fullness of his consciousness but we can know the link which we have with God. Call it the soul, if you must, or the Overself if you prefer, but to catch a glimpse of this link is to be reborn.

87

The glimpse gives him a journey to a land flowing not with milk and honey, but with goodness and beauty, with peace and wisdom. It is the best moment of his life.(P)

88

When a man's consciousness is turned upside-down by a glimpse, when what he thought most substantial is revealed as least so, when his values are reversed and the Good takes on a new definition, he writes that day down as his spiritual birthday.(P)

89

What better thing can he find than the divine Overself! That would be the decisive moment of his entire bodily existence, as establishing himself permanently in its fullness and finality would be the grandest sequel.

90

There is no higher happiness than this discovery of the real man.

91

We must look upon these glimpses as sacred ones, not less religious than those which bibles and ceremonies may furnish us with. And this is so even if they rise of themselves in our best moments or can be traced to some layman's art, music, or speech. For in these times we, and especially the younger ones among us, need wider definitions of such matters.

92

These moments, when spiritual presence is distinctly felt, may be rare or frequent, misunderstood or recognized, but they are moments of blessing. And this is true even if they open the door only slightly and let in merely a chink of light.

93

In these moments of a glimpse, he discovers the very real presence of the Overself. They provide him with a joy, an amiability, which disarms the negative side of his character and brings forward the positive side. These are precious moments; they cannot be too highly valued. And though they must pass, some communication with them is always possible through memory.

94

The glimpse is of supreme worth morally, helping to free him, bestowing goodwill and humility, uplifting his ideals however fleetingly.

95

Instead of being an escape from life, as some sceptics foolishly think, they are its fulfilment.

96

Although life is really like a dream, some phases of the dream are more worthwhile than others—those which bring the Glimpse, for instance.

97

It is far better than being ignorant to know what is read in books or heard at lectures on this topic, but far better than both of these is to *feel* vividly the Overself's presence and reality, to know the truth of It with complete certainty.

98

No better fortune can come to a man or woman than this serene inward well-being and this certitude of universal truth.

99

"He that loseth his life shall save it." Those who would translate Jesus' words into generous emotion and not into metaphysical insight have never known the real meaning of those words. For the philanthropic service of others is a noble but secondary ideal, whereas the mystical union with the Overself is a priceless and primary achievement.

100

The freedom he feels in such moments and the consolation he gets from them are indications of the value of the distant goal itself.

101

Try to describe a colour to someone who has never been able to see any colour at all. Your words will have no meaning for him, however accurate and expressive they may be. In the same way, most mystics are sceptical about the use of describing their experiences to those who have not already had some such experience. This is where the "glimpse" is of such tremendous value.

102

He will know at the time, and come to confirm when the greater part of his life is already past, that the sacredness which infuses them and the beauty which permeates them make these his best moments.

103

Those rare moments of exaltation and uplift, of spiritual glimpse and inward freedom, are of inestimable value. They show the aspirant what he may become, affirm the reality of the ideal and reveal its possibility.

104

This is the one experience which is unique, the most important of all, simply because it throws new uncommon light upon all experiences.

105

There is a pure happiness in these moments of release which no earthly happiness can surpass.

106

The Japanese gurus do not consider what they call *Satori* to be a lasting state but rather to be only a glimpse. Yet, even the achievement of this glimpse is regarded as a very high one.

107

To become conscious of infinity is no mean achievement for a man even if he does so only for a single hour and cannot keep the glimpse longer.

108

The primary value of life lies in these beautiful but brief moods when we lose touch with the world, and fortunate is that person who recognizes the higher authority of their accompanying clear insights.

109

These glimpses come upon us unawares, inadvertently as it were. There is no higher experience in our past to compare with them, and no lovelier.

110

These mystical moments are the most priceless human experience, did we but know it.

111

Instinctively he knows it to be one of the most beautiful, most important of experiences he has ever had.

112

These glimpses scintillate within the dark chamber of man's life like stars in the night sky.

113

We need these occasional confirmations from the Overself of its own existence.

114

We all need the calmness and the love associated with this experience.

115

If he can penetrate to this inmost region of consciousness, he will penetrate also to the secret purpose of the few decades of earthly life.

116

Some kind of awakening is the usual prelude before people take to the Quest in real earnest. The glimpse provides it.

117

There is an image of God within each man; once seen, he will forever after court union with it.

118

It is a blessed state unequalled by another experience, unexcelled by any other satisfaction.

119

It is such glorious moments—refreshing to the will and revelatory to the mind—which alone can compensate for (or justify, if you prefer the word) the long littleness, the recurring torment of living.

120

An experience so lovely, yielding a memory so precious, is worth the effort of seeking.

121

What we know is so little that it ought to make us intellectually humble. But that little is nevertheless of the highest importance to us. For we know that the Overself *is*, that the passage to its stillness from the ego's tumult is worthwhile, and that goodness and purity, prayer and meditation help us to find it.

122

The fact or absence of enlightenment measures the real value of a person.

Their frequency and duration

123

There are exalted but rare occasions when inspiration, peace, and spiritual majesty conjoin their blessed presence within us.

124

It is with him for the flicker of a second—an unfathomable tranquillity, an indefinable beauty—and then gone.

125

Some enter into this experience only once in a lifetime; others repeat it a few times. Only a rare individual here and there enters it frequently.

126

How many have asked in puzzlement why the glimpses of reality cannot remain with them, how many have deplored its brevity! Plotinus long ago gave them his answer: "Man can cease to become man, and become God; but man cannot be God and man at the same time."

127

He can hold himself in this egoless state for a brief while only. The ego soon rises up again and the glorious presence retires, for the two are incompatible.

128

Such periods are short and uncommon but they lift us up and draw us in. We feel then that there is peace and joy for us as ultimate possibilities, even if they are not immediate actualities.

129

It is true that the felicity and freedom of such glimpses are too often too momentary. Yet immense forces lie hidden beneath their brief but intense existence.

130

All glimpses are not of equal duration nor of equal degree. One or the other or both may differ from person to person.

131

These glimpses of Reality which wake us out of the world of illusion come to us only at intervals. We cannot hold them, but we can repeat them.

132

The glimpse may last only an instant, or it may last a year.

133

The glimpse lasts a moment, a minute, an hour, or a week—who can say, for it is a mysterious grace? But in that while, the oscillation of human thoughts is stilled and time takes a rest. It cannot be shared with others—although they may notice or sense some of its fruit—and to that extent it is a private experience.

134

It comes to us only in gleams whose disappointing brevity is balanced by their overwhelming beauty.

135

Such moments rarely come to flower in the arid wilderness of a man's life today.

136

There will even be rare and brief times when these serene glimpses will dissolve into wonderful ecstasies.

137

The glimpses are usually quite short in duration, quite sudden in onset. This is why the *Kenopanishad*, a very old Hindu text, likens them to "the splendour of lightning" and says of them, "They disappear within the twinkling of an eye."

138

Such experiences can be sustained only in small homeopathic doses.

139

But glimpses, as charming to the mind as scented blossoms to the nose, are fugitive. They cannot be kept. They are ephemeral.

140

These glimpses are rarely sustained and should be accepted without surprise or disappointment for the short events they usually are.

141

During the years when I investigated such matters—collecting data from several hundred cases, including my own experience, and combining it with the more authoritative teachings of highly attained and highly respected top-rank persons—I found that in a large percentage of persons who feel too preoccupied with the work of starting to build a career, earn their livelihood, and build a family, the initial glimpse may have been the first and last for a long period of many years. But in some cases they stay in this period of disinterest because of disillusionments.

142

The bliss of the glimpse must pass—and often quickly: its confirmation of unworldly values must diminish.

143

He does not expect to feel often these great moments when he passes through an archway opening on the infinite and enjoys the Best.

144

These glimpses are fitful and their content is fragmentary.

145

It is true that the glimpse comes seldom to most people, but it is all the better remembered for that rarity.

146

The fleeting beauty of these moments veils the harsh greyness of the long periods between them.

147

These moments of spiritual nearness shine in his life, but the glorious feeling they induce does not stay.

148

But the glimpse comes to an end. The glorious new identity which he took on for a while will be shed.

149

These glimpses are often unexpected, usually isolated, and mostly brief.

150

A brief release from the burdens of living, peace-bestowing and mentally illumining, a healing suspense of all negative traits—but soon gone.

151

These moments are rare and beautiful. They can never come too soon nor stay too long.

Glimpses and Light

152

The energy which appears to us as light is the basis of the universe, the principle from which all things are made.

153

The first aspect of God is Light; the first contact of man with the Supreme Being is Light.

154

The pure and primal life-force appears, if seen in vision, as golden sunshine.

155

The light streaming from a table lamp proves the existence of electricity. The light streaming into the mind in these exalted moments proves the existence of the Soul.

156

Whoever approaches the Divine Source of all things comes into the aura of its Power and the perception of its Light.

157

This is not ordinary light: it is holy, transcendental, and awe-inspiring.

158

The experience of divine Light is no hallucination but an actuality, an entirely real one, even a thrilling one.

159

If the Light is not resisted, by timidity, ignorance, or egoism, it will work upon the entire human being, radically transforming his outlook, life, and consciousness.

160

In its Light man begins to see what he has not seen with the body's eyes, the intellect's understanding.

161

If he can hold himself in the Light steadily and unfalteringly, his consciousness will be raised to a higher plane.

162

The inner light will give him a glimpse of an ennobled and purified life and inspire him with the urge to realize it.

163

Generally the seeing of light during meditation is a favourable sign of present experience or good omen of future experience. It indicates that meditation in depth is being attained, or will be later. The light may seem spread out in space or as a thin ray alone. It may appear as a tiny black-centered sun or as a large round ball. There are still other forms—such as lightning and stars. Generally, too, there will be a living dynamic quality in it, a movement, a winking, and a fiery flickering.

164

Light manifestations: (a) throbbing with Energy, (b) as Overself, (c) thought-free Peace or Joy.

165

The Light is felt as energy pulsing in space and tingling in the body; it is seen, usually with the mind's eye but sometimes with the body's, as an unearthly radiance; it is intuited as a glory filling the whole of one's inner being.

166

The Light is seen visually as a golden ball, a brilliant ray or shaft or beam, and finally as a vague radiance diffused in all directions.

167

It may stay within the orbit of vision quite motionless and still. Or it may quiver, throb, and pulsate. Or it may shoot forward like a lightning flash.

168

One who beholds the Light may be grateful for several reasons. First, it is the only occult experience of which it may be said that it is entirely without risk or peril. Second, it is the loftiest of all clairvoyant visions. Third, it confers the feeling of perfect felicity, not in the worldly sense, but of an ethereal unearthly kind. Fourth, it is a direct manifestation of God to man, being the first of his outpourings, hence an uncommon blessing, a grace. Fifth, if it appears in consciousness as Power, the recipient may feel a tremendous force, unknown otherwise, throbbing all around and within him, or a sudden lightning-like flash of complete comprehension: he understands what neither bodily sense nor intellectual faculty can understand—the supernatural meaning of Spirit, of eternity, of transfiguration, and of reality.

169

The Light may be sent forth as a ray to touch the heart or head of any particular person to uplift or console, pacify emotions or exalt ideas; it may also be sent to encircle a person protectively.

170

Light is also symbolic. Contrasted with darkness, it suggests redemption and knowledge as against sinfulness and ignorance.

171

It is significant that not only is night the time when human crime and passion are at their maximum but it is also the time when worrying thoughts are at their blackest. The day with its brightness has ever been a symbol of spirituality, the night with its darkness a symbol of materiality. For he who has found his own spirit, finds peace and is freed from fear, and consequently from its child—worry—too.

172

The very nature of sunshine—all light—and the very condition in which sunrises and sunsets occur—stillness—help us to understand why Light and the Overself are bracketed together. *"Your own consciousness shining, void, inseparable from the great body of radiance, is subject neither to birth nor death, but is the same as the immutable light, Buddha Amitabha."* (Buddhist Sutra)

173

"Use the light that is within you to revert to your natural clearness of sight."—*Tao Teh Ching*

174

Among those who have seen this light, some Christians have named it "the glory of God." Some Hindus termed it "the self-effulgent light."

175

Saint Makarius the Great (fourth century Egyptian) in his *Instructions for Monks* wrote: "The Light is a shining of the Holy Spirit in the soul. Through this light, God is truly known by the worthy and beloved soul."

176

On this point of the Light phenomenon, the Russian Orthodox Church writer Bishop Brianchaninov explains that it is a spiritual light which is seen inwardly but that it may also be seen physically at times. He considers it identical with the Holy Spirit, and that it reveals the reality of that Spirit while sanctifying the person.

177

(LIGHT) Psalm 27: "The Lord is my Light."

178

What the Old Testament writers called the *shekinah* is a sacred and luminous appearance.

179

More than a hundred years ago, Konko Daijin founded a new religion in Japan. Called Konkokyo, "the religion of golden light," it enjoined its followers to live in dependence on "the God of heaven's brightness."

180

One of the states of *samadhi* in Tibetan and Chinese Buddhism is called "Pure Light." One of the Attained Ones in this religion is Amita, or Amitabha, the "Buddha of Boundlessly Diffused Light."

181

That there is actually a light emitted by the divine world of being is indicated by the following excerpt from, I believe, a Mahayana Buddhist: "There are four successive stages of piercing in reality, identical in sleep and dying. The first, 'Revelation,' is experienced in the earliest period of sleep, and appears as a moonlit cloudless sky. The drowsiness deepens and 'Augmentation' is reached. It appears as brilliant clear sunlight. Few can go beyond this into the third stage, 'Immediate Attainment.' Here there is total darkness. It vanishes when sleep gets deeper still; then the Void is penetrated, called 'Innate Light,' the first clear radiance. The student thus passes into Reality and Enlightenment, whether in the nightly death of sleep or the end of human life."

182

The Quakers believe that what they call the Inner Light is a supernatural thing.

183

Saint Brendan saw, while at ceremonial prayer in the presence of other celebrated ancient Irish holy men, a bright flame-like light rising above his head and continuing until the end of the ceremony.

184

Meister Eckhart: "If God is to be seen then it must happen in a Light, as God himself is Light."

185

LIGHT: The seventeenth-century Welsh poet Henry Vaughan expressed the same idea in his lines:

I saw Eternity the other night
Like a great Ring of pure and endless light.

186

(Light) The blind Milton could write, "Hail, holy Light."

187

A young, innocent, well-educated girl of good family found herself pregnant after being seduced by a sophisticated man. She was too ignorant to know what to do, and too ashamed to confess to her parents. In despair, she decided to kill herself. When the fatal day arrived, she called out several times in prayer and agony to whatever God there be, to give some evidence of Its existence so that she should not feel utterly alone and to help her. About one hour later, to her astonishment, the room became filled with an unearthly light for a few minutes. With it came the feeling of being in the presence of the Higher Power, of not being alone any more, and an assurance of help. She slept heavily the rest of the day and all that night, and next morning awoke with a clear guidance of what to do. She went to her parents and in great calmness told them of the trouble which had befallen her. They treated her well and took appropriate measures to deal with it. Thirty years after this event, she related the story to me, after I had described the experience of a titled English lady, who told me how she was saved from committing suicide (because of the death of all her babies one after another) by the manifestation of Light, along with a Voice that spoke the saving words.

188

Bessie M. Lasky, *Candle in the Sun* (autobiography): "As I lay tucked in bed at night, thinking of the evening, a white light came into focus before my closed eyes. It grew brighter as I watched, until it seemed as tho' all the light in the world was there. I was dazzled and perplexed, wondering what this ray could mean. Where was it coming from? It completely enveloped my whole being and increased as the moments passed. It had come instantaneously. I seemed suspended in a wholeness of life, detached from earth. A part of me was radiating a new joy. I held this radiance for at least 15 minutes. Then it changed and disappeared. I fell into sleep, comforted and blissful for the first time. I decided never to speak about this experience, for they would never understand." (*Comment by P.B.*: Within the next few weeks she made a number of new friends all spiritually minded, or spiritually more advanced than herself: such persons she had never known before.)

189

(a) G. saw a descent of light over P.B. It expanded and everything was finally in it. (b) F. saw a small light, felt she was a priestess offering to it. There was great power present. P.B. was there. (c) A Czech once saw himself, in meditation, surrounded by "fluid gold" and with it experienced great peace. (d) Another Czech saw a ball of light coming towards him, again in meditation, and during the whole day afterward felt as if walking on air, so free, light and happily care-free.

190

Mack F. Hewitt, California: "While lying in bed thinking, I was suddenly aware of a blinding brilliance. It was a flash of light that I could feel as well as see. It frightened me and instantly it disappeared. I went to sleep immediately. Other occasions followed this first one and I seemed to observe that the light I saw was bluish-white at the outer edges and intensely white at the centre. It was just a little to the left of me and somewhat above me. I had the sensation that I could feel, sense, that I was on the threshold of all knowledge. The experience of light only lasted one second the first time and somewhat longer the other times. It was all-enveloping and came several times during two years. It came at night when retiring and left behind exhilaration and upliftment."

191

"When I was eighteen years old I had a mystical glimpse. In this experience I was surrounded by light and inwardly felt a strengthening peace. Its support led me to my acceptance of what was then a very difficult situation. I understood its meaning and the lesson it taught me. With time and patience it came to an end but it left me more developed."—a medical secretary

192

The Light dazzled a man on the Damascus road; it changed his mind from anti- to pro-Christian, his name from Saul to Paul. The radiance of the same Light, long before, appeared in a bush to Moses and brought him the uttered message of Jehovah.

193

Saint John of the Cross, held unjustly as a prisoner, found his cell filled with light as he dreamed one night that the Virgin appeared to him promising help if he escaped. Martinus, the Danish mystic, told me that Jesus appeared to him in meditation surrounded by a ball of light.

194

"After I had been with the guru (at first meeting) a little while, I became aware that I was sitting very still. I was motionless. I did not seem to be breathing. A white light appeared, seeming to fill the entire room. I became a part of that wondrous light."—the late Swami Lynn

195

Mr. A. had the experience of light three times. Each time it happened at night when he actually saw sunshine. Usually he couldn't sleep after going to bed and again after the light appeared he could not sleep. However, he felt such peace coming from the light that it was some kind of a compensation for the lack of sleep. After an interval of several months devoid of incident, the experience reappeared. At night he saw the Light shining powerfully but briefly. He deliberately shut his eyes to test if it were only physical, but still it persisted. And another phenomenon began, for in his official life he had to meet very important personages; at such times he found his thoughts wandering away into a sensation of great uplift and great peace. He had to stop the experience by sheer will so as to attend properly to the conversation. When he did so the feeling of great power came too, so that there was a transformation rather than a loss. During the following months all light phenomena vanished, and so did the spiritual exhilarations. But at the end of this period, he felt ready to take up regular practice of meditation, and did so. The results were favourable, if undramatic, bringing an immensely relaxed feeling, a tremendous peace, a stillness of thought, and firsthand knowledge of spiritual reality.

196

The Vision of Mr. A. (a) "I went to bed and was on the verge of nearly falling asleep when, through my closed eyes, I saw a round shape of light to the left of me. It moved towards me, growing larger as it came, until I was surrounded by it. So brilliant was the visual effect, that I received the impression that the room itself was lit up. At the same time there was a powerful pulsating vibration going on around me, as if dynamic energy accompanied the light. With it all, there was a strong feeling that P.B. was present, or somehow associated with it, and with him, strong peace. But as I had never before had any mystic experience or any, in my ignorance, intellectual familiarity with the subject, I became alarmed as to what would happen next, and quite frightened, got up and brought the experience to an end. A week or two later, while sitting at a crowded public function, the peace returned very markedly but briefly, yet I saw no light. A couple of weeks later I stayed awake in bed for some time unable to sleep. Then the light appeared to the left of the bed. It expanded until the whole room was full of it. I got a feeling of boundless energy being at my command, with its centre in the region behind the navel. Another few weeks and a third experience happened. I had just switched off the bedside lamp and in the darkness that fell with eyes only half shut I saw a vertical shaft of light in the distance. I felt myself drawn out of the body and propelled forward at jetplane speed into space. There was peace and power but in two or three minutes it was all over. The light remained in the distance all the time I moved towards it." (b) "Generally the experience started with inability to sleep at night causing a restless feeling, but around midnight a throbbing of the solar plexus started and this powerful force was felt there. It mounted and then there was a kind of change of consciousness, a feeling of not being the body, almost of being out of it and separated from it, of being weightless and in space yet near to the body, developed. The dynamic character of the experience was followed by a sense of utter peace. Nevertheless I seemed to know that there was something beyond this which I had not attained. I wanted to attain it so I resolved to continue the meditation practice regularly if possible."

197

"A Writing Mystic in Uniform" by Monique Benoit (notebook includes cutting with a photo of Walter H. Cronk): We met in the elevator of the

Chronicle building one day. As I was talking with someone, the man behind me asked where I was from in France. "Paris." "Do you remember what you were doing on August 24, 1944?" "Certainly. I was greeting and kissing soldiers from the French Second Armored Division who had entered Paris." "Did you kiss American soldiers, too?" "Quite a few, on that day," I smiled. "Then we may have kissed. I was with Patton's Third Army and entered Paris with the Leclerc soldiers." One thing led to another—all very respectable—and Lieutenant Colonel Walter Cronk, a reserve officer in the Air Force, invited me to lunch at a later date, when he would be at Travis Air Force Base for two weeks. Walter, who is advertising sales manager for Pacific Telephone in Los Angeles, left with me his book, *Golden Light*, which was published recently. I read it and was puzzled. The rugged-looking man didn't appear to be a mystic, yet this was a spiritual book. It described how on Easter, 1953, he was struck by the "Golden Light," which paralyzed him for a few minutes while a thunderous voice asked: "Is This What You Want?" Some time later, in Rome, he had another ecstatic experience, beholding the Star of the East. "Why did you write that book? I don't mean to sound cynical, but even if you experienced those spiritual revelations, why write about them? Isn't spirituality, like love, a very private thing?" "Since I was eight, I have had a strong spiritual awareness. Later, I met a man who was my teacher for many years. He said that when he would leave his physical body, he would be 'as close to me as the paper on the wall.' Since then, a little voice has been with me constantly to guide and protect me. One night I had a call from a mystic. He didn't know me but had been told to call me to say that a sick person would come to see me. Through my prayers I would heal this person, whose name would be Evans. The caller didn't know whether it would be a man or a woman. This would be a sign that I should write a religious book. It all happened as predicted, and I felt compelled to write the book. Its purpose is to show people how the "Golden Light" is there for everyone to see." "But don't you think that when people don't get struck by that light and don't hear the thunderous voice they feel cheated?" "But it can happen to them, too. I explained how through meditation we can all experience spiritual ecstasy. This book is meant for people who cannot be reached by the chaplains, ministers, rabbis, or priests. They need to be shown that there is something besides materialism, and that when our spirit leaves our body it is not the end. We are here to realize Oneness with God and will come back until we achieve this." "Don't you think 'humanism' is a more positive answer, one that pleases God just as well as all that spirituality? Many people aren't spiritual, yet are good and compassionate." Walter reluctantly agreed it might be true. In *Golden Light* the author describes how he was also compelled to give up meat when waves of golden lines appeared before his eyes as he read a passage of the Dead Sea Scrolls. "My 'Little Voice' bugs me at times. It has made me give up cigars and Scotch. I wonder about what it might ask next. If it's wine and sex I think I'll rebel," said Walter, laughing. Ah ha—not altogether spiritual, after all.

198

Walter Cronk, *Golden Light* [excerpts]: (1) My legs and arms became rigid in cross-form. I was astonished to see a brilliant golden light, starting at my solar plexus, a foot in diameter. It moved upward and outward until it became tubular. An odor of raw ozone permeated the room. The light shimmered at the outer edges as if it were vibrating. It cast no shadow. I was unable to call out and unable to move. I prayed that I now believed in the force of Spirit, and would never doubt again. I visited Hollywood Vedanta Swami and told him my experience. He replied: "Life is a journey. This will remind you of God's beauty. As you continue your journey you can't keep asking to see the Grand Canyon again if you are traveling from L.A. to New York. God has many faces." (2) Emerson, Whitman, Voltaire, Ford, Emmet Fox, and Franklin expect a series of rebirths on our path toward perfection. (3) The life of Teresa Neumann, Bavarian Catholic mystic, says she saw this heavenly light, and that she lived 30 years without eating, and died in 1962. At 18 she became ill, saw a light brighter than the sun, recovered and developed stigmata. (4) The Maharaja of Burawan invited a woman mystic, Giri Bala, of Bengal, to stay in his palace to test her claim that she has not eaten for many years. She remained in a room there for two months without food, in 1936 emerged with no loss of weight. She is a saint and once prayed to be relieved of hunger. (5) Teresa Neumann had seen the Light many times. I went to visit her in 1958, but in the village suddenly knew that whether she or I had seen the golden Light was not the key at all. I had really come to find out only one thing: "What should a man do to live a perfect life in God's eyes?" (6) I did not speak to Teresa. I knew now that this question and its answer were what I had come here for. I had nothing to say. (7) Teresa had effected healing for many persons. (8) 1 John 1:5 "God is Light." (8a) Professor Edmond Szekely, an authority on the Essenes; is qualified in Aramaic and Greek. His writing is based on ancient *scripts* in the Vatican and other libraries. In his translation, "Essene Gospel of John," I found phrases which were not in apocrypha nor in the Bible. One para vibrated waves of golden light from the pages to me. In it Jesus forbade slaughter of animals for food. I forthwith stopped eating flesh. Even the desire was taken away at that moment. I asked Professor Szekely to explain the experience. He theorized that perhaps I put myself in the same thought vibrations as he who wrote the words. (9) Dr. Lewis, of San Diego, who died in 1960, recommended that I face east when sitting to meditate, because cosmic rays emanate from east to west and this polarizes me. "Simply reaffirm the oneness of your soul," he said, "with the Infinite Soul. Meditation means to know that you are one with God." I did this, and a blue light, ringed with gold, appeared several successive times. Dr. Lewis told me he had been waiting for me to describe it, and now to meditate longer, and not once a day: early morning and late evening. (10) I attended a Mass. As it progressed the golden light and the heavenly blue light appeared, bathing the spirit in Infinite Love. A beautiful white star appeared in the blue light another time during my meditation. (11) Practical exercise in meditation is simply to recognize oneness with God, omnipresence of God, and activity of God within one here and now. (12) Here Churches become country clubs. (13) If few Mount Athos monks attain the light, it could be that they are too proud of the experiences which they've had already, that is, they may lack humility. (14) How close is Christ when we call on him! (15) If only Churches would encourage worshippers to look within as the only place to find God! (16) Light is only the opening of the door, the beginning. The final state is oneness with infinite intelligence. (17) In everything we do we ought to think of God, and thus reduce ego to nothingness. (18) That which is behind our eyes, never dies.

199

Oxford Dictionary of Christian Church History on Hesychasm ("Quiet"), a fourteenth-century Mount Athos mystical system: Its chief tenet was that by perfect quiet of body and mind man is able to arrive at vision of the "Uncreated Light of the Godhead." The result of these practices was ineffable joy and seeing the Light, which surrounded Our Lord on Mount Tabor. It was held that this Light was not God's essence, which is unapproachable, but his Energy which can be perceived by the senses, and that it was this Light, and not, as Western theologians hold, God's Essence, which is the object of the Beatific Vision. Philotheus Kokkinus in his contribution to the anthology called *Hagioritic Tome*, written at Mount Athos about 1339, states that the Mount Athos doctrine of Divine Light was revealed experientially to the contemplatives who lived there.

Easier methods, therefore more mechanical, to procure this vision of Divine Light, included: (a) breathing exercises, (b) pressing chin against the chest, (c) indefinite repetition of the ejaculation "Lord Jesus Christ have mercy on me." Hesychast theology conceives of God as a compound of essence and activity, whereas Western theology denies the possibility of an uncreated light that was not God's essence, on the grant that any distinction would destroy His unity and simplicity.

200

The Russian Staretz (experienced spiritual guide) Silouan, who lived on Athos for more that forty years until he died in 1938, saw the Christ at the door leading to the sanctuary of a church joining his monastery, saw too a great light all around, felt himself transported to heaven while joy and peace filled his heart. The vision was ever after regarded as the peak of his inner life, but the uplift it brought slowly faded away. It did not exempt him from further struggles and strains of his ascetic existence, as well as dark nights of the soul. These gave him a great humility, which smashed any pride the glimpse might have engendered.

201

R. Fulop-Miller: In the sixteenth century there arose on Athos a controversy which shook the whole Orthodox world. A monk, after a long period of profound meditation on his navel, could see the divine light of Mount Tabor. His example was followed by many other monks who also saw "the Uncreated Light." The question was fought out through a series of Councils and finally decided in favour of the mystics by a Council at Constantinople, which declared the Light was really Divine.

202

Dionysios, the founder of one of the Athos monasteries, lived in a cave as a hermit high up on a mountainside; he saw one day a strange supernatural light shining lower down. He felt inspired to build a monastery at the spot and eventually persuaded the emperor to materialize his inspiration. This was in the fourteenth century and the buildings are still there.

203

The first thing that God gave the created world was physical light. The first communication God makes to the man who has attained His presence is the vision of supernatural Light. This is the doctrine held by the Eastern Church, which calls what is seen "the Uncreated Light." During this rare experience the man feels that he is free from earthly attachments and worldly desires, that the intense peace he enjoys is the true happiness, that

God's reality is the overwhelming fact of existence. This vision is a gift, a grace, so it may come suddenly, unexpectedly, but more often it comes to someone who has prepared himself for it by purification and contemplation. It does not last, the Light leaves him as strangely as it came and as independently of his personal control. But its exquisite memory can never leave him. From that date, too, certain beneficial changes appear in his character and his outlook. The lower nature is weakened, the baser attributes are thinned down. From that date, too, certain spiritual truths are confirmed for him, and certain false beliefs are cancelled. Yet, if the vision of Light brought union with God, intimacy with God, it did not and could not enable him to know God as God knows Himself. He could not penetrate His inmost nature and substance. This, the ultimate beyond the Light, is called "the Divine Darkness" by the Fathers of the Eastern Orthodox Church.

204

Seeing the Light in front of him is one state; being merged into it is another, and superior.(P)

205

This Light is the penultimate experience, the last but one on the mystic's way. He finds himself totally lost indeed but lost in the most dazzling Light. The ego *seems* to have vanished: infinity and universality of being have replaced it. Ecstatic rapture fills him. Is it any wonder that the Greek Orthodox Church mystics of the first few centuries believed this was the ultimate experience of pure Spirit, the final union with God? Yet it may not last, cannot last, must come to an end. It may have held him for one or two minutes only or it may have done so for a longer period. It may never recur again in his whole lifetime—this is so in most cases—or it may come several times more. But it stands as a landmark until the end of his years.

206

Where the Greek Orthodox Church regards the Light experience as the highest point reachable by man, the Indian Philosophic Teaching regards it as the last stage before the highest. For anything which is "seen" implies the existence of a "seer" as separate from it. This is not less so even in the case of the Holy Light. Not seeing but be-ing is the final experience according to this Teaching. "You have to go beyond seeing and find out who is the 'I' who experiences this light," said Ramana Maharshi to a disciple.(P)

5

PREPARING FOR GLIMPSES

How to attract a glimpse

To describe the wonders and benefits, the delights and beauties of these glimpses will whet the appetite of people without satisfying it. Hence they will then be led to ask how such a glimpse is to be obtained.

2

Many glimpses have come suddenly and spontaneously to those who never followed any particular technique intended to bring them on. Nevertheless, it is undoubtedly true that as many if not more glimpses have come to those who follow some technique chosen from the variety which have been transmitted from traditional sources or supplied by authentic contemporary ones.

3

The principle which makes union with the Overself possible is always the same, albeit on different levels. Whether it appears as humility in prayer, passivity to intuition, stillness in meditation, or serenity despite untoward circumstances, these attitudes temporarily weaken the ego and lessen its domination. They temporarily silence the ego and give the Overself the opportunity to touch us or work through us. So long as the ego dominates us, we are outside the reach of the Overself and separated from its help.

4

The notion that it is first necessary to become a monk or to live like a saint before one can hope to acquire this knowledge is erroneous. One must find the inner self, and this of itself will purify us, subdue passions, and tame selfishness. When the magic touch of the Overself falls upon us, our long-held foolishness withers away, and our tightly clutched vices die off and disappear.

5

That which is aware of the world is not the world. That which is aware of the ego is not the ego. When this awareness is isolated, the man "experiences" the Overself.

6

If he will try to perceive the mind by which he perceives the world, he will be practising the shortest, most direct technique of discovering the Overself. This is what Ramana Maharshi meant when he taught, "Trace the 'I' to its source."

7

All that a man knows and experiences is a series of thoughts. There is only one exception and that, in most cases, remains usually as an unrealized possibility. It is when he discovers his *being*. Here thinking is not active, would in fact prevent the discovery if not reined in at the proper point. Here, in this private paradise, knowing and experiencing are one.

8

He should send out experimental feelers in his mental-emotional world until he recognizes an element that seems different from all the others— subtler, grander, nobler, and more divine than all the others. Then, catching firm hold of it, he should try to trace its course back to its source.

The point where the personal ego establishes contact with the Overself is reached and passed only through a momentary lapse of consciousness. But this lapse is so brief—a mere fraction of a second—that it may be unnoticed.

A presence enters his consciousness and comes over him, a benign feeling to which he is glad to surrender himself, a mysterious solvent of his egotism and desires.

9

The value of letting oneself pass this point can hardly be overestimated, even though it be done only during the limited sessions of meditation or the casual periods of unexpected visitations. For from them peace, wisdom, sanity can be emanated. At this point there is the mysterious division between human normal meditation and divine contemplation, between discursive thinking and its dissolution as the divine self takes over, between mental concentration and release into still, timeless being, between imagery and pure Consciousness.

10

Koestler got his glimpse by working out Euclid's geometrical proof of the infinitude of the number of primes. That he was able to learn of the reality of the Infinite by a purely mathematical and precise method, without becoming a vague emotional mystic, so satisfied his highly intellectual and scientific nature that, in his own words, an "aesthetic enchantment" fell upon him. This developed until he became one with Peace never before known. The experience passed away, as it usually does, but it remained to haunt his memory. It inspired his journey to India and Japan several years later, where he spent a year trying to meet holy men and yoga experts. These meetings did not bring him what he sought, but his faith in the authenticity of that earlier glimpse never left him. He knew what few mystics know, that he did not need to violate the integrity of Reason, nor become lost in generally hazy gushy feelings, to know Infinity, which is the truth of Reality.

11

Those who seek this mystic communion with the Overself, this sublime glimpse of its hidden face, must make the Quest their chosen path.

12

If you have enough confidence to trust in the teaching, and to move in the direction toward which it guides you, sooner or later the future will be lighted by these small fugitive glimpses.(P)

13

What, it has been asked, if I get no glimpses? What can I do to break this barren, monotonous, dreary, and sterile spiritual desert of my existence? The answer is if you cannot meditate successfully go to nature, where she is quiet or beautiful; go to art where it is majestic, exalting; go to hear some great soul speak, whether in private talk or public address; go to literature, find a great inspired book written by someone who has had the glimpses.

14

The fact that we know our bodies is a guarantee that we can know our souls. For the knowing principle in us is derived from the soul itself. We have only to search our own minds deeply enough and ardently enough to discover it.(P)

15

When you begin to seek the Knower, who is within you, and to sever yourself from the seen, which is both without and within you, you begin to pass from illusion to reality.(P)

16

The mind's chief distinguishing power is *to know*—whether the object known is the world around or the ideas within. When this is turned in still deeper upon itself, subject and object are one, the thought-making activity comes to rest, and the "I" mystery is solved. Man discovers his real self, or being—his soul.(P)

17

Without learning, studying, or practising yoga, Heisenberg, famed nuclear physicist, formulator of the Law of Indeterminacy, unwittingly entered what is a high goal to yogis, Nirvikalpa Samadhi. This happened at times at the end of the deepest abstract thinking about his subject. Thoughts themselves ceased to be active. He found himself in the Stillness of the Void. He knew then, and knows today, his spiritual being.(P)

18

Hugh Shearman: "There is no self. But, when told this, we still remain ourselves; and the utterance of this truth is again only a thought-form in a world of other thought-forms. What, then, is to be done? There can be no ending of karma by karma, no ceasing of thought-forms by creating counteracting thought-forms. The only effective thing is to come self-consciously awake at the point within ourselves at which thought itself is set in motion, to discover in ourselves the thought-producer, to find the fundamental answer to 'Who Am I?'"

19

It cannot come to those who live on the surface of things, for merely to discover and recognize its existence requires the deepest attentiveness and the strongest love. All the human forces must unite and look for this divine event.

20

The affirmations of the true self made by some creeds are contributions as useful as the denials of the false self made by other creeds. Both are on the same plane, the intellectual plane, and therefore both have only a limited usefulness as one-sided contributions only. They do not solve the problem of eliminating that false self or of uniting with the true self. Only the Quest in all its integral many-sided nature can do that. It uses every function of the psyche in the effort to change the pattern of the mind— not the imagination alone, nor the intellect alone, nor the intuition alone, nor the will alone, nor the emotions alone, but all of them combined.

21

If he has freed himself from the ego's domination, he is entitled to receive the Overself's benedictory influx.

22

His contemplation of the Divine has to become so absorbing as to end in self-forgetfulness.

23

A woman gazing at her child with continued joy may unwittingly lead herself to the glimpse.

24

While most glimpses come naturally and unexpectedly, it is possible to develop the experience systematically by the technique of meditation.

25

Later I intellectually pulled my own inner experiences to pieces to show them to others in the hope that it would help them either obtain or understand such experiences for themselves—and to do this in a scientific way by cultivating a habit of precise observation which rigorously sought to exclude personal prepossession and imaginative intrusion.

26

If the glimpse is not to remain an isolated event, he must try to put less of his mind on himself and more on the Overself, less into emotional reactions to it and more into pure contemplation of it.

27

It may come upon you without warning at any time and in any place. But it is more likely to come if you provide conditions which are proper and propitious for it.

28

Once a man has had this sacred experience he will naturally want to provoke it again. But how? He will find meditation to be part of the answer.

29

If he is tempted by these sudden glimpses to enquire whether there is a method or technique whereby they may be repeated at will, he will find that there is and that it is called meditation. If he wishes to go farther and enquire whether his whole life could continuously enjoy them all the time, the answer is that it could and that to bring it about he needs to follow a way of life called The Quest.(P)

30

It is a useful exercise, to bring the experience back to mental sight and emotional presence, to evoke the glimpse as vividly as he can.

31

The Glimpse is to be recalled frequently and enjoyed reminiscently. Let it help him in this way to dedicate the day to greater obedience of intuitive urge. Let it bring forth afresh that love of and aspiration toward the Overself which are necessary prerequisites to a stable experience of it.

32

If few attain the wonder of Overself consciousness, it is because few can lift their minds to the level of impersonality and anonymity. But what all cannot do with their minds, they can do much more easily with their hearts. Let them approach enveloped in love, and the grace will come forward to meet them. By its power, the ego which they could not bring themselves to renounce will be forgotten.

33

These glimpses will last longer and come more easily, hence more often, if the mind and the feelings are properly balanced, and if, at the same time, the body is purified, its organs co-operated with, and its forces regenerated.

34

When the glimpse happens, a man comes out of himself. It may follow his admiration of a beautiful scene in Nature or his appreciation of a beautiful poem or his simple relaxed mood, but in each case he lets go of his taut self-consciousness. This allows the entry of grace.

35

He will be blessed with such glimpses if he works intensively on himself according to the prescriptions of philosophy.

36

I have given, in *The Wisdom of the Overself*, an exercise for recapturing the Glimpse by reproducing it imaginatively with all effects and details associated with its appearance. It may be added now that not only should the mental and emotional features be reproduced but also the physical. Whatever he can remember of the condition of the muscles, limbs, mouth, eyes, and spine should be faithfully copied.

37

Peering down into those mysterious depths of the "I" which are far deeper than its human and bestial layers, he will come to a region where personality becomes essence. The psychoanalyst cannot reach it by his intellectual and hypnotic methods, but the mystic, by his intuitive and contemplative ones, can.

38

The Soul has its chance to have its voice heard also when the conscious self is too fatigued by the troubles of life to offer resistance.

39

If he understands that the origin of these mystical moments is his own best self, he will understand too that the shortest and quickest way to recapture them is to go directly to that self, while the surest way to keep their happiness for life is to keep constantly aware of that self.

40

Only when the heart has been utterly emptied of all its ties can the divine presence come into it. If you can empty it only for a few moments, do not lament in despair when the visit of the presence comes to an end after a few moments.

41

Sometimes he is lifted up by the beauty of Nature's forms or man's arts, sometimes by the discipline of moral experience or religious worship, sometimes by the personal impact of a great soul.

42

Some people have even felt this calmness, which precedes and follows a glimpse, in a warm-water bath; while enjoying or luxuriating in its comfort, they have half-given themselves up to a half-drowsy half-emptiness of mind. Some Japanese are able to pass from this calmness to the deeper stage, or state, of the glimpse itself.

43

If he understands the process whereby he arrived at illumination, he will know how to recover it if and when it fades away. But if he arrived at it by an unconscious process, then when he loses it he will not know how to help himself.

44

Is it possible, if the Divine is formless, motionless, voiceless, and matterless, to recognize It when the quest brings us to a glimpse of It? The answer is Yes! but either intuition well-developed or intelligence well-instructed is needed: otherwise it happens by faith.

45

Whether it be a mountain scene or a peaceful meadow, a distinguished poem or an impressive opera, the particular source of an unaccustomed exaltation is not the most important thing. Such a visitation can also have its origin in no outside source but within oneself.

46

It should be remembered that whatever kind of meditation is adopted, the glimpse which comes from it comes because we have provided the right condition for its appearance, not because our own doing makes the glimpse appear. For it comes from the realm of timelessness with which we come into some sort of harmony through the intuitive nature. What we do is in the realm of time, and it can only produce effects of a like nature.

47

In contacting the Overself, he does not really sense a bigger "I." He senses SOMETHING which *is*. This is first achieved by forgetting the ego, the personality, the "I." But at a later stage, there is nothing to forget for then he finds that the ego, the personality, and the "I" are of the same stuff as this SOMETHING.

48

All thinking keeps one's awareness out of the Overself. That is why even thinking about the Overself merely produces another thought. Only in the case of the sage, who has established himself in the Overself, is thinking no barrier at all. In this case, thinking may coexist with the larger awareness. So it is not enough to be a good thinker; one also has to learn how to be a good non-thinker. Of course, the way to do this is through the practice of meditation.

49

Tantrik Kashmir—How a glimpse may come: (1) Between two breaths, as then the small self vanishes, the universal pause taking over. (2) Imagine the divine Self's light moving up spine. (3) Mind's attention between eyebrows, without thoughts. (4) Let external beauty melt within you or let any point in space or on a wall dissolve. (5) When everything external dissolves into you, then your wish for another comes true. (6) Meditate with face covered by hands, or with fingers touching eyeballs very lightly. (7) Concentrate continuously on the sound of waterfall, or similar sounds. (8) Intone A-U-M *slowly* and move with the sound into harmony of soundlessness. (9) Bring mindstuff below in your heart. (10) Consider your form as space. (11) Saturate body with cosmic being. (12) Bring senses into heart. (13) Never mind thoughts, keep in the centre. (14) In worldly activity, keep attentive *between* breaths. (15) Concentrate on withdrawing into heart when going to sleep and thus direct dreams. (16) See all things converging into your being. (17) When eating or drinking, become the taste of the food, or become the eating. (18) Abide in a place endlessly spacious, clear of habitations and hills, then undo mind's pressures. (19) Whatever kind of satisfaction is enjoyed, actualize this everliving presence. (20) Just before falling into sleep, being is revealed. (21) See as if for first time a beautiful person or an object. (22) Let yourself swing in slowing invisible circles and thus experience. (23) Close eyes, find blackness. Open eyes, see blackness. So faults disappear. (24) Just as you have impulse to do something, stop. (25) When some desire comes, consider it, then suddenly quit it. (26) Realize; feel your form as made of consciousness. (27) When exhausted physically, drop to the ground, be whole. (28) Both enlightened and unenlightened persons perceive objects, but former remain in subjective mood, not lost in thing. (29) When hearing ultimate teaching imparted, keep eyes still, unblinking, thus become free. (30) Contract rectum, withdraw inwards. (31) Nothing else exists than this consciousness. (32) Enter space, supportless, eternal, still. (33) This consciousness is the guru, be this one.

50

It is not by any kind of privilege that anyone obtains the glimpse but by preparation and equilibration, with some amount of purification. To equilibrate is to calm feelings as and when necessary and render them deeper, exquisitely delicate.

51

To suppose that you are going to be wafted into this lofty awareness of the Overself without having to work very hard and very long for it, is to be a simpleton.

52

The glimpse comes and the glimpse goes, suddenly or slowly, and this coming and this going are independent of his will. This does not, however, mean that he is totally helpless in the matter. Instruction or experience or both can teach him what those conditions are which assist the onset of the glimpse and those which obstruct it.

53

In *The Spiritual Crisis of Man*, a chapter was devoted to the topic of glimpses. It was also touched on briefly in earlier books although not under that name, but when dealing with meditation. I tried to tell what could be done to get more out of a glimpse and mentioned recapturing the memory of it as part of an exercise. It ought to be added that the best time to do such an exercise is before falling asleep at night and on waking up in the morning. It is then easier to recapture such a memory.

54

If we want to hear the voice of the Overself, we have to create a quiet all around us and all within us and we have to listen and go on listening with patience.

55

To enjoy a glimpse it is better to be alone, undisturbed, and undistracted, better to be with nature than with people, better to be among the woods and lakes and mountains than in the offices, the drawing rooms, and the factories of society.

56

Some, like the poet Keats, find Truth through beauty while others, like the poet Dante, find it through suffering.

57

That is a valuable meditation which, whether at odd moments or for fixed periods, returns again and again to dwell on the nature of the Overself and disregards all lesser topics. Such frequent remembrances and such fixed meditations become indeed a kind of communion and are usually rewarded sooner or later by a glimpse.

58

The contemplation in memory of those glimpses will help him to weaken the power of negative thoughts and to weaken, however slightly, the very source of those thoughts, the ego.

59

The Lightning-flash may occur either after reason reaches the peak of its performance and has been exhausted, or by deliberately abandoning intellectual activity for the utmost faith and devotion. In both cases, one has to let go and sink back into the Nothing and stop further efforts on one's own. Sometimes, by destiny, the Lightning-flash can occur unexpectedly when no effort is made.

60

If he can come to this belief in the reality of his own higher self, he can come into all the knowledge he needs, all the help he needs, by heeding its guidance (felt intuitively) and by applying its injunctions to his daily life.

61

If the ego would be willing to abdicate its rule for a short period, the way to a glimpse would be opened.

62

The paradox is perfect: when he is most empty of petty ends, the shining glimpse reveals itself.

63

He must look ardently forward to, and eagerly await, each time when the Overself takes over more and more.

64

Ever drawing us toward Itself, Its power to attract blocked by the layers of thoughts, emotions, desires, and passions which compose the personal self, much time and many lives are needed to unblock a passage to It.

65

Follow the self's track within, not slipping down into its muddy bogs but ascending up to its diviner sources.

66

Is it possible to recapture these wonderful sensations? Long intervals of aridity may inspire a negative answer to this question, but adequate knowledge of the laws at work and the mental processes involved inspires a positive one.

67

Know Consciousness without its objects—and you are free!

68

If he is willing to take the training of his mind seriously in hand he can, either during or at the end of his course, live again in such experiences.

69

In that condition of passive emotions and paralysed thoughts, consciousness can receive That which otherwise it shuts out.

70

When he retreats to his centre, he has retreated to the point where the Glimpse of truth may be had.

71

An event, a book or a person, a piece of music or a piece of landscape may bring the mind to brief spiritual consciousness.

72

The evanescence of all these glimpses is saddening to most of us, but the causes once understood, the remedy is at hand.

73

It is harder to find amid the din of city streets, and when found, easier to lose in the press of thronging crowds.

74

Believe in the higher Self and look up to it.

75

Sometimes one word may flash a light into his mind which goes far and wide. At other times a short phrase may do the same work for him.

76

He realizes that he has had an important experience which will be followed at intervals by others, when he stands on the fringe of cosmic consciousness. Through proper metaphysical study, meditation practice, and philosophic action, it will not be difficult for him to come into the awareness of his own Overself to some extent, although it is difficult to acquire full consciousness in the present age, when the opposition of a materialistic society is so strong and intense. However, even to enjoy a fraction of this wider consciousness is to transform his life in every way.

77

Look back in imagination upon those wonderful glimpses and try to recapture the feeling they produced.

78

Just as the lotus flower opens its buds bit by bit, so should he open his mind to this great truth.

79

In becoming conscious of the not-thinking hinterground of my personality, I attain true being.

80

What peace fills the mind when its thinking faculty is put out of gear in the proper way! What ever-remembered moments of illumination this happening may produce!

Essentially grace-given

81

Everywhere in the Orient as well as the Occident, men and women seek for this glimpse but most of their attempts to gain it are unavailing ones. The explanations usually offered them for this frustrating result fall into four categories. First, they need to look harder into themselves and persevere longer at the practices. Second, they need to get God's grace. Third, they need to get a Master's grace. Fourth, their destiny was unfavourable in this matter or, if favourable, was due to maturate at a later time. All these explanations seem to have some truth in them, but which aspirant knows with any certainty which one of them—or which two in combination—apply to his or her own particular case? It seemed to me that, as with every other major event in human life obeying some law of nature, some process operated by infinite intelligence, there must be an invisible pattern behind these mystical happenings too. And when the truths of the higher philosophy were unveiled to me, I found that this was indeed so.

82

These revealings of inner life, which put its truths before the mind so vividly, seem to come by chance to some, by working for them to others. Faith in a divinely-ordered universe tells us, and philosophy confirms, that we may be sure that they follow certain laws even when we know nothing about those laws.

83

The glimpse is as much subject to grace as the Enlightenment which endures forever. It happens outside the man's own will, although inside his consciousness.

84

Such a glimpse represents a bestowal of Grace. This is why it comes unsought and unworked for, and why some who inwardly work hard fail to experience the Glimpse.

85

One can no more *make* the Glimpse come by personal endeavours than he can make himself fall in love.

86

The gifted—rather than achieved—nature of the glimpse is much more frequent and may be seen from its unexpected manifestation at unforeseen times.

87

The glimpse does not necessarily have to come to you during meditation, even though the work in meditation helps to bring about its occurrence. It may come at any time.(P)

88

Many Yogis are made but some are also born. Destiny transcends all training and often it needs but a mere touch of an illuminate's finger to release the pent-up stores of secret power within a soul.

89

These glimpses come on rare occasions, for the mind's tumult is hard to still—only the Overself's Grace can do so.

90

The glimpse is a blessing which is given to those who have earned it, or those who have sought it in the right spirit.

91

These illuminative glimpses do not come at will or at once. They do not come once for all or when it pleases us. They come and go like the wind and when it pleases them. For they come by Grace.

92

The belief that mystical illumination is solely luck or accident or destiny must be refuted.

93

That a man must work his way into this experience is one view. That a higher power must *induce* it in him is another.

94

Such a mystical experience is not an after-effect of illness but the latter is used by the Overself to open the way for its reception in the conscious mentality. It is an uncommon experience, a visitation of the Overself, and a manifestation of its grace. Why it occurs could only be explained in terms of the theory of reincarnation.

95

There will be a precise moment when he *knows* with a certitude totally and unequivocally unwavering, but until then it will more likely be unplanned, uncertain explorations. This may surprise some persons but it is still true that "the wind bloweth where it listeth. Of such is the kingdom of heaven." Or, going still farther East, in Hindu terms, "The Spirit enlightens whom it chooseth." Of course the human element of seeking and trying must be there, but in the end it is the divine element which wins out.

96

Out of visible light which rapidly increased in intensity and drew nearer, the face and form of Jesus appeared in this twentieth century of ours to two mystics, Sundar Singh in India and Martinus in Denmark. They saw him plainly, heard him speak clearly. In both cases they were already familiar with his name and story. Out of a not very dissimilar light, Jesus appeared to Saul on the Damascus Road. He too was familiar with them. A part of the source of these visions is to be traced back to the suggestive power of the thought-form already implanted in the mind; but the other part, the sudden and dramatic and total change of heart and shift of outlook, has still to be accounted for. What is the secret? It is contact with the Overself, Grace.

97

The divine moment happens. It is the gift of grace. Its arrival is unbidden. Yet the previous longing and working for it have not been futile.

98

The significant flash of insight may come at any moment, the sacred presence of the Overself may be felt when it is not being sought, and the noble peace of reality may even visit one who has never practised any technique at all. For as the New Testament has warned him, "The wind bloweth where it listeth," and as the *Katha Upanishad* has informed him, "Whomsoever the Divine chooses, by him alone is It reached."

99

The Glimpse is sometimes given to him and sometimes created by him. Sometimes the connection between his effort and its appearance may not be visible and yet it may be there.

100

"O Nachiketas, only by the Divine lovingly possessing thee can this transcendental knowledge be got" is an ancient Upanishadic statement of this same truth.

101

The glimpses are not directly caused by his own endeavours. They are experiences of the working of Grace, gifts from the Overself, echoes from former lives on earth, or belated responses to his knocking on the door.

102

It is essentially a grace-given experience.

103

One day there will be a response to the search of his mind for its creative inspirational source.

104

His "I," hemmed in by its ignorance and limitations, is a small affair compared with the "I" which is drawing him onward and upward through the quest and which he must one day become. His personal self, controlled and purified, kept in its place, humbly prostrating itself before the Overself, can gratefully receive even now glimpses of that day, momentary revelations that bless the mind and put intense peace in the heart. Whoever does not feel that these affirmations apply to him but who is yet able to believe in their truth, will be befriended by grace at the time of death.

105

The good karma or God allows him this glimpse of a loftier world in which he could live and thus put his personal turmoil to flight.

106

If with the purpose of seeking to disidentify himself with the ego a man practises the necessary self-denial, makes the requisite sacrifices, and trains his thoughts and feelings, after a certain time and at a certain point of his path the forces of heaven will come to him to complete the work which he has started.

107

One should be profoundly grateful for even a single glimpse. It is a grant of grace.

Accepting, cultivating the glimpse

108

When the sacred moment comes, let him not hesitate to let himself go, to adore the Overself ecstatically, and to let his heart be ravished.

109

The rapt return to mental indrawnness may come to the practising meditator quite unexpectedly and suddenly. It may find him engaged in some ordinary daily activity or caught speaking in the middle of a sentence, but whatever it be, he should instantly surrender himself and his time to it. In the result, the meditation will gradually deepen into a mild ecstasy.

110

The Overself throws out a clue to its existence and presence. This comes in various ways to different persons. One form is a delicate feeling drawing him inward either to deeper thought or to no thought at all. If he goes along with it even though hardly aware and half-involuntarily, he will be led by this clue to a glimpse.

111

He should learn to recognize that these moments, which come so suddenly and so delightfully, have a special value. As soon as they come he ought to suspend all activities, put aside whatever it is that he is doing, even stop what he is speaking, and concentrate all his attention in a passive submissive way upon the delicate feelings and deep understanding that come with them.

112

Once caught up in the glimpse, keep quite still; any physical movement may break its delicate gossamer thread.

113

He may feel his attention being suddenly but gently drawn inwards. The moment this occurs, he should at once pay the fullest heed to this subtle whisper from the Overself, which it really is. It will pay him handsomely to drop for a few minutes whatever else he may be doing at that time. For if he does turn inwards, as he is directed to do, the whisper will grow quickly into a loud call, which will overwhelm his whole being. And as he gives himself up utterly to such listening, he will—and here we are speaking metaphorically only—be led into the sacred precincts of the Overself. The visit may be very brief, but it will also be very beautiful, finely refreshing, and greatly enlightening.

114

There are moments when the Overself gets at a man's consciousness, and rarer moments when he gets at Its consciousness. It is his profit to extend them, if he can, or to dwell long and often on their memory, if he cannot. What he needs to cultivate is both the facility and the capacity to expand the slightest premonitory movement of the door of intuitive awareness to the widest opening of it. Whenever he notices the very slightest indrawing to the Overself, whenever the least feeling of Its onset appears, he should *at once* begin to wrap himself around with the felt influence to the exclusion of everything else.

115

Let go, let thoughts come to rest, let the ego go. This is the best preparation to receive the glimpse, to invite and feel its bliss, wiping out the memories of suffering.

116

Whenever a glimpse is given to him, he should stretch its duration to the utmost. This can be markedly helped by being very careful to keep his physical position unchanged, by not even slightly moving hand or foot or trunk. The perfectly still body offers the best condition for retaining the perfectly still mind. If attention is to be placed anywhere in the body, it should be placed in the region of the heart.

117

The sudden but gentle drawing away from outer activity to the inner one, "the melting away in the heart," as Oriental mystics call it, felt actually inside the middle-chest region, may make itself felt occasionally, or, in an advanced or regular meditator, every day. In the last case it will tend to appear at around the same hour each time. This is a call which ought to be treated properly with all the reverence it deserves. But before it can be honoured it must be recognized. Its marks of identification must be studied in books, learned from experience, gleaned from the statements of other persons, or obtained from a personal teacher. When it comes, the man should heed the signal, drop whatever he is doing, and obey the unuttered command to turn inwards, to practise remembrance, or to enter meditation.(P)

118

The significant points in this matter are three: first, it is a call to be recognized and understood; second, it is a command from the highest authority to be obeyed instantly, as disregard brings its own punishment, which is that the call may not come again; third, it is an offer of grace. If the call is heeded and its meaning known or intuited, the aspirant should first of all arrest his movements and remain utterly frozen, as if posing for a portrait painter. Let the mind be blank, held as empty of thoughts as possible. After a while, when adjusted to this sudden suspension of activity, he may with extreme slowness and with utmost gentleness assume a bodily posture where he will be more relaxed and more comfortable, or perhaps even a formal meditation posture. He may then shut his eyes or let them stay in a steady gaze as if he were transfixed, or he may alternate with both according to the urge from within. If everything else is dropped and all these conditions are fulfilled, then a successful meditation bringing on a spiritual glimpse is sure to follow.(P)

119

If we heed their earliest beginnings and do not ignore their smallness, glimpses can be cultivated. They can grow. Look for them in the feelings—these light delicate intuitions—for that is what they mostly are.

120

What is strange is that the experience which comes with the Overself visitation assumes any one of a wide range of feelings, from the most delicate to the most overwhelming. With time and growth it may become well settled, or—though rarely—its light may shine from the beginning. There are even other possibilities. It is safer to keep out the preconceptions and the expectations, safer too if the ties of books and bibles are left outside for a while. That is, accept the freedom of utter surrender to the Overself, of dissolving in it and letting the wind blow where it listeth.

121

The Overself's summons is immediate, so the response must be immediate too. A king ignored will not wait around.

122

The experience is capturable not by the self's grasping hand but by its loving surrender. This is the paradox.

123

It must be something which *possesses him*, not something which he possesses.

124

These glorious moments must be appraised for what they are, and not received with just casual enjoyment. They are gifts from heaven.

125

Anti-technique: If he regards it egoistically as a new "experience," then it will have to share the transient character of all experience and come to an inevitable end. If, however, he has been taught and trained by metaphysical reflection to regard it impersonally as a realization of something which was always there, which always was and shall be, and if he is morally ready for it—if, in short, he recognizes it as the experience of his own self to which he did not attend before—then it may not lapse.

126

As he receives an influx of light from the Overself, the Glimpse is experienced. But only to the degree that he has previously prepared, molded, and purified himself will he experience it correctly, completely, and safely.

127

The Glimpse is either the result of a certain sensitivity to intuitive feelings and ideas, or else brings him to it.

128

The ego's imagination soon gets to work recreating its past or extending its desires for the future, whenever a glimpse of spiritual calm suspends those memories and desires for a time. It is this restless picture-making faculty, among others, which is used so actively by the ego to keep us out of the kingdom by wrenching us out of the eternal into the temporal. We must beware its operations, or renounce its results, if we would keep this calm a little longer.

129

The less he lets anything disturb the full impact of this experience, the deeper will be the impression it makes. The glimpse requires a complete concentration.

130

Meet these first moments of the Glimpse's onset with instant acceptance and warm love. Then you cannot fail to enter the experience itself.

131

When this glorious feeling comes over him, whether at a gentle pace or with a lively rush, he should accept the gift straightaway.

132

He may sit or stand there, where it caught him, mesmerized by the glimpse, permeated by its tranquillity.

133

When the personal "me" stops the endless struggle for a while and remains quiet, inactive, and passive, the impersonal "I Who Am" arises and, little by little, gently suffuses it with new life and heals it with great love.

134

When the feel of this unusual and ethereal presence suffuses the heart, the first duty is to drop all attention elsewhere and respond to it. This response is not only to be immediate, unhesitating, and unquestioning; it must also be warm, loving, grateful, and joyous.

135

Once he catches that feeling of happy stillness, he should not let himself leave it on any excuse whatever—for thoughts will invade him and try to drag him away. He should refuse to disturb his tranquillity even for thoughts about the nature, working, and effects of the stillness itself! One objective alone should be with him, and that is to become absorbed more and more deeply in this happy state, until every idea, concept, decision, or impulse is dissolved in it. Any other objective will only invite loss of the Glimpse.

136

If it comes without preliminary meditation, then it will probably come unexpectedly and suddenly. Therefore a certain amount of either knowledge or experience is required to recognize the authentic signs of its onset and to detect the precious opportunity which offers itself.

137

He must first identify its real character when he feels its presence, and then be passive to facilitate its onset.

138

Even with the first feelings of this peace-bringing awareness, he should be careful, first, not to ignore them but on the contrary recognize that their importance exists in what they lead up to and, second, to let himself be carried away gently by them. The first he must do quickly but the second slowly.

139

In this experience, the more he can let himself be lost in the feeling of ecstatic peace and egoless understanding, opening his total personality to it, the more will it become a milestone on his road. As such he will look for its inspiration again and again in memory.

140

Sometimes it is necessary to rest a little while to take in more fully the sacred Presence one becomes aware of.

141

Sometimes sleep must be sacrificed to let the glimpse become more than a flash, to let it expand and settle a while in all its healing serenity. This is important, for it is a special opportunity although seldom understood at its true value.

142

Acknowledge the inner call when it comes by simply dropping whatever you are doing and relaxing, be it for a minute or a half-hour. Let consciousness turn away from the world to Consciousness, attend to Attention, but do it all passively, receptively.

143

The glimpse may open delicately, quietly, even faintly; but if we give it the full patient attention which it deserves, it can grow and grow into a great vision.

144

These glimpses do not come often enough to be treated casually. Their importance is easily missed in their subtle outset, but the intuitive mind will begin to learn to recognize the signs of these beginnings, to consider them sacred, and to let them do their work unhindered. This work is something like a magician's throwing of a spell over the mind.

145

The beginnings of a glimpse may be vague, dreamlike, faintly suggestive; but if we let it work and remain passive it will grow into a vivid consciousness, peaceful or joyful, wise and strengthening.

146

Surrender to it as to a piece of music. Let it take possession of you while it lasts, for it will not last. The music reaches its finale and so does the glimpse. The oscillation that is life in the body, the movement to-and-fro between the pairs of opposites, cannot be kept still, inoperative, for more than a fraction of time.

147

When the glimpse starts, it is best to remain still, and in the same bodily position whether sitting or standing, with eyes fixed at the same point.

148

The feeling may be so slight at first that it may easily remain unrecognized for what it is. But if he pauses in whatever he is doing at the time, and gives heed, it will become stronger and stronger.

149

Anyone who is just beginning to feel this presence, however briefly and intermittently, needs to learn how to guard his feeling against large dangers and small encroachments, or it will quickly be killed.

150

Socrates had entered a battlefield along with his friends when suddenly and unexpectedly he caught his breath because he found himself falling into a spiritual Glimpse. It was so wonderful an experience that he denied all other calls on his time and so sunk deeper and deeper into the glimpse. It was not until twenty-four hours later that the glimpse came to an end of itself. There is a lesson here. Such a chance may not repeat itself, it may not be possible to get it again. Advantage should be taken of it because of its all-importance. No one knows how deep the absorption of a glimpse will carry him nor how long a time there will be before it comes to an end.

151

The moment he feels this inner hush, the possibility of developing it is presented to him. But will he use it? Or will he ignore it and thus remain unmindful of his divine source?

152

The glimpse is too delicate and too elusive to be held by force.

153

Those first delicate feelings which betoken the Glimpse must be accepted at once or they may quickly retire and vanish altogether.

154

Be passive and let in the Glimpse. For a while he loses his self-identity but the event happens as if it were quite natural.

155

When this mood comes upon him, he ought to chain himself to it.

156

He should appreciate the worth of these moments and not let them slip by without giving himself up wholly to them.

157

When such moments of grace come to him he should appraise them at their real worth and not turn away to the next activity. Rather should he pause from all activities and wait with hushed thoughts, watchfully, patiently, reverently.

158

If the signals show the probability of an impending glimpse, it is an error to neglect them just because he is preoccupied with something. Better to lay aside the immediate activity and wait, relaxed and receptive, to welcome the likely visitation.

159

He should catch such moments just when they are there and not let them vanish into nothing through inattention or failure to recognize their importance.

160

He should pause at the first faint impression that something unusual and lofty is happening to him, should stay just where he is, stilled into inaction like Socrates standing motionless in the battlefield.

161

In other words, all he has to do at such a moment is to *receive* passively: no other action is needed. Thoughts of any other topic, however elevated in character, would get in the way of such reception: so he should ignore them.

162

The glimpse or Grace bestowed on him, whether by a teacher or by God, must be fully utilized and fully recognized for the opportunity, guidance, help, and inspiration that it is. Otherwise, it will remain only transient emotional experience, which has left behind a tantalizing saddening memory of a joy he is unable to catch again.

Factors hindering the glimpse

163

In the case of persons who are not consciously seeking for the reality or truth, the glimpse may also come but may be turned away, refused, and rejected. This may happen because of their earthy character, materialistic belief, or excessively outgoing orientation. The first faint beginning of the glimpse is suppressed and its importance simply unrecognized. Even if its hushed gentle beauty is momentarily felt, it will be pushed aside as mere daydreaming. Thus these people deny, unwittingly, the messenger and lose what could have been a precious chance to discover what is best in them.

164

Beware of keeping out these beautiful spontaneous intuitive moods through the over-intellectualizing of the path to them and of the truth behind them.

165

The Glimpse will be at its best when his ego is not present to interfere with it. Such interference can not only come from its misinterpretations and distortions, against which philosophy so constantly warns its disciples, but also from the self-consciousness which wants him to notice how the experience is happening, to analyse what effect it is having, and to observe the reactions of other people to it. All these may be done but not then, not at the same time as the glimpse itself. Instead, they may be studied afterwards, when his consciousness has resumed its ordinary state. During the glimpse, he must let himself be completely surrendered to it.(P)

166

Why try to predetermine what, by its very nature, is beyond your reach? Why not let the Overself reveal its existence in its own way? For the moment you introduce your own conception of what it ought to be and insist that it shall be allied to, or governed by, this conception, in that moment you become diverted from the pure and true mystical experience of the Overself into an adulterated and imperfect one.

167

The way in which he got his first glimpse, especially if similar to subsequent ones, becomes a fixed form in his belief about it or in his search for a repetition of it. This may become a handcuff, an unnecessary restriction which the finite self puts upon infinite being. Those who have been instructed in philosophy and therefore in the way glimpses, with the reactions to them and the interpretations of them, happen are not likely to make this mistake; but those who know only religions, aesthetics, and other mysticisms may do so. Let them not dogmatize but leave the Infinite its freedom.

168

The concentration upon the glimpse must be full, complete, and sustained. If, for only a single moment, he allows his attention to be diverted toward some outer thing or person, or to be divided with some inner idea, the glimpse may instantly disappear.(P)

169

It is not that they are wholly insensitive to the touch of the Overself, but that they keep on pushing it away from themselves. And this they do for various reasons, according to their individual nature and situation.

170

The moment you seek to keep the glimpse as your own, it is gone.

171

If he complains that the glimpse does not last, he should understand that it cannot last. Unless the mind and the heart are previously put into a properly prepared state to receive it, they will soon reject it. The process of rejection, however, is an unconscious one, for the active agents in it are the restlessness of his thoughts, the negativity of his emotions, the identification with the body, the strength of his desires and, in fact, all those things which constitute his ego. The forces which keep him apart from the higher state are within his personal self and not within that state. If he is unable to retain it, it is because he needs further purification and preparation, and its departure is really a signal indicating this need.

172

The glimpse is hard to get but easy to lose. It slips away if he interferes with it by becoming intellectually analytic or emotionally conceited during its brief reign.

173

It is the easiest of things to lose the glimpse. For when attention is transferred from it to any physical activity whatever, and however necessary, if it is NOT guarded with the utmost care, it will slip from you.

174

In the glow of the experience any attempt to analyse it destroys it. Let it explain itself. Do not bring it within the narrower walls of the intellect. For then you bring in the ego and unwittingly dismiss the Overself.

175

It is less likely that the glimpse will come if the prerequisite conditions do not exist, if hidden negative traits and mental-emotional imbalance tend to act as a short-circuit and prevent its manifestation.

176

In those first few moments of its beginning the glimpse is so fragile, so vulnerable, that even a small movement of interest elsewhere is likely to bring it to a premature end.

177

The quicker he begins to think about the experience, the quicker does the glimpse go. For by reflecting upon it he unwittingly moves out of it to observe, wonder, and then to analyse it.

178

It is a moment of blessed quietness when earth is deserted and paradise regained. He cannot, perhaps dare not, be himself but must fall into step with all the others. He is imprisoned within their banal patterns of routine, within a life without real awareness.

179

This inward feeling may easily be lost if he gives himself up wholly to the world, if he lets life's trivialities or difficulties absorb it.

180

These moments must be caught as they come, or they will turn their back on us and be gone.

181

The more eagerly he tries to hold the glimpse, the more anxiously his thoughts surround it, the more quickly it leaves him.

182

Many have experienced the early beginnings of a glimpse but, failing to recognize it, have aborted it unwittingly by inattention to this delicate feeling.

6

EXPERIENCING A GLIMPSE

How a glimpse comes in

These glimpses come at the most unexpected of times and in the most unexpected places. It is not possible to be dogmatic about their appearance and be correct at the same time. Reports have been received which reveal that they may come abruptly during the strain and pressure of business or professional activity, as well as during the relaxation of leisure hours, at the beginning, the middle, and the end of the day, during pleasurable periods or amid great suffering.

2

The Overself's take-over is not always the same but changes with the time and the occasion, the person and the place. It may be gentle, quiet, almost unmarked at first, or it may be like a tremendous force, commanding and irresistible.

3

The experience may come on gently in moods of relaxation or flash abruptly after a period of emotional or intellectual tension.

4

Sometimes he will definitely feel that he is being led into an experience, a mood, or an idea. At other times he may feel himself being drawn inward quite deeply as if the very roots of his egoic being were penetrated; more rarely as if he has been drawn beyond the ego itself.

5

When this consciousness takes hold of a man, it takes him by surprise. Infinity is so utterly different from what he was experiencing a few minutes earlier that its wonder, its truth, its beauty, its love fill him abruptly, as if in descent from the skies.

6

The element of surprise and the delight of novelty are present and give the Glimpse its rapturous turn.

7

The glimpse may come to him with a suddenness which makes the surrounding circumstances quite incongruous.

8

The glimpse takes you unawares.

9

When the humour of a particular situation or scene, happening or idea strikes a person he may burst out into *sudden* laughter. It is not long-forming but explosive, not built-up like a wall brick-by-brick but flashed across the darkness like lightning. His mind has this possibility of an abrupt move, an unexpected leap. Just so does it still possess this same possibility with regard to the discovery of truth.

10

Enlightenment is always "sudden" in the sense that during meditation or reverie or relaxation the preliminary thought-concentrating gestatory period usually moves through consciousness quite slowly until, at some unexpected moment, there is an abrupt deepening, followed by a slipping into another dimension, a finding oneself alive in a new atmosphere.

11

A passing sign of progress in arousing latent forces and a physical indication that he is on the eve of noteworthy mystical experience may be a sudden unexpected vibratory movement in the region of the abdomen, in the solar plexus. It usually comes when he has been relaxed for a short time from the daily cares, or after retiring to bed for the night. The diaphragmatic muscle will appear to tremble violently and something will seem to surge to and fro like a snake behind the solar plexus. This bodily agitation will soon subside and be followed by a pleasant calm and out of this calm there will presently arise a sense of unusual power, of heightened control over the animal nature and human self. With this there may also come a clear intuition about some truth needed at the time and a revelatory expansion of consciousness into supersensual reality.(P)

12

These moods descend without invitation and depart without permission.

13

This is the crucial point when ordinary compulsive mental activity fades away and stillness supervenes, perhaps very briefly, perhaps for some minutes.

14

For some time he is tense with the feeling of being about to receive a new revelation.

15

Each glimpse is not just a repeat performance; it is a fresh new experience.

16

Each time the glimpse comes, it is as if it had never come before, so fresh, so sparkling is its never-failing wonder.

17

The higher awareness comes on imperceptibly and little by little. But as it silently gathers itself, like a cloud, it also breaks like a renovating cloud—vehement, sparkling, and splashing.

18

The belief, which prevails in Japan, China, and other lands, in a sudden abrupt enlightenment when one thinks quietly or says aloud, "Ah! so this is IT," has a factual basis. This *satori*, as the Japanese call it, may be either a temporary or a permanent glimpse.

19

Robert Louis Stevenson wrote, "The most beautiful adventures are not those we go to seek." Such is the coming of a glimpse—at the moment of arrival, unsought.

20

Although such glimpses come mostly when a man is alone, come in quiet solitude, they need not do so. They have sometimes come to him in a crowded street or on a well-filled ship.

21

The signs of this visitation are not always the same. It may delicately brush him with the feeling of its presence or forcefully stimulate him with the strength of its being.

22

The beginner usually has to go through an emotional experience in order to receive a mystical experience, but the proficient is under no necessity to do so.

23

It comes into the orb of his awareness as an unstruggled and unsensational happening, so easily, so smoothly, that there is no dramatic emotion.

24

The sensitive informed and experienced person may get intimations, may feel the glimpse coming even before the actual joyous event.

25

In that moment he feels on the very verge of eternity, about to lose himself in its impersonal depths.

26

When the opportunity to gain a glimpse of his Overself draws near, it will be foreshadowed by certain happenings, either of an inward or an outward nature, or both.

27

The glimpse often comes unexpectedly and suddenly. If it comes while he is outdoors and walking a city street, he will automatically and unconsciously slow his pace and sometimes even come to a complete standstill.

28

They may come quite abruptly, those intensely lived moments of true vision, those spasmodic glimpses of a beauty and truth above the best which earthly life offers. The mind then rests and there is a gap in its usual activities, a Void out of which these heavenly experiences come to life as they overcome our ordinary feelings.

29

In those earlier days when I was struggling to get established, the glimpse would come upon me in the most incongruous as well as the most likely occasions. One of these frequent but strange times was when I bent down to tie or untie the laces of my shoes.

30

The Overself takes over his identity not by obliterating it but by including it through its surrender.

31

The glimpse state may come on in different ways. Sometimes it disinclines the man from moving. But if he must attend to some matter which requires him to go across a room or out of the house, his feet will seem to move of themselves, but very, very slowly.

32

Before the glimpse can occur, the aspirant may have to pass through a major crisis of his inner life, sometimes of his outer life too. The mental pressure and emotional strain may leave him feeling utterly confused, perhaps even utterly forlorn. But its sudden culmination in the glimpse will replace darkness by light, chaos by direction, and blindness by sight.

33

It comes unexpectedly in relaxed moments, when enhanced physical or mental ease suspends the ego's activity.

34

Caught by the grace, and drawn into its stillness, he may find the physical body reproducing the same conditions by becoming quite immobile.

35

It may give him a catch of the breath, if not of the heart, when the stillness is first felt if it comes unexpectedly and abruptly.

36

The Divine Power is without shape, is pure Spirit; so the worshipper who accepts or creates any concept of it, or who sees it in spectral celestial vision, himself furnishes a vehicle for it. In the case of the concept, it arises from association of ideas: in the case of the vision, by expectancy or familiarity. In both cases, mind speaks whatever language, assumes whatever aspect appeals to the man thinking about God!

37

The idea, ideal person, inspired prophet, or human redeemer whose image is best established in a person's mind by custom and familiarity is in most cases the channel used by the Overself when bestowing the glimpse.

38

Little by little the stress dissolves, the clamant duties to do this or that fall away as the recognition that this is a benedictory visitation comes closer.

39

The glimpse may move so gently into awareness that the beginning is hardly noticed. Or it may move in with a rush that overwhelms him. With it, knowledge, understanding, meaning, nobility, and divinity fill the aura around him at the moment.

40

It is the awareness of a Presence, a felt but hushed benignity, which signals this kind of entry, this glimpse; but there are other kinds, more forceful yet not more superior.

41

If the glimpse comes unexpectedly in most cases, it comes unaccountedly in others.

42

It is the beginning of what he really wants to happen, this feeling of an inward-drawing presence. This awareness is a new experience so it flickers on and off, unadjusted.

43

Who knows? It may come to you so quietly, so devoid of sounds and expectations, that so many smile at what begins to happen to you. But then it may come like a cloudburst.

44

The glimpse may come in the depth of meditation where expectancy places it. But it may also come at unexpected moments.

45

Either gently and slowly the ego is taken over or violently and quickly the "I" is seized. This may happen during meditation or at any time when he is somewhat relaxed, out of it.

46

And then the long looked-for event will happen. A presence, nay a power, will suddenly make itself felt and control him out of himself by an irresistible impetus moving like a tidal wave.

47

It will come to him as quietly as the moon comes into the sky.

48

The glimpses are not controllable. They come or go without consulting us.

49

The glimpse may come only once or twice in a lifetime to one quester yet repeat itself twentyfold to another person.

50

There are scattered moments of inner rapture underived from earthly things, although they may be started off by earthly things.

51

The beauty of these glimpses is heightened by the delight of their unexpectedness.

52

Bartolommeo della Gatta, fifteenth-century painter, who was himself a monk, made a picture (for a Confraternity in Castel-Fiorentino) of Saint Francis in which the latter appears half-standing, half-squatting, caught in mystical rapturous adoration.

53

The coming of a glimpse is not predictable, although it may be encouraged by contact with Nature, appreciation of art, or practice of meditation. It is less predictable than the clearing of haze which so often hovers over the nearby Swiss lake. "The wind bloweth where it listeth," said Jesus in this connection.

54

There are moments when all his acutest thought-movement is stilled and he finds himself bereft of power, forced into utter submission to the divine Overself.

55

If it starts with a faint awareness of being caught in a still moment, it ends in a full experience.

56

The glimpse shows up something of his higher identity. What is interesting also is that its advent is unpredictable, its form changeable: but it is always fascinating.

57

I do not know the name of the ancient Chinese poet who wrote these lines but they refer to the glimpse:

> For about thirty years I wandered
> Searching for the real Tao everywhere . . .
> But at this moment, seeing the peach blossoms,
> I am suddenly enlightened, and have no more doubts.

58

They come in their own mysterious seasons, stay with us in all their brief beauty, and depart as mysteriously and as elusively as they came.

Characteristics of glimpses

59

The glimpse is what the name purports to be and should not be regarded as something more, as the fullest opening of the mind to divine truth. But naturally, because there are different capacities and temperaments in different persons, one glimpse may be wider than another, or take a less similar form.

60

The Glimpses are not completely uniform in their details. In each one there is different emphasis on a particular aspect, such as its Beauty, Power, Impersonality, or Emptiness.

61

Since no two human beings are exactly alike, whether in body or mind, the kind of glimpse which each one gets, the way in which he or she feels and finds the Overself's pressure, is entirely according to personal needs and not according to a fixed stereotyped pattern for all.

62

All men who win through to the world of their higher self, enter the same world. If their reports differ, as they do, that is not because the experiences differ but because the men themselves differ. Nevertheless a comparative examination of all available reports will show that there is still a golden thread of similarity running through them, a highest common factor of perception.

63

The first occasion when this happens brings a thrill of wonder. This is of course due in part to the tremendous nature of the Overself's discovery, but it is also due to its novelty, to the fact that it was never previously experienced. Hence the thrill cannot come again, cannot be repeated even though the experience itself may be repeated several times; but the wonder will always remain.

64

There is the deepest feeling in the glimpse, but this does not at all mean it is hysterical. It may be extremely quiet. It may be strongly passionate, in which case it will be completely under control—not by the ego but by the higher power.

65

When he begins to know himself as he really is, when he experiences this wondrous touch of the Untouch, he feels truly alive.

66

The amazing clearness of the whole revelation and the certainty beyond all possible doubt which accompanies it are only two of its features. An extraordinary inspired elation—emotional, intellectual, and intuitive—is a third feature, with a diffused sense of well-being as its consequence or its corollary.

67

The points of this experience are the difficulty of describing it precisely, the joy it yields and the peace it brings, the feeling of a finer self and the sense of a higher presence, the appraisal of its preciousness and the fading away of worldly desires.

68

In that blessed moment he finds himself *free* in a way never before felt. For he finds himself without the perplexities of the intellect and without the schemings of the ego.

69

When the two are one, when ego and Overself no longer remain at a distance from one another, man experiences his first illumination. What will happen thereafter is wrapped in mystery.

70

In this brief interval when he feels himself to be in the presence of the Overself, when goodwill, peace, and wisdom become living eternal realities rather than mere mocking words, the littleness vanishes from life and a sacred grandeur replaces it.

71

In extreme cases, he may even feel as if this is the first time in human history that anyone has had such a glowing experience.

72

The tremulous happiness of these contemplative moments attains its zenith with an inarticulate breathless stillness.

73

He feels elated, lifted up beyond his normal self, intensely happy without having any particular physical cause to account for his happiness. He feels too that there is goodness at the heart of things and an urge to share this goodness with all others. And lastly, the burden of past sins and ancient errors falls from his shoulders. He has become cleansed, purified, made whole.

74

These splendid moments, so filled with flashes of beauty and goodness, so tremendous in meaning and perspective, are like peeps into Paradise.

75

All through his spiritual career he has dreamt of this first blissful and unique moment when he would enter the Overself's awareness.

76

In these blessed moments he loves God and knows that he is loved by God.

77

The experience is feeling blent with knowing, but the feeling is as delicious as peach-blossom and the knowing is as certain as sunrise.

78

In finding the godlike within himself, he finds also the Good. And from that stems forth goodwill toward all. It is really love active on a higher plane, love purified of self and cleansed of grossness.

79

Glimpses vary much in their nature. Some are soft, mild and delicate, quiet and restrained; others are ecstatic, rapturous, and excited. All give some sort of uplift, exaltation, enlightenment, or revelation and also to varying degrees.(P)

80

I remember the first time I had this astonishing experience. I was fond of disappearing from London whenever the weather allowed and wandering alongside the river Thames in its more picturesque country parts. If the day was sunny I would stretch my feet out, lie down in the grass, pull out notebook and pen from my pocket—knowing that thoughts would eventually arise that would have for me an instructive or even revelatory nature, apart from those ordinary ones which were merely expressive. One day, while I was waiting for these thoughts to arise, I lost the feeling that I was there at all. I seemed to dissolve and vanish from that place, but not from consciousness. Something was there, a presence, certainly not me, but I was fully aware of it. It seemed to be something of the highest importance, the only thing that mattered. After a few minutes I came back, discovered myself in time and space again; but a great peace had touched me and a very benevolent feeling was still with me. I looked at the trees, the shrubs, the flowers, and the grass and felt a tremendous sympathy with them and then when I thought of other persons a tremendous benevolence towards them.(P)

81

In this mysterious moment the two are one. He no longer abides with the mere images of reality. He is now in the authentic world of reality itself.(P)

82

There are three stages in each glimpse. The initial one brings a soft feeling of its gentle approach. The second carries the man to its peak of upliftment, enlightenment, and peace. The final one draws him down again into a fading glow which occupies the mind's background and later survives only in memory.(P)

83

It is a state of exquisite tenderness, of love welling up from an inner centre and radiating outward in all directions. If other human beings or animal creatures come within his contact at the time, they become recipients of this love without exception. For then no enemies are recognized, none are disliked, and it is not possible to regard anyone as repulsive.(P)

84

The mood is exhilarative without being excitable, centered in reality without losing touch with this pseudo-real world.

85

He may find himself lost at times in short periods of absent-mindedness. It may be in the sound of a bubbling brook or some lovely music or some striking lines of memorable prose. With that he forgets cares and peace wells up within him. Such an experience comes close to the mystical glimpse, only the mystic's consciousness moves on a higher level. He seeks a diviner life, a finer soul, inner peace.

86

For a fraction of the hour, time suddenly and uniquely steps aside, Isis is unveiled and the real beauty of Being exhibits itself: All is suspended in this glimpse, all is stillness and grace.

87

The memory of a first glimpse is imperishable. It is a love-experience along with a birth of knowledge, all under an enchanter's spell.

88

When the highly personal egocentric attitude is first displaced by the Overself, there is a sense of sharp liberation and utter relief.

89

In those glorious experiences, he seems to live a charmed existence, above all that distressed him before, beyond all the hideous negatives which the world obtrudes on his notice, secure in a spiritual ivory tower shimmering with inner light all around.

90

It is an experience which happens deep inside the heart.

91

The glimpse is fresh and direct, it is both a vision and an experience and above all it is spontaneous, for it comes by itself.

92

There is the peace which comes from having a well-filled stomach. There is the peace of the graveyard. But a glimpse gives us the highest peace, the *Shanti* of Indian sages, that *which passeth understanding* of the New Testament.

93

The world's dirt seems so remote from these moods of complete goodness as to seem non-existent, or a mere vaporous mist at most.

94

With the glimpse a feeling overspreads his heart of benevolence towards all living creatures—not only human but also animal and not only animal but even plant. He would not, could not knowingly harm a single one. The Christians call this love, the Buddhists compassion, the Hindus oneness. My own term is goodwill, but all are right. These are different facets, as seen from different points.

95

In this wonderful state he becomes keenly aware of the love that is at the core of the universe, and therefore at his own core too. But he not only absorbs it, he also radiates it. It is not something to be held selfishly, like a material possession. As it is received, so is it given.

96

There is no possibility here of feeling stagnant, mediocre, ordinary. It is their very contraries that he feels.

97

There are exquisite moments when all existence seems elevated to a higher plane, when one's individual being is absorbed in a harmony with all things.

98

The feeling which comes over him at this stage is indescribably delightful. He recognizes its divine quality and rightly attributes it to a transcendental source. No vision accompanies it. Yet the certitude and reality seem greater than if one did.

99

The common youthful experience of falling in love bears some of the leading characteristics of this uncommon mystical experience of awakening to the divine reality. But of course it bears them in a grosser and smaller way. Some of them are: a feeling of "walking on air," a frequent recollection of the beloved at unexpected moments, a glowing sense of deliverance from burdens, a cheerful attitude towards everything and everyone, intense satisfaction with life, rosy expectations about the future, expanded sympathies, dreamy absent-minded lapses from attention to the prosaic everyday round, and new appreciation of poetry, music, or Nature's beauty.

100

There is a self which he feels within him yet it is not himself. Something unknown yet joy-giving.

101

Some dynamic force streams though the blood in his veins, the feeling in his heart, and the will in his innermost being. It is no ordinary force, for he knows that never or rarely has he experienced its like before. There is magic in its movement, enchantment in its effect.

102

The things of the world fall far away from you and a great spell will seemingly be put upon the leaping mind till you remember little of name, or kin, or country, and care less. You lie in the lap of a shining mood, granted respite from heavy cares and given relaxation from corrosive thoughts. You become aware of the secret undercurrent of holy peace which flows silently beneath the heart.

103
Although his general experience of it will be of its gentleness, there will be times when he will feel only an authoritative and commanding force in it, when tremendous power will manifest and rule in some episode or event.

104
He may have a vague feeling of some immaterial presence around or within himself, a presence uplifting, ennobling, unworldly.

105
Not only is the kingdom of heaven within us but we are ourselves within the kingdom. We may discover this as a psychic and visual experience, as some do, or simply as a feeling-and-knowing experience that All is God.

106
It is a transparence because he feels open, letting in a rare mood. It is also a transcendence, because he feels lifted out of his ordinary "I" and put down again on a higher level.

107
Reverence for the divine presence filled my heart, awe at the divine wonder permeated my mind.

108
He will feel spontaneous peace that comes from he knows not where, intellectual conviction that the right path has been found, mysterious detachment that takes hold of him during worldly temptations and worldly tribulations alike.

109
When you are in this wider consciousness you are at home. Outwardly you may be without a roof to shelter your head but still you will feel protected, secure, and provided for. Your feeling and your trust are not groundless. For the outward manifestation of this inward care will follow.

110
You will comprehend that while the Overself thus enfolds you, you can never again feel lonely, never again find the sky turned black because some human love has been denied or been withdrawn from you.

111
It is there, in the deep centre of himself, that he finds holiness and liberation.

112
From the physical standpoint, the ego first becomes aware of the Overself as being located in the heart. But in higher mystical experience, this awareness is free from any bodily relationship.

113

A feeling of lightness and freedom, of songlike well-being and perfect harmony, comes with this disidentification from the body.

114

. . . I have felt
A presence that disturbs me with the joy
Of elevated thoughts; a sense sublime
Of something far more deeply interfused,
Whose dwelling is the light of setting suns . . .
—Wordsworth

115

He feels a rightness about the world-plan and a loveliness in some deeper part of himself. It may remain for a little while only but its memory will remain for long years.

116

In this lofty mood, bringing so much goodwill and insight with it, as it does, he is inclined to ignore misunderstanding and hostility from any quarter which caused him resentment or even suffering in the past.

117

The illumination falls into the mind suddenly and I neither will it nor expect it. There is nothing of the "me" in it. That falls off my shoulders as if it were an extremely heavy and uncomfortable garment.

118

In that great light all his ego's affairs and concerns seem of small dimension; beside that ethereal beneficence all the world's evil and madness seems like a quickly receding nightmare.

119

This is his first thrilling discovery of the Overself's existence, his first incontestable evidence of its power. No later experience can equal it in emotional feeling. It is one of the really momentous points of his life.

120

It is a glimpse of heaven, lifting the mind out of this world and liberating the heart from all that ties it down.

121

With the Glimpse comes a trailing glory of loveliness and enchantment, and a vast freedom.

122

This it is to be "born again," to transcend ordinary experience and become aware of a layer of being within the self which is neither sensual nor rational. Nor is it even emotional in the narrow sense except that egocentric feeling is quite definitely and quite richly present. But it is calm, quiet, deep, detached, and elevated.

123

It is an ennobling experience, shaking out for a few minutes or hours all that is base in a man, all that is mean, small-hearted, and narrow-minded. But perhaps even more marvellous than that is the enormous contentment with which it fills him. Desires dissolve, and with them the frustration, the anxiety, the hopelessness, and the expectancy that accompany them when they remain unfulfilled.

124

For a short time he loses himself in this beautiful consciousness and lets go of the continual routine which makes up his usual day. He gains a healing rest in nerve, mind, feeling, and even body. Such a glimpse comes of itself—"The wind bloweth where it listeth," declared Jesus.

125

These glimpses are encounters with divinity. There is a quality about them which separates them from all the other contacts and encounters of life.

126

This Stillness is called, in the New Testament, "the peace which passeth understanding." It is perhaps the chief feature of the glimpse.

127

That memorable moment when he first opens the door of Consciousness will clear doubt, sanctify feeling, and balance the entire life.

128

This new sense of being liberated from the confining measurements of his own ego, unimpeded by attachments and embroilments, carried beyond the vicious passions to inward equipoise, is unimaginably satisfying.

129

In those moments of inward glory all his life expands. His intelligence advances and his goodness perceives new vistas of growth. Heaven opens out for a while in his emotional world.

130

When he steps forth from the ego's timed life into the Overself's liberating timelessness, the feeling of confinement falls away like a heavy cloak. He enjoys an unimagined exhilaration.

131

Just as a blind person suddenly recovering his sight is carried away by a rush of joy, so the mystical neophyte suddenly recovering his spiritual consciousness is carried away by emotional ecstasy. But just as in the course of time the former will become accustomed to the use of his sight and his joy will subside, so the latter will find his ecstasies subside and pass away. His endeavours to recapture them prove fruitless because it is in the nature of emotion that it should suffer a fall after it enjoys a rise.

132

This wonderful and exquisite feeling is really within himself, only he transfers it unconsciously to the scenes and persons outside himself and thus perceives goodness and beauty everywhere.

133

If it begins quietly and unassumingly, it ends deeply—with the sensation of having entered briefly and memorably a higher world of being.

134

If the intercourse of man and woman is the most intimate act in the lives of both, the conscious contact of a human being with the Overself is even more intimate still.

135

His consciousness is lifted up into another world of being; his little self is in communication with the Overself; his perception of truth is instantly translated into power to live that truth.

136

It is as if one climbed to a high observation post and from there saw what was before utterly unexpected and incredible.

137

The peace of these moments, whether achieved by meditation or received by grace, yields a rich satisfying happiness. Why? Because all those thoughts, desires, attachments, and aversions which compose the ego fade away and leave consciousness free.

138

In this experience he loses consciousness of his own personal identity, a state which begins with a kind of daze but passes into a kind of ecstasy.

139

These first experiences of feeling raised to transfiguring peaks should not be expected to reproduce themselves often. They are necessarily rare sensations. Nor, when they do repeat themselves, can they come in precisely the same form and with the same initial intensity.

140

Something of the rapturous emotional reaction is lost by repetition of this experience, but nothing of the wonder and awe is ever lost.

141

At such moments he is filled with a flowing inspiration, a splendid hope, a vivid understanding.

142

With both the brief Glimpse and the lasting Fulfilment comes a strong feeling of release. This refers to release from all the various kinds of limitation and restriction which have hemmed and oppressed him heretofore.

143

Like a prisoner emerging from a gloomy cell after many years or an invalid liberated from long confinement in a hospital bed, he will feel an overwhelming sense of relief as the glimpse deepens and all cares, all burdens, fade away.

144

There is an air of *effectiveness* in the experience which accompanies the glimpse, a feeling that here is real power ready for use and easy to use, in the way that the Overself directs, of course.

145

It is like the feeling of returning to a well-beloved home after long absence, a joy whose arisal is spontaneous and unavoidable.

146

When the glimpse is at its most, he hears within him the harmony of things like a joyous song.

147

The Stillness made him feel as religious and reverential as could be, yet he remained unpraying, even unthinking.

148

The base, the mean, the unworthy, and the low seem alien and far from him: the noble, the high, the true, and the ideal seem to become his own very nature. From this rare contact he draws an unspeakable peace, a divine upliftment.

149

Too many lives have a hard grey colour about them. The glimpse changes this, for an hour or a day, and puts a delicate pastel beauty in its place.

150

All that is negative in his character fades away for the time of this glimpse, as if it had never existed. For he feels that there is pure harmony at the heart of things, within the universe's Mind, and that he has momentarily touched it.

151

In these enchanted moments, all life takes on the shadowlike quality of a dream.

152

The gulf between the impersonal calm of his present state and the egotistical emotion of his earlier one, is immense.

153

The sudden Olympian elation which the glimpse gives, the unfamiliar feeling that it is like looking through a window on an entirely different and wholly glorious world of being, the inner knowing that *this is reality*—these things make it a benediction.

154

When he is in that consciousness, there is nothing either in place or time which he wants. For his mind is in peace.

155

It is a strange paradox that in this experience although a man becomes infinitely humbler—for he has to be passive to surrender, if it is to happen at all—he finds at the same time an immense dignity within himself.

156

In these glorious moments the awareness of evil in the world fades out; by contrast the continuity of original goodness stays unbroken.

157

The sense of well-being which comes with a glimpse spreads into the body, lights up the mind, glows in the emotions.

158

In its enfolding peace, he will lose his earthly burdens for a time; by its brooding wisdom, he will comprehend the necessity of renunciation; through its mysterious spell, he will confer grace on suffering men.

159

As its beauty seeps into him and affects his entire feeling-nature, all his grievances against other men, against life itself, dissolve.

160

All regrets for the past, complaints about the present, and grumbles over the future, pass away. Even more, all contempt or hatred for other men passes too.

161

The glimpse brings a feeling of enchantment. It is the opening of a secret door. The effect is a magical release from burdens and a flooding by hope.

162

With the discovery of this higher self, there comes a conviction of truth gained, a sense of perfect assurance, and a feeling of happy calmness.

163

The glimpse will affect each individual in a different way, although the feeling of stepping out of darkness into light will be common to all.

164

It is not merely feeling to which he gives himself up, but being into which he settles.

165

The conception alone of a peace which is out of this world is simply daring: its realization is utterly gorgeous in beauty and joyous in remembrance.

166

Mostly as a result of meditation, but sometimes during an unexpected glimpse, a mystical experience of an unusual kind may develop. He feels transparent to the Overself; its light passes into and through him. He then finds that his ordinary condition was as if a thick wall surrounded him, devoid of windows and topped by a thick roof, a condition of imprisonment in limitation and ordinariness. But now the walls turn to glass, their density is miraculously gone, he is not only open to the light streaming in but lets it pass on, irradiating the world around.

167

Those mysterious divine moments are as the sudden arisal of a bridge flung from time into eternity.

168

He feels the presence within him of the mysterious entity which is his soul.

169

This wonderful experience bathes him in wonder, penetrates him with deliciousness, and swings him out into infinity.

170

In those moods he will journey far from bodily conditions and environmental influences, far from human sins and social strife, to a place of sanctuary, peace, blessing, and love.

171

He touches the Permanent, feels that his true self is part of eternity and this other self is a foolish thing he is glad to be rid of.

172

It is an ecstasy which takes complete possession of him for the time; even after it leaves him, there is a kind of twilight glow.

173

There is a presence at such times which lovingly holds the heart and serenely rests the mind. In human relations its effect is towards harmony with others, and in moral relations towards selflessness. If he will only respond to it, even a bad man will feel its goodness and be good accordingly while the spell lasts.

174

There are several causes of this joyful feeling, but the primary one is that the prodigal son has returned to his father. Each is exceedingly happy to see the other again.

175

Something of the quiet joy with which one greets the first faint swelling of green buds on bare trees, comes into the heart with these moods.

176

There is something in man which does not belong to this world, something mysterious, holy, and serene. It is this that touches and holds him at certain unforgettable moments.

177

The inner glow is unique, the emotional transport sublime, the intellectual enlightenment exceptional.

178

Such exalted moments give a man the feeling of his ever-latent greatness.

179

There is no experience in ordinary life equal to it, no joy so perfect.

180

Such are the sweeter moments which come as the "herald of a higher Beauty which is advancing upon man!"

181

A full glimpse gives a self-free experience and a stilled mind.

182

Such is the overpowering effect of its beauty that, when we are admitted to its presence, every egoistic thought is dropped—even the search for truth, since that too is self-centered.

183

The sense of ever-continuing being into which he has been drawn and with which he is now identified overwhelms him.

184

The glimpse is an experience in fascination. The man's mind is allured, his attention firmly fastened, his feelings captivated.

185

The glimpse puts him for a while—a moment or a day—beyond melancholy, misery, fear, and the other negative emotions.

186

There are certain intervals when the mind drifts into a kind of half-reverie, its attention diverted to some high theme, its most delicate feelings gently engaged in it. The common world is then far away. An ethereal rarefied atmosphere has taken its place.

187

Life is halted, time is stopped, mind is stilled, imagination is caught and held.

188

Time is absolutely still. Mind is absolutely at peace. He feels in the midst of a miracle, one which embraces the whole world.

189

The discovery of timelessness, of its reality and factuality, is both a thing to wonder at and a joyful experience.

190

To call it an eternal moment may loosely describe it, but to call it timelessness does so more accurately.

191

It is in these moments when the glimpse happens that we find new strength, new inspiration, and are able to put our weaknesses, for the moment, at least at a distance.

192

The glimpse gives a person, for the short period while it exists, a different way of thought, a different attitude towards others, and a different measure for what the world cherishes or despises.

193

As his inner self is illumined he feels the nearness of God, experiences a loving relationship with God, knows the deathlessness of his own being, and accepts the rightness of all that is throughout the universe.

194

One feels gathered into the depths of the silence, enfolded by it and then, hidden within it, intuits the mysterious inexplicable invisible and higher power which must remain forever nameless.

195

Its coming is an emotional, intuitive, non-physical, intellectual, and spiritual event. It happens, this experience of a transcendental Presence, here, in the place that Jesus mentioned—the Heart.

196

It is an experience of complete security—so rarely found among people in the world today.

197

As he sinks inside himself, his inner being seems to open out into ever-receding depths.

198

When the impeccable peace of the Overself inundates a man's heart, he finds that it is no negative thing. It must not be confused with the sinister calm of a graveyard or with the mocking immobility of a paralytic. It is a strong positive and enduring quality which is definitely enjoyable. We actually get a momentary and much-diluted sample of it at such times as when a hated object is *suddenly* removed from our path, when a powerful ancient ambition is *suddenly* realized, or when we meet a greatly beloved person after long absence. Why? Because at such moments we are freed from the infatuation with the hatred, the ambition, or the love simply because they have achieved their object and the desire-thoughts become still. The freedom passes almost in a flash, however, because some other infatuation replaces it in the heart within a few moments and thoughts begin their movement again.

199

Whatever negative ideas and destructive feelings, whatever harassing doubts and muggy confusions he may have had before the Glimpse comes, disappear in its great joyous peace and vast buoyant certitude.

200

It is not a merely abstract concept in the brain but a piercing experience in the heart.

201

When these rare moments come quietly upon him, he feels himself humbled and subdued.

202

In these moments the air seems warm and pleasant, the universe charged with friendliness.

203

These moments of divine glorification exalt us like moments of hearing fine music. They come with the force of revelations for which we have been waiting. They hold us with the spell of enchantment made by a wizard's hand. Their magical influence and mystical beauty pass all too soon, but the memory of them never does.

204

The ecstasy of that state is rare, the abundant happiness it yields is unforgettable.

205

Those who have lifted themselves up at times into the higher Mind know the paradox of the air in which it dwells. For if beneficent gentle peace is there, so too is invigorating immeasurable strength.

206

The Glimpse comes as a benediction and as a grace. The heart should be grateful, immensely grateful for its visitation. It possesses a beauty which is not of this world, which gives joy to the heart.

207

Psalms 16:11 "In Thy presence is fulness of joy."

208

It is a feeling of unearthly and unlimited peace.

209

The world stands still, the sense of time passing and events happening is suspended. Nothing exists but this Oneness.

210

Some are ready to enter the light and when—through the mediumship of Nature or Art, a man or a book—that happens, the experience is as enjoyable as entering an orchard of ripened apricots.

211

The joy comes upon him out of the unknown, gently, mysteriously, and sunnily.

212

As this wonderful feeling steals over him, there is a clear and unmistakable sense that the Overself is displacing the ego. Hitherto he has obeyed the rule of the flesh and the brain and consequently has shared their pitiful limitations. Now he becomes acutely aware that a new sovereign is taking his place on the throne.

213

As he approaches nearer to awareness of the Overself, he approaches nearer to a cloistral inward stillness.

214

He feels that he has reached the very edge of another self, another world of being.

215

In its newly discovered presence, we are relieved of cares, immune to anxieties about the future, and liberated from regrets about the past.

216

It is not the unspeech of morbid taciturnity but a mysterious hush which falls on the soul.

217

If he or she is fortunate there may come to the waiting seeker a sense of uplift, an exalted mood, a feeling of support from a vast mysterious source.

218

There is a unique bliss in this new-found freedom of the second self, a sublime peace in this dissolution of old restraints.

219

He feels something of that sacred presence within him and around him. Its effect upon the mind is to leave a glow of benign goodwill to all beings.

220

It hovers on the edge of indefinable awareness.

221

What is the mystery of that state when the body sits, stands, or reclines without moving, when the thoughts come to rest and the feelings enter an exquisite calm? It has been given a variety of names, for it takes a man out of this familiar common world and puts him into a most mysterious one.

222

The ego slides from off his shoulders like a heavy overcoat and he feels delightfully free.

223

At the ordinary level he has the ordinary outlook, the habitual desires; but there are times when he finds himself at another and higher level where he is unsympathetic to both.

224

No theological difficulties can trouble this happy state, no religious doubts can enter into it.

225

The glimpse is like a first airplane ride. Looking down at the earthly scene far below, with its patch-like landscape dotted with black specks called houses and autos, and thinking of those millions of living creatures who live in one and drive in the other, one is overcome with humility.

226

It is the glorious moment when Adam re-enters Eden, even though he is only a visiting guest and not a permanent dweller therein.

227

The Glimpse operates to cast an actual spell over him. He is enchanted not merely poetically but literally.

228
Hours that are so far from the common ones, so timeless in their quality, make him feel like an ageless Sphinx.

229
Time itself is suspended, and with it go the fears and worries, the unhappiness, which beset living in this world at this hour of its history.

230
It is a feeling of being right with the universe, with Life itself.

231
It is as if years spent living in a dark cellar are abruptly ended by moving to a bright sunny apartment.

232
In this beautiful mood he becomes possessed of perfect leisure. He has all the time now that he needs. There is no need ever for hurry, strain, anxiety.

233
For a moment or a morning, a day or a week, the confusions of life vanish.

234
During these wonderful glimpses ordinary existence seems suspended.

235
He finds a new joy deep within himself, a new and higher meaning deep within life.

236
Whether he thinks that he has strayed by chance into this starry world or believes that God's grace has fallen upon him, he feels its beauty and peace.

237
The encounter with the Overself may be hushed and gentle or thrilling and dramatic. But it will certainly be absorbing.

238
In that beautiful mood, he is wafted upward because his mind turns away from the earth, its interests and desires which ordinarily hold him down.

239
The glimpse is unquestionably a sort of spell put upon the mind and encircling the self, benign and healing and protective. It imparts a feeling of well-being.

240
How inadequate are constructed sentences to tell anyone the total wonder of a glimpse, of the I's departure and the Overself's arrival!

241

The peace descends, the cares are gone, the fears are shed, the avid desires enfeebled.

242

The experience of liberation yields a peace which lifts him into a detachment from the world never felt before, untouched by sights, persons, incidents, which hitherto produced repulsions, irritations, or rage.

243

Joy glows quietly on the face of one who is experiencing a glimpse.

244

The experience will flood his whole day with sun.

245

He will experience a profound sense of release, a joyous exaltation of feeling, and a lofty soaring of thought.

246

It would not be wrong to use a word from gustatory experience and describe these moments as delicious.

247

It is almost entirely an intense and internal experience.

248

The glimpse carries either a quiet intellectual rapture with it or a seething emotional one.

249

In such a benignant mood, it is easy to forgive one's enemies their vile conduct or to look at faithless friends in a kindlier light.

250

It lifts the egoistic out of their egoism for a while, the fearful out of their fears.

251

When we turn inwards, we turn in the direction of complete composure.

252

It is the first streak of sunrise on his inner life.

253

The discovery of the soul's truth carries with it an excitement which only those who spend their lives seeking it know.

254

The glimpses have various qualities—religious, aesthetic, perceptive, and so on.

255

In such moments of intimacy with the Overself, as we let go of our pettiness, we feel enlarged.

256

It gives him, for a short while, an equanimity which he does not have at other times.

257

His heart is filled with the sense of this Presence and, for the few or many minutes this lasts, he is a changed person.

258

Some persons get their first glimpse by surprise, quite unexpectedly, and from then begins their quest. But others get it during the onward course of their quest, while searching or waiting for it, and hopefully expectant of it.

259

When the mind moves inward from everyday consciousness to mystical being, the benedictory change is both ennobling and sublime.

260

During these short glimpses no anxiety and uncertainty can affect him.

261

It is but a pause in the constant oscillation of life, a stilling of the ego's pursuits.

262

But first a hush of peace, a soundless calm descends;
The struggle of distress and fierce impatience ends;
Mute music soothes my breast—unuttered harmony
That I could never dream till earth was lost to me.

Then dawns the invisible, the Unseen its truth reveals;
My outward sense is gone, my inward essence feels—
Its wings are almost free, its home, its harbour found;
Measuring the gulf it stoops and dares the final bound!
—Emily Brontë

263

In these hushed moments a happiness steals over him, a glory is felt all around him.

264

This is his real being. He sought for it, prayed to it, and communed with it in the past as if it were something other than, and apart from, himself. Now he knows that it was himself, that there is no need *for him* to do any of these things. All he needs is to recognize what he is and to realize it at every moment.

Overself displaces ego

265

He enters into a state which is certainly not a disappearance of the ego, but rather a kind of divine fellowship of the ego with its source.

266

There is still a centre of consciousness in him, still a voice which can utter the words or hold the thought "I am I." The ego is lost in an ocean of being, but the ego's link with God, the Overself, still remains.

267

He loses his ego in the calm serenity of the Overself, yet at the same time it is, mysteriously, still with him.

268

With this displacement of ego he enters into the very presence of divinity.

269

It is neither the ego thinking of the Overself nor the Overself thinking of itself. All thoughts are absent from this experience. It is rather that the Overself contemplates and knows itself in the moment that the ego is withdrawn into it.

270

A point may be reached at rare infrequent intervals where he retreats so far inwards from the body's senses that he is wholly severed from them. If this happens he will of course be wholly severed from the physical world, too. This throws the body into a condition closely resembling sleep, from the point of view of an outside observer, yet it will not be sleep as men ordinarily know it. It will either be more graphic and more vivid than the most memorable of all his dreams or else it will be entirely without visual incident or pictorial scene. In the first case, it will be perfectly rational and highly instructive yet unique, strange, mystical. In the second case, it will be conscious awareness of the Overself alone, with no personal self for It to inspire.

271

For the brief period in which it prevails, the glimpse destroys the ego's dominance.

272

His old centre in the ego has mysteriously gone. His new centre in the Overself has taken its place.

273

It is an experience without any awareness of an experiencer. There was no one present to note his own reaction to it. It was a state of non-ego.

274

The consciousness will deepen and, while vacating the personal ego, will take in the higher ego and feel a unity with it.

275

This is a new dimension of consciousness, where it is coming to itself, demesmerized from the limitation imposed upon it by the ego.

276

In that moment man has come to himself. Before then he has been dwelling in alien things, in his passions, his thoughts, his emotions, and his desires.

277

In this ecstatic mental silence, the personal will is given up, the impersonal Overself is given mastery.

278

His personal identity is taken away for a while, to be replaced by a higher one.

279

To be born again, in the sense that Jesus used this phrase when speaking to Nicodemus, means to leave the ego's limited and outward awareness for the Overself's infinite and inward awareness.

280

Within the ego's life there comes to birth another, utterly dissimilar and outwardly unnoticeable.

281

It is literally a going out of his little self into the liberating enlightening Overself.

282

The search is at an end. The Overself has come toward us even as we went blindly toward It.

283

In that blessed moment he sinks his identity into the Reality which he has reached.

Revelation, exaltation, confirmation

284

This glimpse of a state he has never before seen is an effective revelation. For he has now understood, felt, and experienced—lucidly—the exact meaning of that vague word "spiritual."

285

There is no confusion here of many different and differing cults; the intellect is not presented with contradictory theologies or rival organizational claims. The stillness lifts him to a stratosphere above all such nonsensical choices.

286

The glimpse gives a man either a revelation or a confirmation that something exists which transcends this ordinary life, that it is holy, beautiful, satisfying, and that he may commune with it.

287

The glimpse is a man's personal revelation of his divine possibilities. It is breath-taking and beautiful. He eagerly seeks its repetition.

288

He will see what he really is—the "I" of everyday experience with the mysterious being behind it.

289

Only when he knows his ego as it is known in the Overself can a man be truly said to know himself.

290

The Overself's light enters the understanding and enables him to perceive what men like Jesus really meant when they spoke.

291

The divine self reveals itself for a few thrilling moments and then draws back into the void where it dwells. But the glimpse is enough to tell him that a higher kind of life is possible and that there is a being beyond the ego.

292

The glimpse gives him a slight inkling of what the term Overself means. It shows him—not as intellectual idea but as realized fact—something of the ideal toward which he shall strive.

293

It is in these highest moments of indescribable bliss that a man may know what he truly is and how grand is the relationship that he bears to the Infinite Being.

294

It is from such paradoxical moments that man learns both how insignificant he is and how great he is!

295

It is a message of assurance, a communication of knowledge, and a whisper of trust in the Universal Mind.

296

In these few glorious and luminous moments the truth reveals itself, not to the intellect, but to the inner being.

297

With this experience of his own divinity, he discovers a meaning in life. Henceforth, he is able to take part *consciously* in the higher evolution which is inherent in it.

298

Life announces its divine intention only in the deepest, most secret, and most silent part of our being.

299

It is not felt as just another experience only but also as a truth, so illuminative is it.

300

The Glimpse provides assurance that the Soul exists, that God is, that the purpose of human life must include spiritual fulfilment to be complete, and that the Good, the Beautiful, and the True are more enduring and more rewarding than the Bad, the Ugly, the Lie.

301

Yes it is a wonderful feeling, this which accompanies a glimpse of the higher self; but when it is also merged with a knowing, a positive perception beyond the need of discussion, interpretation, formulation, or judgement, it gives the philosophical seeker a certitude which is like a benediction.(P)

302

Every man who passes through this experience and holds its memory, verifies for himself that there is an Infinite Life-Power pervading the entire universe—also that it is ever present, perfectly wise, and all-knowing. Its point of contact with him is his Overself.(P)

303

In that sudden moment of spiritual awareness, or that longer period of spiritual ecstasy, he identifies himself no more with the projection from

Mind but with pure Mind itself. In that severance from its projection, the shadow becomes the sun.(P)

304

During such unforgettable moments the Soul will speak plainly, if silently, to him. It may tell him about his true relationship to the universe and to his fellow creatures. It will certainly tell him about Itself. It may separate him from his body and let him gaze down upon it as from a height, long enough to permit him to comprehend that the flesh is quite the poorest and least significant part of him. And perhaps best of all it will certainly fill him with the assurance that after his return to the world of lonely struggle and quick forgetfulness, It will still remain beside and behind him.(P)

305

A glimpse may exalt the man and give him inspiration, but above everything else it attests for him the fact that he is fundamentally Spirit. This is the commonest kind of Glimpse but there is another kind which, in addition to doing these things, opens mysterious doors and provides inlooks to the working of secret laws and occult processes in Nature, the world and the life of man. This kind of glimpse may fitly be termed "a revelation."(P)

306

He sees the universe as he might see a great mosaic picture opening before him.

307

This knowledge best comes to a man by interior revelation rather than by exterior instructions.

308

Thus the existence of a higher possibility for man, which our ethical sense demands and to which our metaphysical reasoning points, is confirmed at last by our best experience.

309

All that he now experiences will be seen by the glow of its better light, while the memory of all that he experienced in the past, however distressing or vile, will be transmuted into effective educational forms.

310

The light of truth removes the falsities in his world view, and diminishes the feebleness in his character. It brings him a new strength.

311

He knows that he has a place in the cosmos, that he is part of the World-Idea.

312

In this mood there is knowledge without thoughts, understanding without words.

313

What goes on within his ego could be better seen, and judged, if he could climb above it for a short time. This is just what the glimpse enables him to do. It clears the sight.

314

In some way that he cannot tell, or technically define, by pure intuitive feeling authoritatively transcending the intellect's action, he *knows*.

315

The experience explains a man to himself for the first time, lights up the fact that he lives in two planes at one and the same time. It reveals his ego as the illusion which envelops his consciousness and his Overself as the reality behind his consciousness.

316

The Real was not only always present but always known, but unconsciously. It was the "I-myself," the little ego, the separate person that he thought himself to be and ignorantly superimposed on the Real. All this he comprehends quite plainly now.

317

This world is the unreal dream, *that* is the real and substantial one. So the glimpse teaches him. He views this world temporarily as if he stands behind a theatrical stage and watches actors perform set roles in a play and sees properties which are merely painted representations. He is conscious how utterly illusory it all is and, in dramatic contrast, how the awareness by which he knew this was alone real.

318

The experience will either confirm what he has already vaguely felt or else it will contradict what he has wrongly believed.

319

Whatever religious belief it is made use of to confirm, it can only validate those beliefs which are universally held by everyone who is at all religious, not those which are found only in sectarian theology. The attempt to put into it previously held dogmas should be regarded as suspect. It can confirm the existence of a Higher Power, the fact of the soul, and the possibility of communion with it.

320

These glimpses are moments of truth in a life founded on a conception which is so narrow as to be actually misleading, or even false.

321

These are the only moments in life when we catch hold almost at once of truth as it is, unspoiled by implantations from the ego.

322

It is in those uplifted moments that one has the possibility of coming near to confirm the Pythagorean belief that the human soul is an emanation of the Universal Divine Mind.

323

He will understand the meaning of this beatific experience without need of formulating it into thoughts. There is no necessity for him to tell it to himself in words.

324

These short glimpses do not belong to ordinary life; indeed, they glaringly show up its pitiful meanness and confusion, its miserable aimlessness and unsatisfaction.

325

He needs no religious authority to interfere with, or interrupt this glorious glimpse, no theologian to bring it down to the intellectual level and probably lose it for him.

326

If he will compare those rapturous and illumined moments with his prosaic ordinary days, he will have an excellent clue to what his life's goal should be, what his true self really is, as well as how and where he should look for both.

327

There are some who, while reading inspired pages, may suddenly find that for a few brief instants the veil will fall from their eyes and the ideas which had formerly seemed so remote or so impossible will come alive with actuality.

328

As the light shines, showing the glory of the Overself, it also shows the inadequacies of the ego.

329

It tells him quite directly, quite intuitively, without the interference of logical thinking, what life is for and what man is here for.

330

He feels that he is absorbing the entire meaning of all human lives, all the world's operations, in one crystal-clear insight.

331

He feels that this is the fore-ordained moment of revelation, which is implied by the mystery of the quest, and must eventually be fulfilled.

332

When he reaches this high level, he feels that he is an integral part of the cosmos, rooted in and supported by the illimitable Reality. But the glimpse is only momentary for he is forced by some powerful attraction to return to his body and with it to his ordinary self.

333

He has come-to-life, an experience which reconciles all the contradictions of thought and faith and which explains some of the most puzzling enigmas of human destiny.

334

The Glimpse provides overwhelming confirmation of the belief in a divine principle, positive certainty that it rules the world, and renewed assurance that one day all men will obey its benign prompting towards goodness and wisdom.

335

These moments of spiritual insight give him more than much study could give him.

336

He learns then that there is another part of himself not the ego which has hitherto dominated his thoughts and days—a delightful beautiful unpressured part. He knows then what peace of mind really means. He sees that he has lived only as a fraction of himself, and even that has been made miserable by inner or outer friction.

337

It is a mysterious condition of the mind, when the normal doubts and hesitations vanish, when certitude is complete and understanding direct, when he knows that truth has visited him and feels that peace has held him.

338

He perceives that this is a new kind of experience, a new way of knowing, a new level of happiness, a new quality of life.

339

The proper use of mystic experience is as a counter to the merely intellectual and theoretical stages which usually come before such experience.

340

With the coming of this climax he may experience a profound sense of liberation, which later justifies itself, as the problems which had beset his mind slowly begin to dissolve and vanish under its wise tuition. He may think of Keats' joyful lines: "Then I felt like some watcher of the skies when a new planet swims into his ken." For there will be present all the magnificent exhilaration, the intellectual intoxication which is born when the mind alights upon new-found truth guidance or inspiration.

341

He who has tasted the immeasurable joy of the Overself's peace will not care to shrink back again into the little self's confines. For he will know then that the Infinite, the Void, the Transcendent—call what he will the loss of his ego—is not a loss of happiness but an unlimited magnification of it.

342

Each glimpse generates afresh confidence in the existence and wisdom of the World-Mind.

343

He has now a revelation which throws its vivid light on humans, their lives, characters, and histories. There is now a spacious meaning in existence.

344

The Glimpse may be different from any experience he has known, as well as overwhelming in its several implications. But if he has been exposed to the full power, he will trust it, and can hardly do otherwise.

345

It is as if his inner being clears up, becomes transparent, and obscurities covering his essence roll away.

346

It is like light being enkindled in the mind.

347

It is the will to believe and the determination that backs up its belief. We need a vision of the things to be to light up the rough pathway of the things that are. Without it no great work would be done.

348

If the glimpse is accompanied by a revelation, then he will understand more on the particular subject or subjects it concerns than he has ever understood before.

349

Each glimpse brings a grace. It may be a message or an awakening, a revelation or a warning, a reconciliation or a confirmation, a strengthening or a mellowing.

350

Sometimes the mind slips into a dazed beatitude as Jacob Boehme's did in those famous fifteen minutes of mystical enlightenment.

351

Here in the heart is He who witnesses to your divine identity, and in the head comes the confirmation.

352

Such mystical experiences will open to him the true meaning of his humanhood.

353

In these brief but glorious moments we discover that we are divine beings. If most of us are worse than the front we present to our neighbours, *all* of us are better than they think through our affiliation with divinity.

354

In these hallowed moments he learns his essential oneness with the Universal Mind.

355

The experience is neither an abstract supposition nor an intellectual series of thoughts. It is felt in a quite intimate and very personal way. It is immeasurably more convincing than any thought-series could be, however plausible and logical they were.

356

He knows of what divine stuff he is inwardly made, in what starry direction he is daily going, and on what self-transforming task he is constantly working.

357

It can only reveal to him one or two facets of its nature at each glimpse. The power can touch his will, and the grace can move his heart, but that is all.

358

Men are so wrapt up in themselves that even when the glimpse happens, they look at the experience as their own, in origin occurrence and result. They seldom look at it from the other side. For it is also an attempt by the Overself first to reveal Itself, second to communicate with them.

359

His outlook becomes more spacious, his understanding more lucid, his intuition more immediate.

360

In those revelatory moments the "I," the essence of personality, is found to be only the *thought* of itself.

361

It is the difference between trying to know and actually knowing.

362

To see this truth for the first time is to experience something which will be long remembered. To find some higher meaning in his personal existence is to fortify his will and to buttress his ideals; to ascertain the fact that there is a link between this universe of time and space with a Mind which is above both, is to experience an indefinable satisfaction.

363

With the glimpse there comes a curious feeling of absolute certitude, happy certitude, utter doubtlessness. The truth *is* there plainly before him and deeply sensed within him.

364

This experience of the ultimate oneness of all things and of one's own part in that oneness is, of course, well known in mystical experience—especially in nature mysticism but also in some kinds of religious mysticism, and certainly in philosophic mysticism. The first effect is to make one feel that one is not alone, that the universe is behind one and that one does not need to be crushed by anxieties, worries, and fears—all pertaining to the little self. Such an experience is indeed an excellent counter to them.

365

The fact is that all actual enlightenment is self-enlightenment; it is given to a man by himself, that is, by his own best self. It is generally brief, but enough to provide a glimpse of that self and a touch of its revelatory energy.

366

They are "glimpses of the eternal" and "peeps into timelessness," a development which we could not get as animals but only as humans. It is then only that man, interwoven with the World-Mind, deep in holy happy adoration, is *sure*.

367

A glimmering of what it means to see with the intelligence that there is a Higher Power and that it plays a role in human affairs not less than in the universe's, comes to him.

368

We read in the *Bhagavad Gita* of Arjuna's cosmic vision. He was given a glimpse of a part of the universal order, the World-Design, the World-Idea. Others who have had this glimpse saw other parts of it, such as the evolution of the centre of consciousness through the animal into the human kingdom, an evolution which is recapitulated in a very brief form by an embryo in the womb.

Consciousness may expand into infinity or contract into a point. Some have had this experience through mystical meditation and others through physical chemical drugs, but the point is that they are temporary experiences of the fact that we live in a mind-made world, that the time orders and space dimensions are mental constructs and are alterable, that consciousness is the basic reality, that it can assume many different forms, and that ordinary, average human consciousness is merely one of those forms. This tells us why the insights of the seers like Buddha differed so greatly from those of ordinary human beings.

369

With a glimpse comes revelation. He feels that he belongs to an immortal race, that there is an inner Reality behind all things, and that the ultimate source is a beneficent one.

370

By means of this light in his mind, he will begin to understand scriptures, all the world's scriptures, with a new ease.

371

With this awakening he begins to relate his own purposes in life to the universal purpose.

372

Like the falling of a bandage from the eyes of a blindfolded man, there will come plainly into his understanding the recognition of his past misdeeds, foolhardiness, and failings—all of them the consequences of his ignorant clinging to the ego. This is the vision which may come to him before he begins to purify himself.

373

A vivid, intense, and self-critical revelation of how "sinful" he has been may precede, accompany, or follow the glimpse. It may shake him to his core. But it cannot be said that he feels he has betrayed his best and higher being any more than it can be said a child has betrayed the adult it has not yet grown into. He understands this at the same time and so forgives himself.

374

That glorious glimpse wherein the All becomes bathed in the light of meaning, when the reality behind comes through and leaves him enriched: it is as if a web of illusion spun around the mind falls away.

375

From that time he will look out on the world with clearer eyes.

376

In the mystical happening of the Glimpse, the man gets the intuition that *this* is what he belongs to; here he can find rest.

377

In the sunlit tranquillity of such moments, he recognizes his true stature.

378

In short, he possesses a kind of double entity, harbouring at times within his breast a life and consciousness that seem higher than what was originally and still is normally his own.

379

In this moment of illumination he is able to look into the image of his own self, to see what is best and highest in it and accept that as his goal and ideal henceforth.

380

He will know only that he stands in the presence of authority and love, truth and power, wisdom and beauty.

381

The experience tells him vividly, luminously, and memorably that there is an existence beyond the physical one and a consciousness beyond the personal one.

382

Another reason why glimpses are given to man is to show him—as in a magic mirror—that there is such a thing as the Overself.

383

These brief enlightenments give us clues to both the true way and the true goal. They point within.

384

As the picture of the True comes forth, it obliterates the picture of the False which *held him* so long.

385

The glimpse gives him an untrammelled consciousness of this freer and higher self.

386

Disjointed fragments of comprehension may be picked up now and then, when the world-scene is lighted up by some grace.

387

The passing from hope to certainty comes with the glimpse.

388

As the glimpse lengthens, it draws the man to look into himself.

389

It is showing him what he is deep down—a vivid and personal demonstration!

390
From that time life is susceptible of a higher interpretation, and its situations of a psychological meaning.

391
The mind is irradiated with the light of a new understanding. The heart is lifted up into the joy of a new experience.

392
What he now knows, he knows outside all doubting, immovably and unshakeably.

393
He is now sure that there is a higher power behind this world.

394
When this felicitous glimpse comes to a man it brings him *certitude*. He knows now that God IS and *where* he is.

395
The glimpse not only throws a fresh impersonal light on all the episodes of his personal history that went before, but also on those which are happening now.

396
He who penetrates to this inner citadel discovers what Saint Augustine called "the eternal truth of the soul."

397
The glimpse confirms existing religious faith and so strengthens it.

398
At such times he feels the world mystery, for now that he knows so much esoteric truth he knows so little of THAT which is behind it all.

399
The rapture of finding truth comes because it *is* truth.

400
The revelation wells up slowly, quietly, deeply; it is unfaltering and continues so long as he does not interrupt or interfere with it by his own thoughts. It is really his own innermost guide and guru, his higher self.

401
It is in such moments of enlightenment that he comes to see that all these evils may be there, but they will go.

402
"Seeing the point" which solves the problem of existence, suddenly getting the glimpse of what all this means, and noting how it was there all the time staring him in the face, may cause a man to break out abruptly into laughter at himself.

403

He knows from this experience that he is incipient with a love that the world does not ordinarily know, with a goodness that it seldom sees in action, and with an understanding that lights up dark places in the course of life.

7

AFTER THE GLIMPSE

Retain the glow

Each glimpse is a precious gift to be treasured. But we must also remember that it not only comes, but it also goes. This remembrance should make us treat its aftermath very carefully, very delicately, and very watchfully.

2

When these rare glimpses are granted, take from them as they leave all that you can get—all the strength, the wisdom, the support, and the goodwill that they can hold.

3

He has had the glimpse. The after-period is important. For as he returns to his ordinary self and to the ordinary persons around him, the opportunity is offered to make an adjustment, a fresh start by the light of what the experience revealed.

4

The great experience is soon over; the released insight lasts but a few minutes or hours, but its memory lasts long. It is a delectable foretaste and warming anticipation of what his continued spiritual development may bring to man. It lifts him far above himself and out of his ordinary state of consciousness, yielding sharper understandings and creating deeper sympathies.

5

He returns from his first initiation into the egoless life with a rich cargo. He carries the stability of peace. A strange feeling of safety takes possession of him at that time. He knows neither care for the uncertain future nor regret for the unpleasant past. He knows that henceforth the life of his being is in the hands of the higher self, and with this he is quite content.

6

Once he has attained this inner realization, the student should cling persistently to it, for the world's multifarious forces will come to hear of it and seek to drag him away.(P)

7

To get up and move too soon after the glimpse has come to an end is to lose some of its heavenly afterglow. To refrain from any movement, keeping still and being patient, is to enjoy that glow till its last flickering moments as one may enjoy the last moments of sunset.

8

His first need is to immerse himself in the feeling, to preserve as much as he can of the glimpse.

9

Print every detail of the Glimpse on your mind.

10

It is a useful practice to write down every detail of the experience while it is still fresh in the mind. The record will still be there when the joy is gone.

11

The fragrance of this peace lingers on long after the glimpse itself is over.

12

The holy feelings generated by the Glimpse ought to be protected against the world's disintegrating power and shielded against your own tendency to dissipate them by hasty violent movements or needless irrelevant chatter.(P)

13

Immediately after the glimpse no word should be spoken or it may be lost the more quickly.

14

After such a glimpse there is enchantment in the air. The annoying or disagreeable happenings of the day fail to remove it.

15

When the inspiration derived from the glimpse is upon him, the unexpected and the unpredictable may happen for his benefit; but when it is gone, he is no more fortunate than his neighbour.

16

The glimpse goes and the habitual daily self returns. The single and simple largeness of the one is lost in the innumerable trivialities of the other.

17

As the glimpse fades away, he takes the ego back into consciousness again.

18

But the glimpse may not stand alone in its own full purity: he may put his own ideas into it as an accompaniment without knowing that he has done so.

19

The spiritual event, the mystical experience, is there but its presentation to the conscious mind—manipulated by his personal tendencies to an extent which exaggerates their importance—creates a mixed result.

20

But the glow of this transcendence lingers in the heart for long after its actual manifestation. It suffuses him with unearthly happiness and fills him with solemn reverence.

21

When this mood is fully upon him, he may find it hard to talk to anyone for some time afterward.

22

He emerges from the experience feeling surrounded by peace and protected by supernormal powers.

23

The glimpse vanishes, slowly with a few, quickly with most, leaving its effects in his recognition of greater possibilities in life and grander ones in himself.

24

He comes back from the glimpse not only renewed in grace but purged in character, not only less egoistic but more detached, hence calmer. It is only a mood, of course, and may vanish in a few minutes, hours, or days. But whereas most other moods pass from memory and are unrecallable, this kind is unforgettable.

25

This wonderful and memorable experience, call it Void or call it God, will for some time afterwards become a kind of background to the events of his life and to him, himself.

26

Illumination arising from suffering seems to last longer than that arising from happiness because the latter is easier to lose. One is likely to become careless with that which comes from happiness.

27

Whatever the height reached, the glory felt during the glimpse, he still lives on as a human being after it has passed. Thoughts reappear, ordinary emotions are felt again.

28

The uplifted consciousness falls back, the rapturous moments pass away. He must then revert to the ordinary animal-intellectual life of everyday, to all the human implications of his existence. Why try, vainly, to deny them?

29

He has seen some truth and may want to share it. But in what manner can he communicate that which is not intellectually measurable?

30

If the glimpse does not last, if a man discovers, or rather comes back to find, that he still is man, he should be pleased that it came at all.

31

It is not easy and it may need a long period of practice and remembrance, but something of this afterglow may be kept and retained even amid the turmoil of the world's work.

32

In those glorious enchanted moments which immediately succeed the glimpse, almost anything seems possible.

33

The glimpse comes to be treasured in memory as something very precious and quite unique, most intimate and not freely talked about with others.

34

Slowly and dimly he will become aware of his surroundings and his body. Little by little he will struggle back to them as if from some far planet. The recovery of consciousness will be only intermittent at first, only in brief snatches achieved with difficulty. But later it will be held and kept for longer periods until it remains altogether.

35

The afterglow of this experience may be a sensation of its curative power, leaving nerves and heart healed of their troubled negative conditions, or of its purifying power, leaving the mind freed of its undesired and undesirable thoughts.

36

The glimpse leaves an afterglow of truth, a reassurance of support.

37

His heart will be warmed and his will moved as a consequence of this experience.

38

The test will come when he has to descend from the mountain-peak of meditation into the valleys of prosaic everyday living. Can he adjust the greatness he has seen and felt to this smaller narrower world or will he lose it therein?

39

The closer he comes to the Overself the more reticent he becomes about it.

40

Even though the glimpse is so impressive, the subsequent activities of the day put it out of his mind until he is able to relax, perhaps at bedtime.

41

When the spark of inspiration fades out, new ideas often go with it, or if they come, the power to utilize them escapes him.

42

If the glimpse slips away from the great calm, where does it go? Into the ever-active outward-turned thinking movement.(P)

43

From this inner world of Essence we descend to the outer world of Experience.

Possible negative after-thoughts

44

Most questers experience this momentary elation, this cosmic paean of exultation, at some time. In some the wish to re-experience it becomes a craving which causes them to lose their balance, to be repeatedly depressed and unhappy at its loss. Thus what was intended to increase their happiness becomes a source of further misery!

45

If he is young in the life of the Spirit, ignorant of its laws and inexperienced in its ways, he may take the fading of the Glimpse amiss. He may complain too long or bemoan too much, thus inviting that dread experience, the dark night of the soul.

46

His own great joy in the glimpse is natural and inevitable, but if he clings to it to the point where it is succeeded by great disappointment when the glimpse disappears, then it is merely another mood of the personal ego. In that case he will certainly be left feeling empty when it leaves him, and he probably will be troubled by the thought that something has gone wrong.

47

It is a common mistake among those who have this glimpse for the first time, and even for the second time, to expect it to last forever. But when they find that it has no more immortality than the other experiences of the human mind, they suffer needlessly, not understanding, bewildered.

48

To bestow this glimpse upon someone with no previous preparation for it, with an undeveloped psyche and an imperfect character, someone too backward spiritually to profit properly by it, may be to bestow a dangerous gift. It is likely to be misused as it is certain to be misconceived.

49

If the experience is not fully understood, or if it comes to one quite unprepared for it, or if it comes too prematurely, it may be half-misunderstood and its teaching half-misconceived. In that case the will to act may become paralysed, the mind over-conscious of futility and evanescence.

50

These holy visitations ought not to make him conceited or proud or fatten his ego or make him lose his wits. If they do he is in spiritual danger so that what ought to be a blessing becomes a curse.

51

These visitations of a higher presence may deceive him into thinking that he has reached a higher degree than he really has. If so, he may expect their light and strength to abide permanently with him. In that case he may plunge into emotional reactions of gloom and disappointment when they ebb. It would be better for him to receive them gratefully as well as to regard their passing as tests of his resignation to the higher self and of his trust that its inner working is not mistaken. It knows quite well what It is doing in and for him.

52

To have had the glimpse and yet to ignore it in subsequent life, or to utilize it only for the purpose of exalting the ego, is deliberately to tell a lie to oneself, consciously to be unfaithful to truth.

53

When a person gets this experience without guidelines and in total surprise, within a family living in the common ignorance of such matters, he may let bewilderment come in to destroy the new lucidity.

54

After the glimpse has passed away—and a warning that it usually does so is needed by beginners—either thankfulness for the visitation or discouragement by its loss may set in.

55

He waits for an inner event that shall be thrilling and spectacular. He does not wait for one that shall be as gentle, as silent, as the fall of dew, so of course he is disappointed and falls into some kind of negative thought.

56

Such moments are so precious that, when they are found to be irretrievable, a deep melancholy often settles on a man.

57

Since people are not accustomed to these glimpses, they are easily swept off by the first few into emotional extravagances.

58

He approaches these moods with delight but remembers them with despair. They are cored with happiness yet he feels frustrated by their evanescence.

59

A wiser attitude understands that there is no need to grieve because the flash has gone, the ecstasy faded, the light shut out again. It knows that the Overself is still with him, even though these emotional or egoistic reactions try to trick him into believing otherwise.

Lasting effects

60

A few days pass. The experience itself has now lodged in the shadows of memory. What is left to him as the after-effect of the Glimpse? What does he really possess as the gain from it?

61

Only those who have felt it can know the completely satisfying nature of the love which flows to and fro between the ego and the Overself at such enkindled moments. They may be gone the same day but they will reflect themselves in a whole lifetime's aspiration thereafter.

62

The fact remains that the awakening to the Overself leaves great witness and striking testimony that it has passed over a man's head. It brings new and subtle powers, an altered outlook upon people and events, and a deep calm in the very centre of his being. When he is given his primal glimpse of the spiritual possibilities of man, he is immeasurably exalted. When he discovers the dynamic power of the Overself for the first time and hears the beautiful hidden rhythm of its life, his heart becomes as the heart of Hercules and for hours, days, or weeks he walks on air. He begins to price his fleshly desires at their true worth and treads them under foot. He has been permitted to taste of the spirit's fruits, and he knows that they alone are good.

63

A sense of being lifted up from all worldly cares will pervade him for some time as an afterglow of this experience. The gracious feeling swims away again and leaves him not forlorn but forsworn. He will never again be alone. The remembrance of what happened is by itself enough to be company for him the rest of his life.

64

The feeling that he *belongs* to THAT to which all the universes also belong, is with him the moment the glimpse is over. If, as a full realization, it passes away with the experience, an afterglow remains as a residue, a strong conviction persists for years later.

65

The Glimpse which discloses heaven refines the mind as it does so, otherwise the two would remain too far from one another to make vision possible.

66

Whoever has had this beautiful experience, felt its glorious freedom and known its amazing serenity, has had something which he will always remember. Even after he has fallen utterly away from both freedom and serenity, when darkness bitterness or degradation are his melancholy lot, the knowledge that a life of truth goodness and beauty is somewhere and sometime possible will continue to haunt him.

67

The glimpse, when finally it does come, compensates for all the struggles and difficulties of the years that precede it. He can look back upon them with complete detachment, perhaps even smile at them. Even the sufferings seem no longer what they were, but diminish into unimportant little incidents.

68

Yes, the Glimpse will gently go away, its fine exaltation will subside, but neither its lustrous meaning nor its loving memory will ever be forgotten.

69

Even merely knowing that he has had such a glimpse gives him some kind of reassurance about life, some little security within himself, some degree of faith that a higher power is taking care of the universe—and hence of himself.

70

It may seem incredible that so short a glimpse should leave so large an effect, so misty a comprehension should give so profound a revelation, but so it is.

71

The isolated glimpses will have this effect, that they will not only whet his appetite for farther ones but also for a lasting identity with the Overself.

72

Ambition may remain but its objects will not. How could they when their triviality is so glaringly exposed by the Glimpse?

73

If the beauty of his experience penetrates his heart deeply enough, it will not fail to bring about a change in his life. It will also point out the direction in which the change is to be made.

74

The insight, once caught, and however briefly, will leave behind a calm discontent with the triviality of ordinary life, a lucid recognition of its pathetic futility and emptiness, as well as a calm dissatisfaction with the man himself.(P)

75

He will, at the least, win an enlarged conception of life and, at the most, an ennobled character. Better still, he will feel for the first time what it is like to attain an inner equilibrium.

76

The glimpse may give him a dynamic charge of power, or leave him bereft of all aggression—depending on the particular need or phase of the moment.

77

The door of his inner consciousness has opened; the regeneration of his moral nature has begun. The truth will come into the innermost chambers of his consciousness, sometimes abruptly but sometimes sluggishly. And because it comes in this way, because it comes from the god within him, it will be dynamic, creative, powerful. As he becomes aware of this sublime influx, so will he soon become aware that character is altering with it, and so will others become aware that his conduct is shaping itself around nobler standards.

78

When a man discovers that he himself is the bearer of divine forces, he ceases to run hither and thither in search of other men.

79

Once the soul has revealed her lovely self to him, he cannot help adoring her, cannot help the feeling of being carried away in lifelong pursuit of her. The attraction is not of his own choosing. It is as natural and inevitable as the movement of the sunflower towards the sun.

80

If we can gain the power to enter the Presence, it will work silently upon the reform and reshaping of our character. Every such entry will carry the work forward, or consolidate what has already been done.

81

He begins to look on the world afresh, as if for the first time. But it is the beauties, the harmonies, the inner meanings, and the higher purposes that he now sees. He becomes more attentive to the attractiveness of Nature, observes her colourings and forms with new delight.

82

If the glimpse ends, its memory does not and will always be preserved. Those who forget have only let changes in character or circumstance push it down out of sight for a period.

83

For a time the thrill of having had the glimpse inspires him. But it soon fades and then he becomes dependent upon his simple memory of it.

84

Even after he sinks back to his former state, the mystic who has had a flash, a glimpse, a revelation, or a vision of something beyond it can never be exactly the same as he was before. The light cannot fall upon him without leaving some little effect behind at the least, or some tremendous change at the most.

85

One of the purposes of the glimpse is to make the man aspire that he shall be made worthy of its coming again.

86

If the first contribution of memory is an unconscious one, intuitively reminding man of what he really is but seems to have lost, the second is a conscious one. It is to keep up his interest in the establishment of the higher awareness and to stop him from forgetting the pursuit of this goal. That is, it is to keep him on the Quest.

87

These experiences if taken aright will lead him not to spiritual pride but to spiritual humbleness.

88

Because he has been once illumined, the darkness can never again be total darkness. He will know that the possibility of light flashing across it always exists.

89

No one can know in advance how long it will stay with him. It is here out of nowhere and nowhen, and then gone away the next hour. The visitation may or may not be repeated but because it is nothing that he has achieved, the repetition is outside his reach to control. Thus begins a lifelong haunting by what becomes his dearest wish—to repeat, and especially to continue in, this magical transformation.

90

The glimpse is impermanent, its satisfactions fugitive; but it leaves behind a residue of hope and revelation which the impermanent and fugitive pleasures of the world can never do.

91

Those who catch this glimpse are not necessarily better persons than others, not even wiser persons. But, having caught it, the result cannot fail to make them better and wiser. Yet their goodness will not be of a kind that is outwardly measurable by worldly approval, nor their wisdom by worldly success.

92

The rapturous exaltation soon dissolves in the humdrum toil and play of everyday. But its cleansing remembrance does not.

93

It is not only desires and lusts which fade and leave him, but even the prying curiosities which express themselves at every level from mere gossip to the majestic investigations of science.

94

The man who tries for years vainly to transcend his human nature is released by this experience. He no longer tortures himself practising excessive asceticisms.

95

The stillness ends his quest, or rather its struggles and strivings; but if it passes away, as it usually does, he will at least know now what to look for again.

96

It will affect him to the extent that he will always venerate its memory.

97

He must come to see that, by valuing and applying philosophic attitudes to the troubles and vexations of the world, he is truly recalling those moments of uplift and joy which glimpses provide. This is another way, and one of the best, in which they can bear good fruit for him. From these delicate dreamlike experiences he can draw strength and courage to endure either the world's buffeting or his personal difficulties.

98

The remembered glimpse helps him to go on living, because its recapture is both a possibility and a spur. The one gives him hope, the other determination to provide conditions which may renew it.

99

It is a spiritual miracle, for it not only transforms his character but also releases some latent powers.

100

Because it gives new hope, fresh encouragement, and the prospect of eventual relief from trouble, the glimpse is like a rainbow in the sky. It reminds him that a providential love is still behind the world and his own existence.

101

The more glimpses he has, the more will his desires be taken from him.

102

The after-effects of the glimpse are sometimes widely opposite. One person swells with pride, exults in the fact that *he* has been granted it, where another will be made humbler by it.

103

The glimpse will help him to live through the dark periods that may come, when otherwise he might succumb to despair.

104

The remembrance of most of those years spent in the world is dim but the remembrance of these exquisite interludes is vivid.

105

He will remember it as a momentary benediction, something to be saved from the tragic inexorable fleetingness of life.

106

This alone could be the kind of experience which led Omar Khayyam, who was more mystical than Westerners realize, to write: "The more I drink of Being's wine, more sane I grow, and sober than before."

107

What he discovers during these deepest possible experiences becomes a part of him.

108

The more he exposes himself to these moments of alignment of mind, the more will negative outbursts and destructive passions calm down and die away.

109

The extraordinary thing is that this illumination, the most important event that can happen to a human being, lessens his feeling of self-importance.

110

The memory of this day will last longer, mean more, and touch deeper than any other.

111

Ecstasy is not a permanent mark of the mystical experience, but only a temporary mark which accompanies its first discovery. It is the beginners who are so excited by mystical ecstasies, not the proficients. The process of re-adjusting the personality to a future filled with wonderful promise and stamped with tremendous importance naturally moves the emotional nature towards an extreme of delight. Nevertheless, it would be a mistake to regard the mystic's ecstasy as something that was merely emotional only. Behind it there is the all-important contribution of the Overself's grace, love, and peace. When the emotional excitement of the discovery eventually subsides, these will then show themselves more plainly as being its really significant elements.

112

Life can never again be just as ordinary, just as commonplace as before, nor just as if he had never passed through those vital moments of divine uplift. The white-hot point of their inspiration has faded, but it can never be forgotten. It will, nay it must, show itself powerfully in his directive purposes and in the quality of his living.

113

He will want to keep this awakened consciousness at all times. This aspiration will instantaneously or eventually bring him to tread the Quest.

114

In the intellectual deductions which he may make after the experience, and when he is viewing it analytically, he may find corroboration of his true beliefs or contradiction of his false ones. But the ego having closed in upon him again, this may happen only partially, or only slightly, depending on its strength.

115

Every glimpse of the Infinite helps him to let go of the finite, to detach himself from his possessions and passions.

116

Here is goodness and beauty which worldly objects and worldly creatures do not possess. The man who has once glimpsed them can never again be completely satisfied with the world's offerings, for this reason, but will again and again be haunted by, and attracted to, the vision of this higher possibility for man.

117

Either ecstasy or quietude may pervade the glimpse; either insight or intuition may follow it.

118

The glimpse has several results: it awakens sleeping minds, it encourages questing minds, it inspires earnest minds, and it quickens growing minds.

119

The feeling that time can wait is rare these days but it does come when the glimpse comes. Then the realization comes that it is foolish to hurry to appointments, datelines, work, or shopping and better to move more leisurely toward them or even loiter on the way.

120

Those few tranced moments of beatific calm will nourish him for many a month, perhaps even for some years.

121

Some are willing to take up the discipline if it will help them recover the first radiant excitement of the glimpse, the overwhelming greatness of that brief intensified existence.

122

One important effect of the glimpse is to show him how wonderful life could be if there were frequent and easy access to this diviner region. For this spurs him to seek ways and means to bring about its recurrence.

123

Even if it happens only once or twice in a lifetime, such a glimpse acts as a catalyst which pushes the man into making changes.

124

The glimpse will always be an incandescent memory in his life, a token of grace to prove that reality does dwell somewhere behind the seeming fatuity and illusoriness of the world's life.

125

The glimpse brings release from doubts, burdens, fears, depressions, and other negative conditions which may beset the ego. This is most welcome. But only seldom does it last long. It is a momentary or temporary condition. It is never totally or permanently lost; there is usually some kind of residue, if only in memory.

126

Henceforth, either prominent in his everyday consciousness or hidden in his half-buried subconsciousness, there is the ever-present aspiration to renew this wonderful experience.

127

The man who enters this state while still a criminal will abandon crime after coming out of it.

128

The glimpse will fill his heart with a beautiful peace, his head with a larger understanding; but it will end and pass away, for it is only a glimpse gained for a few minutes' space. Nevertheless, memory will hold for years its wonderful afterglow.

129

He has introduced a new principle into his life, one which is going to bear fruitful consequences in several different directions.

130

He may have to weep for a mere glimpse of the soul. But this got, he will certainly weep again for its return. For he knows now by unshakeable conviction and by this vivid demonstration that the durable realization of the Soul is what he is here on earth for.

131

These lovely gleams, which gave him such joy and dignity, will flicker out and the spiritual night in which most men live will once again close in upon him. Nevertheless they have added a new kind of experience to his stock and revealed a new hope for his comfort.

132

But when the years have passed and middle life falls upon him, he will remember those early flashes of something grandly exalted above the daily round, and, remembering, may seek out ways and means of recovering them.

133

A flight into the stratosphere is a strange but fascinating experience for the first time but not so strange nor one-hundredth so fascinating as a flight into a higher level of consciousness. And if it happens not on some mountaintop surrounded by enchanting scenery but on a crowded noisy bustling and tumultuous city street, one is not only keenly conscious of the alteration within oneself but also feels that the world around as well as the people in it have altered in some mysterious way, too.

134

However fantastic may be the practical consequences of this experience, due to its wrong interpretation by the mystic himself, the essential worth and intelligible meaning of the intrinsic reality out of which it arises still remain.

135

It not only brings about a stupendous change in his view of life but also a corresponding change in his moral conscience and character.

136

In that great light he sees his old self as sinful, and so rejects it, his old character as defective and deficient on every side and so amends it. The rejection soon becomes habitual while the amendment is made swiftly enough.

137

The glimpse astonishes some persons by its startling reversal of some of their cherished notions, beliefs, and opinions.

138

The glimpse gives a man the feeling of a newness as if he were beginning a new kind of life with a new attitude and a new ethical code.

139

With this growing feeling for spirituality *may* come, in some cases, a new feeling for refinement, an aesthetic appreciation of the beautiful; in others, it may be some virtue or quality which reflects the sensibility or inspiration.

140

It is a power which affects him in a strange way. At one and at the same time it isolates him from his fellow men, yet unites him with them as well. He is isolated because this functioning on a higher level of consciousness makes him feel like some strange visitor from outer space, just arrived on our ancient planet. But he can enjoy the sense of Being whether isolated or surrounded by others.

141

Although he may quite precisely and clearly understand what is happening to him, an extra-worldly awareness develops in parallel to the spiritual development. It is a feeling of what other persons are, their mood at the time, their general dispositions also.

142

The times when he is brought into memorable awareness and reverent worship of the true God, the moments when the illuminative flash permeates him utterly, may have far-reaching effects on his later years. For he can then see the ego's life as it really is and make new decisions concerning it which could only have been arrived at when out of the ego's clutches.

143

He comes away from these glimpses hushed into peace, awed by their mystery, and filled with goodwill to all beings. This attitude towards them is an absolute imperative, but it does not mean that he is to put himself in their hands, at their mercy, by submitting to their desires, yielding to their faults.

144

The glimpse gives us new life and assists in the process of redemption, of what is called salvation in religious circles, but what happens when it is lost again? Well, something is left over, obviously the memory of it, but something more, difficult to describe, because it is in the subconscious.

145

It is to these glimpses that he must return again and again, or rather to the memory of them, so they will give him support and will help him in his hour of need. He must love them and live by them in their light and not let them get lost in the limbo of utter forgetfulness.

146

Uncertainties and fears beset the ordinary man. They come up in spite of himself, whether they refer to his fortunes or his health, his business or his relationships. In such a situation whatever peace of mind he finds does not last long and cannot unless he has looked for and found, at least from time to time, a measure of communion with the Overself. Even a glimpse, a single glimpse, which may happen only once during several years, gives him a measure of support whatever thoughts appear and disappear during the interval of years.

147

The glimpse goes, but it remains in his mind as a point of reference, a criterion for the future, something with which he can compare his ordinary existence and his ordinary attitudes.

148

The simple discovery of what he really is leads to large implications. He sees his aims in life, his goals and ambitions, his desires and attitudes, under a different light. The glimpse itself passes but the memory remains and the effect upon them is disturbing. He begins to feel a new unease with them.

149

The Truth itself is a cleansing agent, although its work on the emotions and thoughts and tendencies may be quite slow in many cases, because it is on a deep level. In some cases its effect is sudden, dynamic.

150
At the very least the glimpse leaves a beautiful memory, at the most a divine inspiration.

151
In our best moments, we discover that we are not really alone, for with them comes our best self. It is our guide and comforter.

152
The experience may seem to happen by chance, its duration may be little more than momentary, but the impression left may last a lifetime.

153
The glimpse is also a therapeutic experience.

154
How can anyone who has gained entry into this sublime state ever again fall into the error of materialism?

155
It has not even the value of a dream but only that of the memory of a dream! The experience is devastating towards his concept of reality.

156
When the Overself takes full possession of him, it will change his personality and outlook completely.

157
The dynamic inspiration imported by this experience will continue long after the experience itself has ceased.

158
Life will be very different for man when, at long last, he recovers the sense of his own divinity.

159
When man is touched by the power of God, he is called a "Son of God."

160
Nothing can hold the experience. It evades his mental grasp, eludes his emotional hold. The Glimpse falls away and cannot be retained. But the minutes or hours during which he was exposed to it will long be associated in memory with a great joy, a grave stillness, and an acute understanding.

161
He longs to renew the glimpse but finds it beyond his power to do so; without it, the days seem futile.

162
There is this value of these glimpses at least, that forever after the man possesses their standard by which to judge all other experiences in life.

163

The Overself, like the horizon, receded each time he came nearer and claimed it, but gave him sufficient tokens to lure him onward still again.

164

The more he tastes these delightful unions, the less he will be able to endure these inevitable separations.

165

These glimpses are received with holy joy and, in later years, remembered with sweet nostalgia.

166

The years will follow each other and his impressions of this divine day will blur. But its tremendous meaning will never blur.

167

In this supreme moment he feels that so much in his life which mattered greatly now matters little, so many desires, aims, ambitions, and values now fall in the scale of things. The mood passes, his feet descend to earth, but he finds that at the back of his mind he is a little suspicious of them, a little sceptical of their promises.

168

A few minutes of the glimpse compensates fully for the lengthened years of dull mediocrity and triviality, reconciles him to the past's sufferings.

169

The heartbreaks of life may be compensated by these glimpses.

170

Out of the inner quietude have come the great decisions, the miraculous healings, the memorable awakenings, and the end of sorrows.

171

It is an experience he shall remember when all else is forgotten.

172

He who is uplifted by this power will understand where others only condemn.

173

The memory of this lovely foretaste will haunt imagination and taunt desire. He will long to recapture the experience but will suffer under the feeling of its elusiveness and remoteness.

174

Who can forget his first experience of the Glimpse? What a memory of gentleness, beauty, wonderment, and deeper understanding it leaves behind!

175

The glimpse sustains ideals, nurtures hope, and supports faith.

176

This balmy and relaxed experience may nevertheless have drastic and dramatic consequences. For it may drive the man to repudiate his former way of life and to initiate a reorientation of thought, habit, and conduct.

177

To lock awareness to one of these glimpses even for a minute, without wilting, unmoved, is the highest form of concentration. It yields new power for his future life, and leaves an unforgettable stamp on his past life.

178

The glimpse makes him feel exalted and strengthened, even though it thwarts his ego and weakens his lusts.

179

A Glimpse gives him the confidence that he is walking the right road and encourages him to go forward.

180

Even a little glimpse may lead to a momentous decision. For it is the *quality* of consciousness which is important.

181

With each glimpse he will see life differently.

182

When he finds, as all aspirants do, that he cannot keep this feeling or even recover it whenever he wants to, he may become wistfully nostalgic for it or even sadly mournful.

183

The ordinary attitudes toward life suddenly desert him and no longer exist. New and strange ones just as suddenly arise within him.

184

It leaves a firm and ineffaceable imprint on memory.

185

Sometimes experienced, always remembered, the glimpse has marked him for life with some positive and benign signs.

186

These glimpses serve several purposes. First, they uplift the aspirant's heart.

187

It is as if he has turned into another man, someone who still is but no longer seems himself.

188

Most seekers get experiences of mystic illumination at some time or other, but these are not essential. They are transient and they pass. They are intended to entice seekers away from too much materialism and then they vanish.

189

Accept the historic fact that you had these experiences and glimpses—dozens of them—which revealed the Soul. What of worth life has given still stays in the mind, can still be recalled and be found there again.

192

Such is the magic of that passing-over to the higher consciousness, that the most sinful character or the most sorrowful life is transformed overnight. Virtue redeems the one; serenity heals the other.

191

Even if the glimpse does not heighten the feeling that here is a signal from something real, his own further or deeper study and the testimony of historic figures will show him that he is on the right track.

192

Such is the magic of that passing-over to the higher consciousness, that the most sinful character of the most sorrowful life is transformed overnight. Virtue redeems the one; serenity heals the other.

193

The nostalgia which keeps on calling us back to those lovely moments is worth heeding.

194

Man cannot live in memories alone. He will soon or late feel the need to become that glory which he remembers so well. It will not let him forget, whatever pleasurable or painful experiences he passes through.

Marks of authenticity

195

For proof that the glimpse is a genuine fact and not a hallucinatory one, not only ought the experience itself to be analysed but the after-condition ought to be studied and the subsequent behaviour ought to be noted. Does it show less attachment to the ego and more devotion to the Overself, less emotional disturbance and more mental tranquillity?

196

If it is a genuine glimpse, its effect will be seen in his face, his gait, his talk, while the influence, and some of the aftermath, lasts. For his face will be transfigured, his gait will be slowed down, his talk will be restrained and wise.

197

The Glimpse is in very truth a magic spell cast over a man's whole being so that he neither feels nor reacts as he did before. For a short time he is born again, a new person.

198

The question whether someone is a mystic or yogi can be answered easily enough once we understand what is his state of consciousness and what the mystical condition really is. All the annals of the vanished past and all the experiences of the living present inform us that whoever enters into it feels his natural egotism subside, his fierce passions assuaged, his restless thoughts stilled, his troubled emotions pacified, his habitual world-view spiritualized, and his whole person caught up into a beatific supernal power. Did he ever have this kind of consciousness? His words and deeds, his personal presence and psychological self-betrayal should proclaim with a united voice what he is. No man who habitually enters such a blessed state could ever bring himself to hate or injure a fellow human being.(P)

199

What are the signs whereby he shall know that this is an authentic glimpse of reality? First, it is and shall remain ever present. There is no future in it and no past. Second, the pure spiritual experience comes without excitement, is reported without exaggeration, and needs no external authority to authenticate it.(P)

200

The glimpse also does in part for a man what initiation did in some ancient mystical institutions. It sets him on the road of a new life, a life more earnestly and more consciously devoted to the quest of Overself. It silently bids him dedicate, or rededicate anew, the remainder of his life on earth to this undertaking. It is a baptism with inner light more far-reaching than the baptism with physical water.(P)

201

The motives and reactions of a spiritually intuitive man will necessarily be on a higher level than those of a man driven by animal and worldly compulsions only.

202

And once you are reborn in the heart, life will become what it should be—the realization that you are outworking a higher destiny than the merely personal one.

203

Another noteworthy mark of the true glimpse is its purificatory effect. This is usually temporary but in a few cases it has been permanent.

204

When he has this first unprecedented experience, when he knows and feels that he is a part of divine being, he is born "in Christ." But it is not for him to stand at street corners and announce to the multitude that he has had this glimpse.

205

The sustained consciousness of the Overself puts its mark upon a man's face.

206

They are men with "the shine" on their faces, like the one who descended from Sinai.

207

He emerges from the old man that he was, from the ego-ridden nature, as a snake emerges from its old skin.

208

The old self which he has left behind and which once so occupied his interest now seems ugly, bad, and dull. So great is the change in him that it also seems like a stranger, not entitled to bear his name.

209

However cynical and blasé may have been his attitude in earlier days, it will yield to and melt in the sunny light of this second birth.

210

Those who have experienced a glimpse of this blessed Reality or, better, established themselves in it, may share its atmosphere with others in silent communion. But on a lesser level, they may also share with them in phrased speech the thoughts it provokes.

211

The more one becomes familiar with this experience, the easier one can describe it.

212

He who has been touched by the goddess comes out of his sleep, says the Oriental wisdom. For he has a knowledge which appears as a special and unusual kind of awareness that escapes most other people.

213

There comes a time when out of the silence within himself there comes the spiritual guidance which he needs for his further course. It comes sometimes as a delicate feeling, sometimes as a strong one, sometimes in a clearly formulated message, and sometimes out of the circumstances and happenings themselves. Not only does it tell him and teach him, but sometimes it does the same for others. Such is the effect of the Divine Life now working increasingly within him.

214

You are saved the moment this divine power takes possession of you, but not otherwise.

Following through

215

You have been given a glimpse of the goal. Now you must strive to attain that goal. The glimpse itself has enabled you to understand the consciousness and the characteristics to strive for. Both are so subtle that words merely hint at them and may be meaningless. In receiving an experience beyond words, you have therefore been so fortunate as to be favoured with the Overself's Grace.

216

Merely to enjoy such a glimpse is not enough. It must be turned to use, made into a standard for thought and living, applied to every situation in which he finds himself. He must let its beneficent memory shed peace, goodwill, and kindliness on all around.

217

The illuminatory experience may come to one who is without previous preparation, seeking, effort, or self-discipline. But if it comes so unexpectedly it leaves just as unexpectedly. The visitant is transient. The effects are permanent. If it be asked why it should come to such a person, who neither desired nor strove for it, when others are unable to secure it despite years of seeking, the answer must be that he worked for it in earlier lives. He has forgotten himself for an interval but the illumination recalls him to the quest even though it passes away: hence the permanency of its moral and mystical results.

218

What he sees in that sudden flash is to be slowly worked out in his character and conduct during the hours and months of subsequent years. Indeed, every minute offers the chance to transform himself by the smallest of degrees.

219

What he feels during those moments he has to become during the years that follow.

220

All his life has to converge upon this divine focus, all his experience has to draw its supreme significance from it.

221

What we are ordinarily conscious of are the thoughts and feelings of the ego, but there is much more in us than that. There is the true self, of which the ego is only a miserable caricature. If we could penetrate to this, the fundamental element of our selfhood, we would never again be satisfied with a wholly egoistic life—the call of the Quest would come again and again in our ears. And indeed it is through such rare glimpses, such exalted moments, when they become conscious of a presence, higher and more blessed than their ordinary state, that men are drawn to the Quest in the effort to recapture those moments and those moods. The recapturing is done, not by taking possession of something but by allowing oneself to be possessed, not by a positive and affirmative movement of the will, but by a yielding to, and acceptance of, the gentlest and most delicate thing in man's psyche—the intuition.(P)

222

Another purpose of these glimpses is to show him how ignorant of truth he really is, and, having so shown, to stimulate his effort to get rid of this ignorance. For they will light up the fanciful or opinionative nature of so much that he hitherto took to be true.(P)

223

The bestowal of a glimpse is not merely for his pleasure and satisfaction: there are certain self-cleansing duties and self-improving obligations which follow in its train. The light it throws into him is thrown on his sins and weaknesses too. He sees them more plainly for what they are, as well as the amendment he must make. But he sees also the forgiveness which grace grants.

224

The glimpse affords its own proof, supplies its own evidence, certifies by itself the truths it yields. But if its experiencer falls back into his ego and lets its prejudice, opinion, and expectation intrude into those truths, that is his own fault, not the Glimpse's.

225

A single glimpse will offer all the evidence his reason needs, all the proof his judgement demands that there is a kingdom of heaven and that it is the best of all things to search for.

226

One of the first consequences of the glimpse ought to be—if it is properly received and sufficiently understood—a resolve to improve himself, to be more truthful and less excitable, for instance.

227

The effect of a Glimpse upon character may show itself as a passing feeling but it is the business of a quester to show it as a habit of life.

228

It is of particular importance to every man to whom a glimpse has been vouchsafed, that after it he is summoned to begin his life afresh, to try a new start. If he heeds the summons no matter how unpromising his circumstances are for such a start—and this requires both faith and courage—eventually help will come, a change for the better.

229

During the glimpse he left himself and found a being within which transcended it. After the glimpse he has the chance to create a conscious relationship between them. His outer life ought to carry the mark of this extraordinary event.

230

What was seen in the glimpse must now be taken into the heart and mind, the thought and memory, the whole being of the man. Henceforth he is to live and act among other men as one who is marked for a higher destiny then semi-animal, incompletely human, blind existence.

231

The more glimpses he gets, the more will he want to become like the ideal in all its beauty, and the longer each glimpse lasts, the longer will he seek to use its light and strength to make himself a better man or build a better world.

232

The glimpse is a memorable experience, but it is not enough. It shows him a possible future, gives him a new world-view, but he must henceforth bring all that into his everyday life and into his whole being. This needs time, practice, patience, vigilance, self-training, and more sensitivity.

233

Wisdom does not come overnight. It needs time to ripen. But Revelation can come in that way. But its recipient will still need time to adjust to it, and to integrate with it.

234

What he has learned from the glimpse must be applied to life, to action and attitude. It is not enough merely to enjoy its memory, as if it made no difference.

235

Most glimpses *got through meditation* are followed by the surfacing of egoistic tendencies and weaknesses. This is only that their existence may be more clearly seen and an attempt made to get rid of them.

236

Whatever happens to himself or to others, whether he rises or falls, whether they hurt or help him, let him keep the hope that the glimpse gave him and continue to love the highest, remote though it may seem.

237

Sometimes the glimpse may pass unrecognized for what it really is, but in later years this is usually rectified.

238

He can make his little world reflect something of the goodness and beauty he has glimpsed.

239

Some among us must seek a higher quality of thought and being, a better way of life and action, in obedience to this call which is heard most clearly during the period of a glimpse.

240

Now and then if the glimpse is granted in response to his patient endeavours, his trust will be strengthened and he will know that he is neither crazy nor wrong to follow this quest.

241

He feels a personal obligation to carry into everyday living what he has deduced from these golden moments.

242

When a glimpse comes to a man, from whatever cause and in whatever way, its effects show themselves variously. One very important effect is that whether he wants to or not, and despite negative passing moods of frustration or depression, if the man to whom it has come has consciously entered on the Quest he cannot desert it but must sooner or later enter upon it again.

243

It is possible for a man who knows of the Quest only through emotional faith or intellectual conviction to turn aside from it for the remainder of his incarnation, but it is not possible for a man who has enjoyed this Glimpse to do so. He may try—and some do—but each day of such alienation will be a haunted day. The ghost will not leave him alone until he returns.(P)

244

These glimpses are only occasional. They take us unawares and depart from us unexpectedly. But the joy they bring with them, the insight they bestow, make us yearn for a permanent and unbroken attainment of the state they tell us about.

245

It is important to remember that such experiences may be expected only rarely in most cases, perhaps once or twice in a lifetime, if the person is not consciously on the quest. It is natural to hope that it will be repeated. The first glimpse is given to show the way, to throw light on the path ahead, to give direction and goal to the person. But if the glimpse is only temporary and rare, the metaphysical understanding to be derived from it is the permanent benefit. So seek to get and clarify the understanding.(P)

8

GLIMPSES AND PERMANENT ILLUMINATION

Some (perhaps too many) believe that the glimpse has permanently changed them, made "the new man" out of the old Adam. But what is to outlast time itself takes time. A pathetic self-deception may delight the ego, but breaks down in the end.

2

That with one breakthrough in awareness, all would be known and comprehended, all questions answered, all personal shortcomings obliterated, is the usual conception of this experience. But there is some wishful thinking here.

3

The misinterpretation of his experience, the belief that his glimpse is the full transcendence of ordinary humanity, often follows it. In no way has he attained perfection, whether of knowledge, consciousness, character, or wisdom.

4

His human condition does not vanish because of this experience: it returns and remains with him as his usual one. Only swollen megalomaniacs assert otherwise.

5

It is true that illumination of itself exalts character and ennobles feeling, purifies thought and spiritualizes action. But if there has been insufficient effort along these lines, then the illumination will only be temporary.

6

Too soon he will find that the rebirth was not a durable spiritual event but a temporary one. It offered a picture of something for which, from then on, he must start working in earnest. It was a glimpse only but it provided testimony, evidence, confirmation.

7

Enlightenment may come suddenly to a man, but then it is usually a temporary glimpse. Only rarely does it stay and never leave him. The normal way is a gradual one. The experience of Ramana Maharshi, Atmananda, and Aurobindo illustrates this rare fated exception, and can only be looked for at the risk of frustration.

8

Glimpses will come to him now and then; they will cheer his heart and enlighten his mind; but a constant level of serene perception will be quite beyond the orbit of his experience.

9

There are two things lacking in these glimpses. They are not full and total nor are they stable and lasting.

10

The mystic or yogi who seeks entry into the divine presence may possibly succeed in doing so. For a while his state is completely changed, transcended, heightened. But after all he is not God; he is a human still and he falls back to the old awareness. The glimpse goes: he is once again what he was, yet with a difference. The experience can be, is, remembered, and may even possibly return. Moreover some kind of a residue is left behind, subtle, not easy to measure or describe, yet appearing in briefly felt and beautifully scented moments.

Is this glimpse the highest anyone may dare to hope for? Let it be said frankly that in his present condition and situation a greater attainment for the human being is uncommon—yet it happens.

11

Neither deep meditation nor the experience can give more than a temporary glimpse. The full and permanent enlightenment, which is to stay with a man and never leave him, can only come after he has clear insight into the nature of Overself.

12

It is not only possible to attain these brief glimpses of the Overself, but also to attain a durable lasting consciousness of it. No change of this state can then happen. The adept discovers that its future is no different from but quite the same as its past. This is the sacred Eternal Now. Only by this abiding light is it possible to see how mixed and imperfect are all earlier and transient experiences.

13

These flashes of light, peace, bliss, and understanding are brief but they have the intended effect. They encourage the aspirant to continue his quest and they implant in him a deep yearning to gain entry into the world to which they belong. They will be brief because the ordinary condition of thought and feeling is still far below the exalted condition revealed during these flashes. In other words, he has still to toil away at self-improvement so as to deserve the treasures which have been momentarily shown him.

14

Between the seeker and the Overself, between his mind and Truth, there is a thick layer of desires, egoisms, passions, opinions, and imaginings. Until he cuts through it—which means until he denies and resists himself in these matters—he may not expect more than Glimpses which fade away.

15

The belief that he can do nothing to hold this glimpse or keep this mood settles on him through repeated experience. But it is not quite correct. Philosophy points out that he can thin down or remove altogether the causes of such evanescence.

16

If it is to be a continuous light that stays with him and not a fitful flash, he will need first, to cast all negative tendencies, thoughts, and feelings entirely out of his character; second, to make good the insufficiencies in his development; third, to achieve a state of balance between his faculties.

17

The glimpse comes spontaneously and outside of his control, but to the master it comes at will and by command.

18

During the Glimpse he feels that he has travelled close to his journey's end, to the fulfilment of his highest purposes. The quest has suddenly become easy and pleasant. But alas! after the rainbow fades and vanishes, he is forced to recognize that he has far yet to go, that what he experienced was only a passing glimpse and not the final goal.

19

If he cannot keep this higher consciousness, it is because his lower and earthly nature is strong enough to rise again and block the way. When the purificatory lessons are learned it will then be possible for him, by self-effort and self-development, to regain this experience—at first temporarily and occasionally, but if he works correctly and Grace sanctions, permanently.

20

In each of these glimpses, his quest attains a minor climax, for each is a step towards full illumination.

21

It is a kind of pre-vision in which he sees, as Moses saw the Land of Canaan, the Promised Land toward which he journeys.

22

It is a mistake to regard it as final illumination when it is in fact only one of many stages toward final illumination.

23

It must be remembered that the glimpse is not the goal of life. It is a happening, something which begins and ends, but something which is of immense value in contributing to the philosophic life, its day-to-day consciousness, its ordinary stabilized nature. Philosophic life is established continuously and permanently in the divine presence; the glimpse comes and goes within that presence. The glimpse is exceptional and exciting; but *sahaja*, the established state, is ordinary, normal, every day. The glimpse tends to withdraw us from activity, even if only for a few moments, whereas *sahaja* does not have to stop its outward activity.(P)

24

To the man who has come along the path of loving devotion to God and finally gained the reward of frequent, joyous, ardent, inward communion with God, equally as to the man who has practised the way of mystical self-recollection and attained frequent awareness of the Overself's presence, an unexpected and unpalatable change may happen little by little or suddenly. God will seem to withdraw from the devotee, the Overself from the mystic. The blisses will fade and end. Although this experience will have none of the terror or isolation and misery of the "dark night" it will be comparable to that unforgettable time. And although it will seem like a withdrawal of Grace, the hidden truth is that it is actually a farther and deeper bestowal of Grace. For the man is being led to the next stage— which is to round out, balance, and complete his development. This he will be taught to do by first, acquiring cosmological knowledge, and later, attaining ontological wisdom. That is, he will learn something about the World-Idea and then, this gained, pass upward to learning the nature of that Reality in whose light even the universe is illusion. Thus from study of the operations of the Power behind the World-Idea he passes on to pondering on the Power itself. This last involves the highest degree of concentration and is indeed the mysterious little practised Yoga of the Uncontradictable. When successfully followed it brings about the attainment of Insight, the final discovery that there is no other being than THAT, no second entity.(P)

25

It would be unreasonable to expect anyone to give up his worldly attachments until he sees something more worthwhile. Consequently his soul gives him a foretaste, as it were, through these ecstatic moments and brief enlightenments, of its own higher values.(P)

26

That glimpse is his initiation into the spiritual life and therefore into the sacrificial life. It is but the first step in a long process wherein he will have to part with his lower tendencies, give up his ignoble passions, surrender his baser inclinations, and renounce egoistic views.(P)

27

Under the emotional thrill of a religious conversion, many people have thought themselves saved and have believed they live in Christ. Yet how many of them have later fallen away! They thought the conversion was enough to bring about a permanent result, whereas it was only the first step toward such a result in reality. The same situation holds with those who have undergone the emotional thrill of a mystical experience. The illumination they have achieved is not the end of the road for them but the beginning. It gives them a picture of the goal and a glimpse of the course to it. It gives them right direction and an inspirational impetus to move towards it. But still it is only the first step, not the last one. They should beware of the personal ego's vanity which would tell them otherwise, or of its deceitfulness, which would tell it to others.(P)

28

Islamic mystics called Sufis differentiate between glimpses, which they call "states," and permanent advances on the path, which they call "stations." The former are described as being not only temporary but also fragmentary, while the latter are described as bearing results which cannot be lost. There are three main stations along the path. The first is annihilation of the ego; the second is rebirth in the Overself; and the third is fully grown union with the Overself. The Sufis assert that this final state can never be reached without the Grace of the Higher Power and that it is complete, lasting, and unchangeable.(P)

29

If illumination does not become permanent, if it does not stay with its host, that is because it does not find a proper place within him for such abiding stay. His heart is still too impure, his character still too imperfect for the consciousness of the Overself to associate constantly with him.(P)

30

He must finish what he has started. He must go on until the peace, the understanding, the strength, and the benevolence of these rare uplifted moods have become a continuous presence within him.(P)

31

We cannot see the Truth and still be what we were before we saw it. That is why Truth comes in glimpses, for we cannot sustain staying away from ourselves too long, that is to say, from our egos.(P)

32

When, through the medium of meditation exercise or the awakening by human skill or Nature's charm of aesthetic appreciation, beginners feel a new joy or an unusual peace, they are too often carried away into extravagant exaggeration of the happening. What seems like a tremendous event may be so in its effect on their inexperienced minds, but mostly it is only a skimming of the surface. To realize its further possibilities, it ought to be used as a starting point for exploration *in depth*.

33

When he is willing to let go of the self-centered ego and the grace can manifest, there may be this union with his higher nature, with the Overself. It is usually not a permanent experience but the possibility of its becoming one is always there. Then the new outlook seems perfectly natural.

34

Let him not be presumptuous. He has not attained the true goal yet despite these noteworthy experiences. For his present knowledge of the Overself comes to him partly through the imagination, partly through the emotions, partly through the intellect, and only partly through the Overself. It is authentic but inferior. He must learn to get it through the understanding which is also authentic, but superior.

35

A continuous insight, present all the time, is the goal, not a passing glimpse.

36

What he has gained is good but not enough, is mystical but not philosophically mystical. For it is now but a flash when it has yet to become constant; it is now partial when it has yet to become full. Its felt presence should be intimate and inseparable as well as clear and complete. When insight continues whatever his occupation of the hour may be, it can be called philosophic.

37

The notion that the glimpse is the goal is a wrong one, usually corrected by time.

38

A glimpse is only a beginning, and those who are willing to follow it up may be ready to study philosophy and learn why this world is only a husk. It must be penetrated, the husk removed and the kernel revealed, for a truer understanding, both of the world and oneself, to be gained.

39

Because they come to an unprepared and unpurified person, these transient glimpses are not adequate, full, and clear. Insight, however, possesses all these qualities.

40

Aspirants should understand that they have no right to expect a spiritual illumination to prolong its brief duration and stay forever with them, much less demand it, so long as they have not made themselves scrupulously fit for such a quest.

41

The glimpse is a precious thing but it is not enough. The man who has had it has also a new problem: how to find it again and how to turn it into an all-time state of mind, continuing through all kinds of circumstances and experiences. And how can he bring his everyday life into harmony with it?

42

The grand realization of his identity with the ONE should support him in all hours. He who gains this consciousness in times when karma smiles must keep it also in times of tribulation. He must liberate himself from the hazards of circumstance and from the bondage to emotional reactions, and at all times realize his best self.

43

How many mystics live on the memory of those rare long-gone moments; how much of their reputation depends on the glory of an illumination which did not last longer than a few minutes or hours, which produced their fame but did not preserve their capacity to be inspired again.

44

He may be lifted up by the light of a great experience or the presence of a great soul, but in the end he falls back to the consciousness he ordinarily has, to the self he ordinarily is. This is not to say that what has happened is without value—on the contrary, such a glimpse is very important—but that under the thrill of its emotional accompaniments he may easily miscomprehend a part of it to the point of self-deception.

45

The error is to believe that he has now been put in possession of all truth, or the highest truth, for all time. But it is only a transient glimpse!

46

If he were pure enough and prepared enough to receive the light in all its fullness and in all the parts of his being, the glimpse would not leave him. But he is not.

47

If the glimpse is intermittent, let him not mourn the fact but remember that he was fortunate enough to get it. If the glimpse becomes a continuous thing, he will accept it humbly because of its very mysteriousness to himself.

48

No glimpse is ever full and complete. If it were, the person experiencing it would be unable to fall into spiritual ignorance again. From this we may understand that however wonderful a glimpse of the Overself may be, it is still only a cloudy reflection of the real thing.

49

This illumination does not make him an adept at the end of his path. He is a seeker still, albeit a highly advanced seeker.

50

These experiences are only foretastes of the farthest one which lies at the end of this quest, and only limited partial tastes at that.

51

The mystical feeling of divine presence and the direct revelation of divine truth for which they long may come but, unless they are among the rare exceptions, will also wane and finally get lost. In most cases the Glimpse is but transitory.

52

Dorje, "the heavenly lightning," is a Himalayan and trans-Himalayan symbol both of the Glimpse and of the final illumination.

53

These glimpses may be looked upon as brief, minor illuminations leading to the final major illumination that will quash the ego's rule forever.

54

These are the ultimate phenomena—that is, appearances and experiences—before realization. They differ at different times, or with different persons, but that is because they come into being as human reactions, as the self's final point of view before its own dissolution.

55

In spite of itself the ego is drawn more and more to the spiritual grandeur revealed by these glimpses. Its ties to selfishness, animality, and materiality are loosened. Finally it comes to see that it is standing in its own way and light and then lets itself be effaced.(P)

56

The failure to sustain this glimpse is not due to his personal demerit but to his system's limitation. For only by passing from yoga to philosophy, or rather by widening it, can permanence of result be had.

57

If it soon fades away, it is a glimpse. If he can stay in it every minute of his waking life, it is illumination.

58

An intermittent enlightenment which comes like this in moments is only a step on the way. He should not be satisfied with it. Nothing short of total enlightenment which is permanent, constant, and ever-present ought to be his goal.

59

The continued existence of this experience, the lengthening of this glimpse into perpetual vision, is something that cannot be brought about without patience, care, effort, guidance, and grace.

60

It is one thing to secure an enthralling glimpse, but it is another thing for this light, native to heaven and alien to earth, to endure through the prosaic routine and belittling affairs of everyday living.

61

The ability to maintain himself in the high state reached during these glimpses is ordinarily lacking in a man, for it requires the whole power of his being.

62

In these glimpses he only looks at the Infinite Beauty, but in the final realization he becomes unified with it.

63

Once he has experienced the glimpse he will understand why his next goal is to experience it again, and why his final goal is to attain it in permanence.

64

That initial realization has henceforth to be established and made his own under all kinds of diverse conditions and in all kinds of places. Hence his life may be broken up for years by a wide range of vicissitudes, pains, pleasures, tests, temptations, and tribulations.

65

If it be asked why these momentary revelations come and go all too quickly, the answer may be given in Sri Aurobindo's own words to the writer: "It is because the nature remains untransformed. Only when fully transformed can it be illuminated. Until the whole nature is transformed, it cannot hold the Light but must let it go eventually."

66

Few can continue in the glimpse, for the lesser nature soon rises to the surface again and overwhelms them.

67

Since there are no negative emotions in the Overself, how can it stay in the same breast as an ego filled with them? This is why the glimpse can be only a brief one, and why it can be stretched into permanency only by first cleansing the nature of all negatives.

68

Let us value these encounters with the divine and be glad and truly grateful when they happen. They are significant and important. But they are special events. The quest does not run through them alone. It runs just as much through ordinary daily life in which our experiences are shared in common with so many people.

69

The momentary feeling of peace he experienced may be an intimation of the still greater peace he may know if he takes the trouble to pursue the opportunity of developing it through the Quest.

70

The luminous understanding of cosmic truths given him by this experience has still to be connected to, and brought into relation with, his everyday human character.

71

What he feels in these beautiful minutes is really a far-off echo from a higher, diviner world. The echo wanes and vanishes but its origin does not. One day, soon or late, he may pick it up again and this time learn of the greatness secreted within him.

72

No glimpse is wasted, even if it does pass away. For not only does it leave a memory to stir comfort guide inspire or meditate upon, but it also leaves a positive advance forward. Each glimpse is to be regarded as a step taken in the direction of the goal, or as a stage in the process of work needed to be done on oneself, or as a further cleansing of the accretions impurities animalities and egoisms which hide the true Self. If his own work is fully and faithfully done, the time comes when the power to prolong a glimpse is at the disciple's command. He is then able not only to bring it on at will but also to extend its length at will.

73

The higher awareness falls like pollen for a few short hours, perhaps, only to be blown away for long years. Yet this intervening period need not be wasted. It should be used to cut down the obstructions in his character and to fill up the deficiencies in his equipment. This done, he will grow more and more into his spiritual selfhood with every return to temporary awareness of it.

74

The completeness of the mystic experience is proportionate to, and measurable by, intensity. So long as it remains a passing and temporary state, so long ought it be regarded by the man who has had it as affording an incomplete enlightenment.

75

The mystic experience is not necessarily complete in itself when it happens to a man for the first time—or for the fourth time. Nor are its effects necessarily permanent. They may disappear even after a whole year's existence.

76

Unless the personal man has matured in brain and heart and balance, the efforts to transcend ego will necessarily be premature and the glimpse, if it happens, will be of a mixed character.

77

Those who look for a magical release from their shortcomings and automatic victory over their weaknesses with the coming of the Glimpse, become disheartened at learning that this desirable result may happen only in a part of their nature, if at all, and is unlikely to happen in the totality of their nature. Others, governed by wishful thinking, even reject the teaching as untrue. That their own co-operative effort will still be needed is a reasonable demand. But reason is what some of these people hope to transcend!

78

The glimpse will be lengthened when he himself develops: it will then no longer be abnormal, or supernormal, but a constant experience.

79

Neither the movements of the Spirit-Energy (*Kundalini*) nor the opening of the *chakras* gives the ultimate enlightenment: usually a glimpse: that is discovered only in the Stillness of the Void.

80

To go beyond the glimpse into the permanent condition of being established requires time to grow up, to develop, until the illusion of time is itself seen through.

81

Although no act of thinking can take hold of That which is utterly beyond thinking—for it is the holy of holies—he may, by pushing attention deeply enough, stand as Moses stood and view the Promised Land as from afar. Or, by being still, in body and in mind, he may do the same. This effect is called a Glimpse. But if the Grace is to wrap itself around him and end his quest then . . . alas! I may write no more. Why is the pen stopped? Because for each person the answer is different, personal, and to be given by God alone, for *He* is the real giver, not another man.

82

A certain type of mystic experience represents a descent of Grace by the Overself. The results are transient, however, because such an experience is given merely as a glimpse of the goal yet to be achieved by one's own personal effort. Through practice of the advanced meditations given in *The Wisdom of the Overself* such an experience may recur from time to time, although its emotional results may seem tamer after a while because they will lack the novelty which they first possessed.

83

The more he gives himself up to the Overself as a consequence of these glimpses of what it requires of him, the sooner will their transience be transformed into permanence.

84

"In carrying water and chopping wood—there is the wonderful Tao." This ancient Chinese sentence is a subtle, clever way of saying that not only in meditation is the glimpse to be sought, but also in the world's work and life it is to be found and kept. Such is the ultimate state, this emptiness of mind amid activity of body. It is possible only by knowledge, the unforgettable recognition and understanding that within this emptiness lies Tao.

85

The translation of the Sanskrit phrase *antardrishti* is literally "inward seeing" in the sense of seeing beneath appearances what is under them. It does not refer to clairvoyance in the psychic sense, but rather to the metaphysical or mystical sense. It can be particularized as meaning entering into the witness state of consciousness. The ordinary person sees only the object; penetrating deeper, he enters the witness state which is an intermediate condition; going still deeper, he reaches the ultimate state of Reality when there is no subject or object, whereas in the witness there is still subject and object, but the subject no longer identifies himself with the object as the ordinary man does.

86

Sometimes the experience got in deep meditation verges on trance and abolishes the normal awareness of time and space. The sense of time may cease altogether so that there is no succession from one moment to the next but an absolute stillness. The sense of space may be so enlarged that there is a feeling of being spread out to immense dimensions or a contrary feeling of being reduced to a single point. The whirling dervishes of the Near East by turning round and round and round for a long time also lose the sense of time and space. But we must remember that the experiences just described have a beginning and an ending, they are only mental conditions which change; they are not the authentic ultimate experience of enlightenment. This latter is called *sahaja*. It is the permanent awareness of the divine presence whether in the midst of activity or meditation.

87

It is not the faint glimpse of truth which reveals all but the full and steady insight. The innate felicity of the one may—and often does—deceive a man into believing that he is experiencing the absolute uniqueness of the other. But the philosophic student, trained to control his ego, is unlikely to mistake these passing phases of his inner life for what they are not.

88

There is a difference between the ordinary glimpse and the philosophical way. Both come to an end; but the philosophical seeker incessantly returns to its remembrance, uses it to work continuously at the transformation of his self and never lets go of the vision.

89

An elementary or obscure knowledge of reality is too often taken by the aspirant as the full knowledge. This is because it so dramatically transcends his ordinary condition. But it is still not to be compared with the firm certitude of clear Insight.

90

It is possible to be open to one's best inner self, aware of its presence, its beauty and peace. And this possibility can be not only realized but also naturalized. It can become one's normal condition.

91

More and more its light will enter his mind, its strength his heart, and its presence his meditative periods.

92

On that day when the glimpse comes, the impact may be strong enough and the man's ambition high enough to make him believe that this is ultimate salvation. Not so, alas!

93

He sees that his quest will not end with the illuminative experience of this first contact with the higher self and that the process so started must continue.

94

Since it is a glimpse only, and not a completed experience, he ought not to expect his own person and personal life to be completely transformed.

95

This is his further task, to infuse the beauty and tranquillity, the un-worldliness and immaterialism of the glimpse into his ordinary everyday life.

96

This beautiful state of heart has yet to become natural and continuous. And that cannot happen until the personal ego is laid low and until the whole psyche of the man engages in the struggle for self-conquest.

97

To glimpse the land beyond is not to reach the goal itself.

98

He who experiences it only intermittently may guess from this how wonderful his existence would be if he were able to experience it constantly.

99

Seeing a man or an object is one thing, recognizing him or it is another. The glimpse is the beginning; recognizing it for what it is, is a further and extended operation.

100

These glimpses come quite fitfully. Rare is the person to whom the Light comes and stays, day after day, year after year. Most have to work on, with, and by themselves to convert this momentary experience into the ever-present feeling of living in the Overself.

101

It is man's highest happiness to stay in this heaven of Consciousness all the time, not merely catch a glimpse of it, wonderful though that be.

102

Enlightenment ripens into Exhilaration if its promptings are faithfully followed.

103

The joyous awareness evoked for a short period is a foretaste of what will one day be manifested continuously.

104

He can then say truthfully, *knowing* whereof he speaks: "A divine element lives in me!" Far though this has taken him from the ordinary good man or ordinary pious man, it is not enough. He needs to go further so that he can attain the place where, obedient, purified, conscious of the World-Idea, he can add: "This element now works in me." With that the ego's tyranny falls away.

105

His impulses, intuitions, and emotional reactions alike will harmonize in time with the true.

106

Flashes of Cosmic Consciousness or glimpses of the higher self could be of one aspect of it only, such as its beauty or its wisdom. You will have to broaden out later.

107

Glimpses of Light

"For some there be that without much and long exercise may not come thereto, and yet it shall be but full seldom, and in special calling of our Lord that they shall feel the perfection of this work; the which calling is called ravishing. And some there be that be so subtle in grace and in spirit, and so homely with God in this grace of contemplation, that they may have it when they will in the common state of man's soul; as it is in sitting, going, standing, or kneeling."
—*The Cloud of Unknowing*

The way is a progressive one only in the largest sense. In actuality it consists often of stagnations and setbacks, falls and even withdrawals. Instead of smooth progression there are fits and starts, rises and falls. Nearly all seekers experience lapses and wanderings aside. Continuous advance without retrogression is likely to begin only after initiation into the ultimate path. The disciple should not worry about the ups and downs of his moods, but should wait patiently while continuing his regular meditation practices and philosophical studies, for if he has a teacher he will come within his sphere of protection, so that advice and guidance are always open to him, and inwardly he will be aware of this.

It is as much a part of the aspirant's experience of this quest to be deprived at times of all feeling that the divine exists and is real, as it is to be granted the sunny assurance of such existence and reality. The upward flights of his novitiate have to be bought at the cost of downward falls. A period of illumination is often followed by a period of darkness. At first the experience of reality will come only in flashes.

Many a student tells of disheartenment at the lack of results, and depression over the long period of barren waiting, despite the faithfulness with which meditation has been practised. They tend to overlook that the path is integral, is a fourfold and not a single one. Often there is something left undone by the student. For instance, no effort in character building may have been made by this student, or in religious prayer by that one.

Until the human psyche is equilibrated it cannot gain durable peace or solid wisdom, and the aspirant must turn his attention to those aspects of his psyche the development of which has not kept pace with those with which he has been most concerned. Balanced living does not overdevelop one phase and underdevelop another. If the student's advance is an unbalanced one, if its various points do not meet on the same even level, then there is no alternative but to go backward and bring up the laggards. If he has purified his emotions of grossness and selfishness but failed to purge his intellect of errors and illusions, then he will have to undertake this task. He has to build up the other sides of his nature, where they have been neglected in the building of the mystical side. And this will enable him in his mystical attainment to "bring it down to earth," as it were, and adjust it to the body, intellect, and environment.

It is very encouraging to him to have the "Witness Self" experience quite a number of times. It speaks more for itself than any descriptive words could do. The student's meditation may have been unfruitful on the surface for many years, yet if he remains loyally patient and persistent, he may have at last in this experience the definite and discernible fruits of seeds sown long before. The experience does help to make the burden— and it is such to old souls—of the body more bearable. It helps in the understanding of what Spirit means, and gives testimony of its existence. It demonstrates what the quest is trying to reach, and how real is its divine goal. It is very important that the disciple should have this experience, and it is a favourable augury for his future progress.

The vision of truth is one thing, its durable realization is another.

The felicitous experience of the Overself may come briefly during meditation. It comes abruptly. At one moment the student is his ordinary egoistic self, struggling with his restless thoughts and turbulent feelings; at the next the ego suddenly subsides, and every faculty becomes quiescent. All the disciple has to do is to be nonresistant to the divinity which is taking possession of him, to receive lovingly and not strive laboriously. The oncoming of this experience will be marked by various other signs: the intellect becomes suspended; will, judgement, memory, and reasoning slip gently into abeyance. A deep serenity unknown before takes possession of him, and an exquisite calm settles over him. In these moments of joyous beauty, the bitterest past is blotted out, and the ugliest history redeemed. With the mind deep-held by the Overself in an atmosphere of exaltation, the harassments and burdens of life beat but faintly at the portals of attention; the troubles of a lifetime recede to nothingness, the fears of the future decline into triviality. The disciple's outlook on the world becomes enlarged, ennobled, and illumined, and is no longer bounded wholly by commonplace interests. The veils hiding truth from him are lifted for a time. The idea that he has a higher self, the conviction that he has a soul, breaks in upon his "little existence" with great revelatory force, and he feels he is emerging into glorious light after a dreary journey through a long dark tunnel.

The Overself is enthroned. The disciple deeply realizes its presence in his inmost feelings. Nothing in his experience, intellectual or emotional, has ever possessed for him such satisfying ecstasy, such paradisiacal contentment. For the delight of the higher levels of mystical experience, unlike the delight of passionate earthly experience, never palls but remains ever fresh and vivid as though encountered for the first time. The world takes on the texture of a lovely half-dream. His feet tread air. Blissfully, wondrously, and overwhelmingly the disciple becomes that which he sought.

These glimpses are accompanied sometimes by a brief ecstatic state, wherein the world is half dropped out of consciousness and the mystic's body wholly held in a fixed attitude. An indescribable lightness will pass through his head. The flash will seem to transfix his thoughts and keep his body rigid for a while in the same position and place in which it found him. The bodily position in which the flash catches him should not be changed in any way. All kinds of excuses for such a change will be suggested by the ever restless lower mentality, but they should be resisted and refused. Even the pretext that it would be better to go to his usual place of meditation should be unacceptable. The contemplation should start and continue to its close in the very spot where the light first flashed.

Delight of these exalted moments and the fragrance of these heavenly visitations will linger in memory for years after they themselves have vanished, and the influence on subsequent life and thought is as long and beneficent as they themselves are short and beautiful. The experience will slip away, but the memory of its certitude will remain.

This all happens deep in the secret places of his own heart. One of the greatest events of his spiritual life-history passes by silently, unnoticed by those around him.

In his enthusiasm and ecstasy, the student may believe he has been granted the ineffable cosmic consciousness and will enjoy it for the rest of his lifetime. But such an event is an exceedingly rare one. He will find instead he has been granted only a brief foretaste of its memorable sweetness, a momentary touch of its awakening hand.

Afterwards, with the return to his ordinary state, the aspirant realizes that the whole lovely, miraculous event was but a single movement, one quick step.

Any man who will desert his present standpoint for the higher one may get the same result. It is the mystical crossing-over from the limited shallow personal consciousness to the wide deep impersonal one. When this happens during meditation there is a clearly felt sense of abrupt displacement, of sudden transformation.

The aspirant should be very grateful for such rich and rare spiritual experiences. They bring him truly into touch with his soul, and demonstrate that divinity is both with and within him. They establish in his consciousness the knowledge of its real existence and the understanding of its real character.

The higher self will not yield to him completely before he has entirely detached himself from his lower nature. And any such deficiency in his character or mentality puts a term to his ecstatic mood and compels him by natural reaction to return to his normal state and set to work to make it good. To encourage him to do this and to strengthen his willingness to turn away from the lower nature, the higher self alternately reveals and hides itself at intervals. Once the Overself has vouchsafed to him its Grace, he must make himself increasingly worthy of the gift.

The aspirant should regard the glimpse afforded him in the glow of his best moments as a working blueprint. He has to make himself over again according to the mental picture thus placed before him. The difference between the Idea and the actuality should shame him constantly into renewed endeavour. The purpose of this brief glimpse is to call him to more serious, more frequent, and sterner efforts, and to arouse in him increased ardours of moral self-improvement. It has shown him his finest potentialities of virtue; now he has to realize them. All elements of personality must be adjusted to the ideal shown by the glimpse, as the whole personality itself has to be surrendered to it. A work lasting several years may be rooted in a flash lasting only a few minutes.

The disciple should remember that the emotional uplifts will eventually subside leaving only the moral, intellectual, and intuitional elements remaining. Therefore this period should be used for cultivating these elements and for rethinking incessantly his whole attitude towards life. The glimpse afforded him is only a glimpse, and therefore transient, but it is enough to suggest new developments in several directions. It is highly important that the disciple should recognize watchfully every such manifestation of Grace and respond to it quickly. The chance to advance is thus given him, but the duty of co-operating with it must be fulfilled. No gross earthliness can be carried into that sublime atmosphere. Hence his glimpse of the supernal state must necessarily remain only a glimpse. If he wishes to make it something more, he must set to work purifying himself. It is true that occasional glimpses and momentary exaltations may occur, but they are quite sporadic and may disappear altogether for a long time. The moral re-education of the self is indispensable to the reception of a continuous and durable experience.

To that diviner self thus glimpsed, he must henceforth address all his prayers; through its remembrance he must seek succour; in its reliance he must perform all his endeavors; by its light he must plead for grace.

For the Overself to give itself wholly and perpetually to a man is a rare and wonderful event. Most often it gives itself only for a short time. This serves to intensify and enlarge his love and attraction for it, and to provide him with beautiful memories to support and sustain him in faithfulness to the quest in the fatiguing long-drawn years of struggle and darkness.

The glimpse is a fleeting one because he is still too unprepared to remain abidingly in such a lofty order of being. The glowing experience is glorious and memorable, but he falls back from it because he is dazzled by its brightness. He cannot retain it precisely because he is unequipped for so doing. But he who has once seen the goal, felt its sublimity, discerned its reality, enjoyed its beauty, and known its security, should draw from the experience the strength needed for the hard upward climb.

Although what the mystic feels is a genuine glimpse of the Overself, it is not necessarily a full or complete one. It reveals the ideal but he is not yet strong enough to realize it. New life has come to birth within himself but it is still in the embryonic stage. These glimpses make him aware of the existence of his spiritual self but do not make him united with that self. They fulfil their chief purpose if they awaken him from sleep in the senses or deceit by the intellect. With this awakening, he becomes aware that his great need of this higher order of being is so supreme that his lower life can no other than be dedicated to its rediscovery. And thus he enters upon the Quest. What he must do henceforth is to fortify and expand the union of his ordinary consciousness with his extraordinary Overself with unremitting effort.

Nobody is likely to be content permanently with but a mere glimpse of reality; he wants also to live it. He is not likely, and he should not be satisfied with these transient inspirations. Constant spiritual awareness should be his distant yet attainable goal. This is not to sway to and fro between periodic unions and separations but to dwell always with and in the Overself.

It is a common complaint that exalted experience of the Overself's presence are not continuous, are indeed utterly beyond the mystic's control. The Overself seems to leave him and the loss brings him back to his ordinary self. These phenomena are not subject to his will. It has no power of itself to repeat them. The heavenly visitations come he knows not how, and as mysteriously they depart. He will never be able to observe precisely the mechanics of this movement of grace. This indicates they are vouchsafed to him by the grace of the Overself. Because they are so exceptional, it is folly to demand their return but wisdom to work for it. The fact that he is unable to control these alternations between pleasurable and irksome meditations, between fruitful and barren ones, should show him that he is in the presence of an unknown and unpredictable factor. It should show him that by no act of his own will alone can he attain success in this labour. Patience is needed. He must wait for further revelations in the Overself's good time, and not his own. And no rhapsody can last. Life itself brings it to an end whether it is musical or mystical.

The momentary glimpse of the true self is not the ultimate experience. There is another yet more wonderful lying ahead. In this he will be bound by invisible hoops of wide selfless compassion to all living creatures. The detachment will be sublimated, taken up into a higher level, where the universal Unity will be truly felt.

108

The glimpse must leave him; only at the end of his road, only in the final Redemption, can all its glorious promises be realized.

109

Even though a glimpse has lengthened through time into permanence, it may not have lengthened through consciousness into completeness.

110

It is not only a question of how much of his mind does the experience illuminate but also what other parts of his personality does it inspire.

111

When the state of egolessness is first reached, it will be in deep meditation. The second stage of its development will be when it is temporarily reached in active life, the third and last when it is established there.

112

When the Grace has led him sufficiently far, he will be distinctly aware of an inner presence. It will think for him, feel for him, and even act for him. This is the beginning of, and what it means to have, an egoless life.

113

Just as the sun's rays are reflected on a burnished silver plate, so the Overself's attributes are faithfully reflected on a purified and egoless mind.

Index

Entries are listed by chapter number followed by "para" number. For example, 6.85 means chapter 6, para 85, and 4.172, 180 means chapter 4, paras 172 and 180. Chapter listings are separated by a semicolon. Please note also that, for the reader's convenience, the first number in the right-hand running heads throughout the text indicates chapter number.

The 28 Categories from the Notebooks

This outline of categories in *The Notebooks* is the most recent one Paul Brunton developed for sorting, ordering, and filing his written work. The listings he put after each title were not meant to be all-inclusive. They merely suggest something of the range of topics included in each category.

1 THE QUEST

Its choice —Independent path —Organized groups —Self-development —Student/teacher

2 PRACTICES FOR THE QUEST

Ant's long path —Work on oneself

3 RELAX AND RETREAT

Intermittent pauses —Tension and pressures —Relax body, breath, and mind —Retreat centres —Solitude — Nature appreciation —Sunset contemplation

4 ELEMENTARY MEDITATION

Place and conditions —Wandering thoughts —Practise concentrated attention —Meditative thinking — Visualized images —Mantrams —Symbols —Affirmations and suggestions

5 THE BODY

Hygiene and cleansings —Food —Exercises and postures —Breathings —Sex: importance, influence, effects

6 EMOTIONS AND ETHICS

Uplift character —Re-educate feelings —Discipline emotions — Purify passions —Refinement and courtesy —Avoid fanaticism

7 THE INTELLECT

Nature —Services —Development —Semantic training — Science —Metaphysics —Abstract thinking

8 THE EGO

What am I? —The I-thought —The psyche